Dark Horses

Karl Miller

Dark Horses

An Experience of Literary Journalism

PICADOR

First published 1998 by Picador

an imprint of Macmillan Publishers Ltd
25 Eccleston Place, London SW1W 9NF
and Basingstoke

Associated companies throughout the world

ISBN 0 330 36832 X

9 8 7 6 5 4 3 2 1

A CIP catalogue record for this book is available from
the British Library.

Typeset by SetSystems Ltd, Saffron Walden, Essex
Printed and bound in Great Britain by
Mackays of Chatham plc, Chatham, Kent

Contents

Preface

THIS IS A second memoir of mine. The first was *Rebecca's Vest*, which was published in 1993, and which came to an end – save for a few flashes forward – soon after its arrival at the point when I started to earn a living. I earned that living by editing magazines and teaching in a university, and the present book undertakes to say what it was like, and to come up with some thoughts on the literature and politics of the times in question. Earlier versions of certain passages have appeared in the following places: the American journal *Raritan*, the *New Statesman*, the *Times Literary Supplement*, the *Independent on Sunday*, *Thumbscrew* and the *London Quarterly*. Chapters 2, 4, 7 and 11 are based on the three Northcliffe Lectures I gave at University College London in February and March 1996. Chapter 5 is derived from a preface I wrote for the Everyman's Library edition (1995) of V. S. Naipaul's novel *A House for Mr Biswas*. I am grateful to the editors concerned, to Richard Poirier of *Raritan* in particular, and to those with whom I have talked about the matters treated in the book – among them my wife Jane, Ian Hamilton, James Fox and Douglas Johnson. I have been advised and encouraged by Alexandra Pringle, and have benefited from the interest taken by Jon Riley, Peter Straus and Ursula Doyle in what I have written. I have also benefited from the views of Claude Rawson, John Sutherland and Neil Berry, with whom I have looked at the bound volumes of my various magazines. The book is dedicated to the writers I have published.

Karl Miller
November 1997

1. Paper Round

MY FIRST PAPER round entailed cycling down Ferniehill Avenue, Gilmerton, Edinburgh, in the early hours of the morning in order to dish out newspapers to the sleepers. On one occasion a kindly woman was awake and had made pancakes, and she fed me a pair. The taste returns to me every now and then, and puts me back on my bike with my pancakes and my papers. But the job was not to last for more than a few days. I dropped out. My second paper round entailed selling the hot cakes of my various magazines. It lasted for the best part of forty years.

This is a book about the magazines I have edited. I have written it in order to describe what they were like, and what literary journalism was like, and to do honour to the writers I worked with. The dreams I dreamed in my bed at night came to respond to a daily life of commas and semi-colons, of overmatters and terrible oversights and terrific pieces, of pages cut to fit and refusing to fit. Of chopping off the fingers of people's articles, as a bandaged Medievalist once complained. My dreams have owed more to such dramas than to any desire to murder my father and marry my mother – a desire perhaps frustrated by my parents' failure to remain married to each other, or to me. The slow business of hot-metal setting was replaced by the chuckling of computer keyboards. Errors could now be swiftly and safely corrected. But they have yet to disappear from the page. Writers and rewriters and editors continue to make them, and infection continues to arise from the cuts which are still necessary. As my dreams suggest, I lived for my pages, for the attempt to turn them into living magazines, with something to say. But I lived for other things too. My torments haven't all been confined to print.

I shall start with the birth of my first child, my son Daniel, in the summer of 1957, at about the time of year when I am writing these words in West London, pleased with the bulging cauliflower blossoms of a shrub which is nerving itself, in the sudden sun, to struggle like some giant panda to get in at my open window, before going on to throw out, when winter comes, necklaces of tiny red berries. I was already living in West London all those years ago, and was reviewing for a weekly, the *Spectator*, where I was about to take charge of the book section. My wife Jane and I lived then in a small flat, rook's-nest-high, in a beetling, overcast nineteenth-century square, Cornwall Gardens off the Gloucester Road; her round soft cheek, that of the Florentine dame in a Piero painting, I used to measure with a sickle-shaped ivory brush. She suspected satire here, but this cheek-measuring was done in high spirits and out of love, the love that made her round with Daniel.

The square rang with the scales of a practising diva, Joan Sutherland, and at one end, in Braemar Mansions, lay the dark tea-taking apartment of the novelist Ivy Compton-Burnett, with her fine old-fashioned name and studied air of austere gentility – a gentility which a biographer was later to find fictive, another of her novels. Ivy's more-than-serious face, framed by its sibyl's braids, peered down one morning into the pram in which I was wheeling my son. She was present to me as a fairy godmother of uncertain good will and of tragic predilection. But I felt that she liked what she saw in the pram, though I doubt whether she summoned an actual smile.

Not very far away lived another serious writer, T. S. Eliot; nearby were a church and an old-fashioned hotel that he frequented. West London was enough to persuade you that the country's writers rarely smiled and wished to belong to an upper class. This impression, of a patrician strain or supremacy in the literary culture, could be taken for granted, even in those circles – such as the Leavisites and the Movement school of poets and novelists – where upper-class solidarity and display were sometimes resented. There was less of all this in the democratic Scotland I'd imagined for myself in my teens, when, in my bungalow outside Edinburgh, I'd known more about literature than I did about the cash economy, and had not identified the writing of books with gentility or grandeur.

Braemar Mansions and Joan Sutherland's Lucia di Lammermoor amused me, as Scots touches amid the more appropriate West Country ones at this end of London, where Western Gate was once a postal district. Having grown up in Edinburgh and attended the Royal High School there, I had done my National Service in Germany as a producer in Army Radio, had gone to Cambridge to read English with F. R. Leavis, and to Harvard as a research student, and had put in stints as an assistant principal at the Treasury and as a Current Affairs television producer at the Lime Grove studios of the BBC. Now I was going to be a journalist.

The Suez invasion, Anthony Eden's bungled scam of a few months before, had pleased the electorate for a spell, and had then driven him from power. Harold Macmillan, the first-in, first-out Suez warrior, was now Prime Minister, and Hugh Gaitskell was leader of the Labour Party. Gaitskell's authority was under challenge from supporters of Aneurin Bevan, and the two main journals of politics and letters, the *Spectator* and the *New Statesman*, were apt, by and large, to sympathize with Gaitskell and with Bevan respectively. Eisenhower's America drew to it a left-wing British youth which had no patience with the Republican Party but was persuaded by a romantic America of the mind, with its plains and deserts, its cars and easy riders, its Forties gangster films, Robert Mitchum's barrel chest, angular suits and Mona Lisa reserve, its science and technology, the problem-solving zeal which was about to launch the *Apollo* space programme, its imaginary absence of class distinction. Some of these people would one day lose patience with welfare-state socialism, and assist its passage to the dark side of the Moon. The Cold War was on, and while there were those on the left who were minded to blame America for that, there were very few socialists known to me, and of my own age, who were other than hostile to Soviet Communism, other than aware of its mass murders and show trials. Socialists of an earlier generation, of the sort who'd retained an attachment to Russia, gave the sense of a last intransigence. As late as 1963 – a year of change and convulsion – one member of that generation, my mother, up in Scotland, declared that 'a socialist dictatorship is the only healthy way out.' I'd never believed that myself, and the late Fifties seemed no time to begin.

Lining my rook's nest in Cornwall Gardens were letters from friends which, when I re-read them now in their yellowness, remind me of the changes which came in with the early Sixties, changes which some may think of as having been, in their restricted sphere, revolutionary, which stood in ambivalent relation to socialism and in inverse ratio to Stalinism, and which had a good deal to do with journalism. Neal Ascherson wrote me inspired letters from exotic parts of the world, and from Lancashire, where he had started work at the headquarters of the *Manchester Guardian*, as it still was. He would descend on London in order, he said, to 'live off the land', like a guerrilla, and to doss down on my sofa. Neal was to advance a theory of child-rearing which spoke, a little reproachfully, to my new situation as a devoted parent. 'Intern all parents,' he enjoined with reference to his theoretical child of eleven, 'and send him (or her) off to pass adolescence under the care of a deaf, offhand old centaur in a cave, and the essentials would be well looked after, supposing plenty of similar caves in the district.' That offhand old centaur now seems like a creature, or a mentor, of the alternative, innovative loose-hanging Sixties that were about to open up – seems like the flower child's or the guerrilla's uncle. 'Well,' went on Neal, half-man, half-beast, 'I expect you are tired of hearing about caves, so I will pass to my own news. I had tonsillitis. Once my balls became strangely glossy and seemed almost to be glowing with interior light.'

An academic friend wrote to say that he was happy, but would be even happier if he were married to a woman. 'The English Department,' he reported, 'is full of gossipy and effeminate temperaments who can't do anything in a direct and manly way.' He could occasionally feel that he was the first man ever to be appointed to that department. But this was a time when gender was on the move, both in Britain and America, and by the early Sixties he had embraced a homosexual life. In Stalinist Russia, freedom was extinct. In the West, sexual freedom was demanded. The freedoms claimed by younger generations are recurrent and are apt to be ephemeral, and they may be, as in the Sixties, just as hurtful and phantasmal as they are ever salutary. Publicists are now engaged in trashing the efforts that were made at that time, and the errors and postures that attended them. An angry nostalgia is expressed for a wide range of ante-bellum repressions and hypocrisies. The struggle continues, between freedom's friends and advocates of restriction, and so does a tension between radically different views of the past.

Another 'Athenian' friend, to employ his own designation, the American critic Marius Bewley, wrote to say that he rarely saw the *Spectator*, 'but am rather charmed by it when I do. I seem always to remember lovely pictures of various English elegancies. I remember seeing a picture of Lord Beaulieu in it once' – a man recently jailed, on the eve of our freedom, for something with a Boy Scout. Marius was thinking of the *Tatler*. But it was for the *Spectator* that he found himself reviewing when I went to work there. He can't have minded. An English elegancy and effrontery have seldom been absent from the modern *Spectator*.

In 1960 my wife Jane and I, together with our wheat-coloured son Daniel and his Babar books, moved to Chelsea, to a house in Limerston Street off the Fulham Road. There was no *au pair* offhand old centaur in attendance, but, as I say, there was Babar, of the apple-green tweeds, the elephant monarch of a welfare state, of Celesteville, whose mother used in his early days to rock him to sleep with her trunk, 'singing to him softly the while', or, as Daniel heard it, 'singing to him softly the wireless'. At Daniel's age, I'd prayed to be delivered 'from Eagle'. Between these two mishearings fell a world war, and they might suggest that we were now living in a gentler time. But Eagle was still around – for all that we could sometimes seem to be singing softly to ourselves in our haven of lily-white brick.

I still live in this same house. It is my crystalline, succinct Celesteville. The house belongs to two facing Early Victorian terraces. A section of the terrace opposite was knocked down by a German bomb, but the house where my mother had a room before the war still stands. More bombs have since gone off in the vicinity, Irish ones. These were merchants', then artisans' houses, and were done up after the war. There are others like them architecturally, but not many, in the north-east of the city. My house was leased for the mild sum of £6,500, and a Labour Government law was to be passed which made it possible for us to acquire the freehold for another mild sum. It has two floors and a basement. A lavishly-glassed, IRA-vulnerable front window is set within plaster lips in a whitewashed front that shows its bricks, and this window is answered at the back by one that looks out on a small garden that has roses and berries in it, forsythia, ferns, pecking sparrows and the odd handbag crow. There's a window in the roof which lets down a Jacob's ladder of light into a stairwell composed of delightfully-attuned planes and volumes, stairs and arches. On one occasion, I plummeted down that ladder, scattering its shafts of light, sailing through the door of the bedroom where Daniel was, and landing at his feet with nothing on. I'd violated his den, meaning to urge him to do his homework, and had broken an admonitory finger. No offhand old centaur would have done that.

One stormy winter's night my brother-in-law, the theatre director Jonathan Miller, climbed a real ladder to staunch a leak on the roof, with its shards of ice and slippery slopes — up over the eaves he went in his clumsy English shoes, twice the size of Robert Mitchum's suit. I felt cheated of an act which I badly didn't want to perform. I thought what it must be like for Santa Claus. I told myself that this was show business, and an extension of Jonathan's telling you about a profound new foreign book in two volumes which you hadn't heard of. But I had to admit it was brave of him to tackle the eaves.

I fear I may be making my dear house loathsome with this praise. But I shall finish. The American novelist Philip Roth called it *très sympathique*: this was the Sixties, and no praise was intended. Roth's sour grapes were to do with his being disinclined to rent it for the summer, and he mistook the character of the house: part of its point is to be elegant without being chic. There's a hospital at the back, and when I go there to be ill I look down at my house, hung with Daniel's paintings and with those of Jane's mother, Ruth Collet, and of my father. There it sits, as in a nineteenth-century street map of swelling London, enfolding its shafts of light and its Handel's arias. After Daniel came two other children, Sam and Georgia. I thought of them as my three little magazines, very soon to be editing themselves. They have gone from the house now, on their editorial courses. But they will never be gone for as long as I am in it. I think of it as a place where children slept and leapt, where Jonathan went up and I went down, where the Sixties showed their promise and their pains.

It feels a bit unlucky, praising your own house. But it would be false to leave it out of any autobiographical account of this kind, mostly about magazines and writers though it may be. From this house I travelled each day, for the rest of my life, to Bloomsbury or thereabouts, by 14 bus or Circle Line tube, to do my work as a journalist and as a university teacher. I was later to write a book called *Cockburn's Millennium*, about the Whig benevolence that designed the Reform Bill of 1832, about one Scotsman's dream of political improvement, a dream which came true and which has also been held – critics being what they are – to fail. I think of the magazines we are now approaching, whose story I'm about to tell, as Miller's millennium, as another of those dreams which came true and which have also been held by some people to have failed. I don't attribute to my millennium any high degree of public visibility. It was not like Parliamentary Reform. What made it a millennium was that my magazines were something I had looked forward to, that there were many others in it besides myself, and that we thought it was something worth doing. When I compare what we did with what is done now in the line of literary journalism, or with the prestigious coterie journals of earlier in the century, I don't feel ashamed. And among my dreams is one which beholds a serious person sitting up in heaven, reading through a wide range of rival backnumbers, and deciding whether those responsible for the magazines impending in the present book should hang their heads. This person then says they needn't.

Bloomsbury is a patch of central London which has the air of a former Latin Quarter subject to Tennysonian autumnal glooms. It has been a region of teachers and students, doctors and nurses, and of government spies. The pin that drops in libraries can be heard there. It has become a bazaar where you can buy the new technology which is believed to be a threat to English literature. It gave its name to an upper-class bohemia of the 1920s which has sometimes been confused with English literature. And it is the environment in which much of London's literary and political weekly journalism has been produced.

I began my long haul as a literary journalist by sending out books for review, pasting up galleys and laying out pages in one of Gower Street's crepuscular houses, as literary editor of the *Spectator*, which has since moved from the Fitzrovian end of Bloomsbury to Dickens's Doughty Street. Many years later I helped to set up the *London Review of Books* in Bedford Square; it was in due course to move to the site of another of Dickens's Bloomsbury houses, next door to the flat where the poet Yeats lost his virginity. In between my terms on these two journals, I served as literary editor of the *New Statesman*, at Great Turnstile, down a lane off Lincoln's Inn Fields, and then as editor of the BBC's erstwhile weekly journal, the *Listener*, which was quartered, not far from Fitzroy Square, in the Langham Hotel as was, and as is again – which is more than you can say for the *Listener*.

The kind of periodical I am writing about is one which has in it both politics and literature, and on which night is sometimes said to be falling. A taste for twilights, for predicting the death of this or that form of literature, and of literature itself, has long been a feature of literary opinion, and few of its prophecies of doom have so far come true. But then this one might. One of the four journals I used to work for has gone, and another, the *New Statesman*, has been in squabbling decline. It has lately been relaunched, however, and new journals continue to be invented. The show goes on. The tent has not been struck. The circus animals have not been forced to desert. Television has shown itself increasingly uninterested in incorporating what journals can do, and is less of a threat than was originally supposed to those journals which refuse to resemble television programmes.

The first two of my four magazines were privately-owned; the third was publicly-owned; and the fourth, while in the main privately-financed, was also in receipt of money from the Arts Council. Three of them were politically-engaged and one of them was politically impartial. They can all be defined in terms of a certain ambivalence. They were all minority journals of general interest which specialized in the two different subjects of politics and literature. They did not seek a mass readership, and their practice dated from a period when the existence of such a readership was still rudimentary.

2. Back to Front

THE KIND OF JOURNALISM I am writing about is often thought to have originated with the *Edinburgh Review*. That journal was founded in 1802 by Francis Jeffrey, among others, and rose rapidly to a print-run of around 10,000. Its motto was lifted by the economist Francis Horner from the literature of Classical Rome: *Judex damnatur cum nocens absolvitur* – the judge who lets the guilty off should be condemned. Just the stuff, some might feel, for a Scotch reviewer on the make to be telling himself at the start of his career.

The journal came out quarterly and consisted of unsigned essayistic book reviews, arranged in no predetermined thematic order. It was a journal of politics and letters: but it didn't have a front half and a back which dealt respectively with these subjects. These were writers who knew everything or aspired to do so, and the format suited such pretensions. Miscellaneous and anonymous, the journal might have been called what a short-lived government of the day was called, a ministry of all the talents, and there were individual savants ready to tackle several different subjects. For Edinburgh Reviewers, the term 'literature' signified a unified field of knowledge which ran from politics to poetry and which included science; and it also signified – as in the phrase 'the literature of this place' – an individually and collectively wide-ranging Northern élite. When Thomas Carlyle set out his journalistic stall in Edinburgh it was that of a mathematician who was shortly to become an omnicompetent, one of the wide rangers of the place. The place had its specialists, of course, and the *Review* was known for its special interest in politics and in what we now know as literature. It is rightly regarded as the Whig journal which fought for an extension of the franchise, for the provisions of the Reform Bill of 1832. And yet the word 'party' was in ill-repute among certain contributors. Matters of Parliamentary politics were felt by them to deserve backgrounding in relation to what belonged to the serious subject-matter implied by the compendious period sense of the word 'literature'. Francis Horner's corner was political economy, but his recently published papers are startling evidence of how wide a field of interests his specialism demanded and commanded.

The idea of a paper which professed to know everything while specializing in politics and literature helped to form some of the leading periodicals of the Victorian age, and helped them to confront the 'damned times' deplored by Matthew Arnold, in which 'everything is against one – the height to which knowledge is come, the spread of luxury, our physical enervation, the absence of great natures, the unavoidable contact with millions of small ones, newspapers, cities, light profligate friends, moral desperadoes like Carlyle, our own selves, and the sickening consciousness of our difficulties'. Arnold seems to use the word 'desperado' here in both an archaic and a modern sense – to evoke both a despairing and a desperate behaviour (the passage confers a title on a recent life of Carlyle by Simon Heffer, *Moral Desperado*, a title which makes the praiser of past times seem like some Leavisian cowboy). And there's a touch of Arnold's desperado about his own complaint on this occasion. It also manages to anticipate a phobic strain, a Cassandraism or canting pessimism, of the literary journalism which lay ahead, and which continued to have to cope with an influx of knowledge and of people.

Victorian periodicals, then, were beholden to Francis Jeffrey's *Edinburgh Review,* and sixty years after Arnold's complaint, and 110 years after the founding of the *Edinburgh Review*, the same conception of journalism helped to form the *New Statesman*. The two journals have a good deal in common, but there was to be an important difference of structure and approach which might seem to reflect an aggravation of the difficulties complained of by Arnold.

Politics and letters were put together in the *New Statesman*, as in the *Edinburgh Review*. But in the *New Statesman* they were also set apart – placed, respectively, at the front of the paper and at the back, where a book section was at one time followed by a section entitled Arts and Entertainment. This separation of the political from the cultural was to be characterized as a pantomime-horse arrangement, and the *Edinburgh Review* was no such horse, though there were those in its early days who could talk as if it were. 'Independent of its politics,' said Walter Scott, it offered a 'valuable literary criticism'. The remark needn't, in fact, lead one to doubt the element of unity or homogeneity which I've been describing. As a political enemy, Scott saw a difference of direction between the journal's politics and its valuable literary criticism; it was a difference which a Tory might want to see, and to exaggerate. Those who felt that there was a difference, an independence, of this kind can seldom have seen it as profoundly divisive, and it was a difference which became much easier to see in the pages of the *New Statesman*, about which remarks identical to Scott's used frequently to be made.

Literature – in its old sense of a unified and compendious field of knowledge – had long ceased, by the 1920s, to represent a problem-free conception, if indeed it had ever done so. Cracks had appeared. Jurisdictions had become entrenched. The attempt to write, as Edinburgh Reviewers had once aspired to do, *de omne scibile* – about whatever could be known – had become altogether more arduous, and could sometimes appear to have been replaced by the *omne scribile* of journalists who wrote knowingly about whatever came up. It had grown less easy to be a Professor of Things in General – Carlyle's ironic self-description. A siege of categories had begun. Knowing all may now be one of the prime difficulties of the modern world, and an aspect of its anxiety. And the difficulty has been an aspect of its literary journalism. For all the occasional presence of journalists, of bookmen professors, in the academic world of the later nineteenth century, that world was on its way to being seen as a fortress of mutually exclusive disciplines, and the professions had darkened their doors against amateur intrusion.

Estrangements of this sort help to account for the difference in layout between the two journals.

The pantomime-horse effect was an attribute of the *New Statesman*'s successive heydays, and could give the impression of a brace of editors, and of a degree of rivalry and a difference of outlook between the front and the back. The bi-part format was both a departure from and a deference to the old project of a unified field of knowledge; a division of editorial labour was applied to what was experienced as an increasingly intractable subject-matter – to the accommodation, within a single discourse, of a wide range of preoccupations. As in the cases of some other journals, the arrangement was often to work well, and could lead to a productive tension between rival viewpoints and priorities. But the drawbacks are obvious, and it took a strong editor to overcome them. There was a risk of huffs and quarrels, and the paper's identity could become slurred or smudged. What remains in Britain of the bi-part journal is mostly vestiges of a former practice which could appear, even at the time, to have something provisional about it. It is better to have and to be a single editor, with an undoubted overall responsibility. Nevertheless, dual control has its advantages, and all journals have a measure of it, together with a measure of contradiction and internal struggle.

The quarrel of 1962 between C. P. Snow and F. R. Leavis broke out when the latter's splenetic Richmond Lecture in response to Snow's opinions concerning the 'two cultures' of literature and science was published in the *Spectator* shortly after I left that paper. It was to raise a question which the weeklies had already had to face –

this question of a unified field of knowledge, and of the single culture which it might assist in sustaining. The quarrel was in the nature of a *Kulturkampf*, a clash of outlooks, with Snow's version of scientific progress opposed by a variety of religious experience, a Lawrentian or Carlylean variety. Neither Snow nor Leavis seemed to feel that the idea of a continuum of knowledge, and of the integration of science in the general culture of the country, was chimerical, but it was evident that the idea was in difficulties: letters to the journal worried about what might happen to a culture which lacked science, and to a science-dominated culture which lacked literature. Periodical journalism was capable of an interest in helping to make these two ends meet – these two among others – and there was space there for such a quarrel. It was unlikely to have originated in any of the quality newspapers which had begun to steal the weeklies' clothes, and to surpass them in respect of their investigative, as distinct from their argumentative, function.

When I crossed the Gower Street threshold in 1958, the *Spectator* and the *New Statesman* were the provinces of former Army officers who had served in the war with the Grenadier Guards and the Rifle Brigade. To the right of me and to the left of me, politically speaking, stood two tall men, with the Guards officer, Ian Gilmour, the more laid-back of a charismatic pair, a Cavalier to John Freeman's Roundhead. Gilmour, who owned and had recently edited the *Spectator*, was later to be a Defence Minister in Margaret Thatcher's first government, and, later still, her cogent antagonist. In 1958, Harold Macmillan was Prime Minister. The Opposition he faced was still somewhat the worse for the battle that had been running for some while between the Labour Party leader Hugh Gaitskell and the Bevanite Left, for whom, as for their supporters in the country, Gaitskell was a betrayer of socialism, neither the first nor the last of such so-called betrayers. Gaitskell's Labour Party and the Conservative Party were in a state of rapprochement so far as certain aspects of economic policy were concerned, a state that was known as Butskellism. 'I am an aristocrat,' said Aneurin Bevan, and Gaitskell was thought by him to be a bourgeois. Bevan's aura could indeed appear to be like that of the patrician Whig adored by Edinburgh Reviewers, Charles James Fox, and Gaitskell was both a socialist and a member of the upper middle class. The same was true of John Freeman, who had been one of the principal Bevanite MPs. But Bevan now had not much longer to live and the affiliation was on the wane.

Meanwhile the Western world had entered the golden age attributed lately by the historian Eric Hobsbawm to the decades that followed the Second World War; we had entered a *belle époque* of prosperity, technological advance and transnational business structures – an epoch not universally apparent at the time, and made altogether less beautiful by the outbreak of the Cold War and the threat of nuclear destruction. In 1969, Richard Crossman, a former Bevanite affiliate, said in the House of Commons what Macmillan had said, in knockabout fashion, ten years before – that we'd never had it so good. Crossman's version ran: 'In the Fifties and Sixties the standard of living of those at work in this country rose far, far faster than in any previous epoch of history.' This was said in the course of an insistence that more be done for the old and the sick and for single parents.

As a Labour sympathizer, a pupil of Leavis's and a deserter from the Treasury and from BBC Television, I took time, fazed by its brilliant articles, to adjust to the *Spectator*, and to its underlying direction, its well-founded politics. It was a jolly sort of paper, compact of Tory residues and Labour leanings – the New Labour leanings, the Gaitskellite revisionism, of the time; and its displays of brilliance and impudence looked forward to the satirical Sixties. To switch to the *New Statesman*, as I did in 1961, was to require no gymnastic leap (and was to afford me twice as much editorial space). The two journals had moved closer together, to the tune of the convergent politics of the time. Nevertheless, their front halves were by no means indistinguishable, and the *New Statesman* was apt to be hostile to such revisionist Labour MPs as Anthony Crosland and Gilmour's friend Roy Jenkins, both of whom wrote for the *Spectator*.

Soon after my arrival there I published a review by Crosland. The book under review was a collection of firebrand left-wing essays called *Declaration*, and the article – editorially headed 'Leftover Left to Kill', in strained allusion to a memoir by Dylan Thomas's widow – spoke of a new socialism which had come into being, and which was due to Gaitskell and, said Crosland, to such confederates as Crosland. 'British socialism,' he wrote, 'now lays much less emphasis on old-style nation-alization and detailed physical controls, and much more on economic expansion, social welfare and social equality; while its pristine semi-Marxist analysis of capitalism has given way to a more subtle revisionist theory of the post-capitalist society.' The emergence of the New Left, and of its journal *Universities and Left Review*, was politely acknowledged in the piece, but the group was held to be out of touch with 'ordinary people', and to be reactionary, in the sense of pre-, or anti-, revisionist. Crosland was interested, in his lordly way, in ordinary people, in a revival and improvement of the welfare state, and in its refinancing on the basis of an assured prosperity. Out of strength would come sweetness.

Four years later I was to publish in the *New Statesman* a searching account of Crosland's writings by George Lichtheim, who said that he thought everybody knew that the Labour Party had always been committed to a social-democratic programme, and who also noted the lack in Crosland's writings of a specifically socialist approach. This was not a case of editorial second thoughts, or of a betrayal of revisionism. As a Labour sympathizer back from a sympathetic stay in America, I had no trouble in recognizing that Crosland's arguments should be heard, and am glad to have published them in both of these papers. But I also felt they should be responded to by those on the left who were not persuaded by them.

Crosland's review of 1958 had a word to say about an essay in the book under discussion which was contemptuous of the upper classes. Something had to be done about them, according to Paul Johnson. His nostrums on this occasion, which were those of a *New Statesman* staff member who had made a name for himself as a fierce and skilful Bevanite polemicist, would not help and might even hurt ordinary people, observed Crosland. But

'presumably it would be worth while,' he joked, 'in order
to rid ourselves of debutantes and guardsmen.' This *New
Statesman* banisher of debutantes and guardsmen went on
to edit the journal, and after that to make the leap that
took him to performing as a Thatcher firebrand; in more
recent times, he has been one of the many people
susceptible to Tony Blair. The same man, the same
fierceness, the same politics of denunciation and reproach,
have been apparent throughout his changes of shape.

Britain's upper class has moved in mysterious ways,
its wonders to preserve. It has also moved to attack itself.
These two tall former members of a military élite,
Gilmour and Freeman, produced journals which were
both of them averse to what was then becoming known
as the Establishment. The *Spectator* was to pioneer the
expression, and the journal's political development had
reached a stage when it was possible for editorials to
charge the Labour Party with having 'allowed itself to be
sucked into the Establishment'. It took an interest in the
New Labour of the day, and in the new America that was
shaping up. Its writers felt, as many others did, as even
Sixties satirists did, a hopeful admiration for John Kennedy, the Young Lochinvar campaigner and Camelot
President. Nixon was 'not the man to lead the free world'.
The journal's political attitude was grounded in a dislike
of the British Government's dissembling Suez War, which
had collapsed in fiasco a few months before I went there.
A new New Right editor of the *Spectator* said not long
ago that it had been the work of cranks to protest against
Suez: not all of his predecessors would have agreed. The
Spectator of the Fifties welcomed Macmillan's 'wind of

change' in Africa, and spoke against racial oppression and injustice, both abroad and at home, on the part both of the South African Government and of the Cambridge University Appointments Board. It approved of Britain's entry into Europe, and of Britain's Health Service. It had been nicknamed 'The Bugger's Bugle' for supporting the Wolfenden proposals for a relaxation of the laws governing homosexual conduct.

In the course of the last forty years public confidence in democratic socialism declined to the point where it sometimes seemed unable to speak its own name. Having passed through the fires of schism and defection, the Labour Party has become the least socialist of Labour Parties since the war, in its latterday search for electability. The *Spectator* played a part in those vicissitudes, a prescient part in certain respects, which contributed ancestrally to the SDP exodus, as well as to the Blair realignment; for all the faults it found with the Old Labour of the time, it can't be charged with helping to administer a starting touch to the Thatcher avalanche. Clause Four nationalization was Labour's albatross, for the *Spectator* of the late Fifties, and the albatross has at long last been shed. Gone too, it would seem, thanks to Thatcher, and to Tony Blair, is the backward and bullying trade-unionism which was another of the *Spectator*'s concerns.

The paper was in favour of tolerance at a time when tolerance could be very hard to argue for, in areas where it was then to be achieved, and enjoyed, and abused. The desired millennium has not arrived. But the freedoms which were sought were worth seeking. Many *Spectator* writers would have accepted what Roy Jenkins was to say subsequently: that a permissive society – an idea much mocked by Eighties thinkers greatly in favour of a permissive view of financial advantage – is a civilized society. Many *Spectator* writers also believed, I think, that theirs was a Christian society. Lord Altrincham, alias John Grigg, who was to be temporarily scandalous for expressing a desire for the more popularly accessible Royal Family we now know so well, 'liked Christ', as he put it, and the paper's proprietor liked him too.

At the Election of 1959 the journal voted Labour, and so did its contributor Kingsley Amis. But the country did not. Another contributor, in a short piece presented as the 'aspirations of a mugwump', said that he 'hoped to see the Conservative Party return with a substantial majority', while not aspiring to 'advise my Sovereign in her choice of servants'. The mugwump was Evelyn Waugh. Mugwumps are persons who stand aloof from party politics, but this one was shortly to be rejoicing at Macmillan's return to Downing Street, after which Amis changed his allegiance. Lucky Jim moved to the right, and would one day take to behaving like, and indeed to looking like, Waugh. Both Waugh and Amis were told off for permissiveness when they were young, but neither can have been displeased by Leavis's attack on the permissive 'new orthodoxy of Enlightenment' at the time of the Chatterley trial. Waugh, though, was displeased by Amis when Amis was young, and Leavis was to be displeased by him too, and to call him a pornographer. All three wrote for the paper when I was there. It was a paper with a right wing and a left, in which Establishment and Enlightenment were conjoined, and in which there were writers who called down a plague on both.

In 1955, Waugh issued a warning which would seem to have referred to Amis, among other university graduates, including the pupils of Leavis. He spoke of 'the new wave of philistinism with which we are threatened by these sour young people who are coming off the assembly line in their hundreds every year and finding employment as critics, even as poets and novelists'. These rodents were to creep inside the citadal of the *Spectator*, where the Movement group of poets and novelists, led by Amis and Philip Larkin, was identified and supported. Linked with, and sometimes confused with, the angry young men and hypergamists, the upstarts and marriers-up, fussed over in the newspapers of the period, the members of the group went on writing in the *Spectator* during my time as literary editor. Their presence was an aspect of the cross-currents and contradictions that had become perceptible in a journal which had its snobs and its prigs, its party politicians, belletrists, university wits and Fleet Street show-offs, its thoughtful and judgmental new-style literary critics, in which Leavis's praise of Lawrence's *Phoenix* coexisted with the tale of an 'infelicitous' journey down from Aberdeen by nationalized British Rail.

In July 1960 John Coleman, who'd been a pupil of Leavis's at Downing College, Cambridge, wrote astringently about Waugh's novel *Brideshead Revisited* at the very time when the paper was serializing Waugh's book about his African travels. Neither book is among his best, and I expect I thought I was doing the right thing by *Brideshead*, perhaps not realizing that there might have been — though there wasn't — a Gower Street uproar. Waugh's books were admired on the paper, even by its prigs, and so were his reviews, delivered in copperplate by post, from the depths of the West Country, to someone whom he may have come to suspect of being a sour young philistine. I remember his felicitously barbed appraisal of a memoir by a former friend in which an ingratitude was revealed on the part of the friend, during his days as 'the lean young Quennell', towards a host, the sumptuous Harold Acton. Acton was a kind of prince who wrote books about the Bourbon kings of Naples and lunched with ex-Queen Helen of Romania. His Florentine servants wore the white gloves of an ancient regime as they dispensed aperitifs to the recorded music of a Beethoven string quartet. He possessed a feline courtesy, and spoke much as one might imagine Henry James to have done. He had that air of a certain sort of English man of letters which seemed to go with an American provenance. His books received, in their time, many a favourable review. But Waugh felt that Peter Quennell had slighted him in his memoir, and here I am myself, a former fleeting guest, compounding the slight.

Before objecting to *Brideshead*, Coleman had objected to Lawrence Durrell's lushly romantic *Alexandria Quartet*, a once-celebrated sequence of novels — a former master-piece — which bore, for the back of the paper, some of the cautionary properties which Eden's Suez venture did for the front. The issues of May that same year, 1960, carried pieces by E. M. Forster, on Lampedusa's *Leopard*, by Philip Larkin, and by William Golding, who was one day to write a piece which expressed a desire to blow up Eton

College. After a slow start the book pages had settled down. They were part of a paper which supplied its readers with opposites and arrant contrasts, which was a mixture of old and new loyalties, old and new blood – Evelyn Waugh, as it were, and Frank Kermode.

On 17 June the Congo crisis entered the paper. It was to embroil one of the most accomplished critics to appear in either of the two papers at this time, Conor Cruise O'Brien, who once boasted of having had 'a foot in both graves', who had written a dissenting piece on Edmund Wilson's support for American Indian secessionism in the *Spectator* of 27 May, and who was now to be faced, as UN Representative in the region, with the mercenary-backed secession of Katanga from the newly independent Congo state. A third grave, as could well have been feared, for O'Brien's foot.

In that same issue of 17 June 1960, the year of Bevan's death, was a leader on Clause Four, together with an article by Roy Jenkins on the 'fallacies' of Bevan's ally, Dick Crossman, with his call for more nationalization, and his view that Western capitalism was in dire straits and headed for defeat in the Cold War, and with his 'passion for semi-permanent opposition', in Jenkins's phrase. The passion was not to be requited. Three years later weekly journalism was to lose for a time, to the wilderness of power, one of its most dynamic exponents. Six years later still, at the end of his period of ministerial office, he would be informing the House of Commons of a post-war golden age. This hardly counts as a betrayal of his previous position, or of socialism, and the 'Double-Crossman' known to certain detractors was a jealous exaggeration. Ebullient, impatient Crossman – no one more percussive when it came to replacing the phone – was always ardently criticized by his fellow politicians, as by *New Statesman* journalists during his brief spell, from 1970, as editor of the paper.

Labour should seek power, Jenkins argued in this piece, and a Labour leader powerful enough to win elections was presently to take the stage. Gaitskell died suddenly in January 1963 – an event which caused Crossman to feel that 'a great light had appeared in the sky' – and the succession went to another of Bevan's old associates, Harold Wilson. This was welcomed by those *New Statesman* editorialists for whom Jenkins and Crosland – rising reviewers and rising political stars – had been objects of horror. The rival rag had profiled Crosland as 'Gaitskell's Ganymede'. No one has less resembled a cup-bearer to the gods.

Wilson has been credited with the joke that his was a revolution which had to be undertaken with a Czarist Cabinet. His Cabinet contained *Spectator* reviewers who did something to extend the record of success in government to which the post-war Labour Party, with its complement of true believers in opposition and in the art of the impossible, is entitled to lay claim. But it's also true that Labourites of all stripes and persuasions took part in this success, and that Aneurin Bevan achieved the impossible when he created a National Health Service. He did so with the assistance of Kingsley Martin's *New Statesman*, of which it can and should be said that it helped to give the British Empire back to its native peoples, and to build the welfare state. The work done by successors in left-of-centre journalism eventually became that of supporting democratic socialism at a time when a left-over Left had resigned its challenge, when morale had failed, a failure due to be polemically entangled with the collapse of democratic socialism's opposite, of the inimical Soviet system, and when the welfare state, and the public interest, were being subjected to assault.

Several back-half contributors moved, as O'Brien did, from the one grave to the other, during my time on these papers, and these two book sections of mine can't be thought very different from one another. Neither went in for the determined application of political prejudice to the discussion of literature. But we were not above the battle. We were not mugwumps. We were with the people, in a number of literary ways, and yet professionally academic too, in temper, as well as bohemian and metropolitan and journalistic. The presence of academics in literary journalism was increasing, and would go on increasing with the arrival of the new universities: but we also wanted to publish, and did publish, 'low-income Glaswegians', in John Redwood's generic expression of recent times, working-class people who might or might not have matriculated at a university, but were less accustomed than such people as Redwood's one-time associates at All Souls to being asked to write articles. These were book sections in which, with the odd plunge into black reaction, a sceptical and multiple democratic socialism took account of a literature which was full of sympathy, and yet full of hatred as well, for such an outlook. They were liberal book sections, in exactly the sense of the word, the permissive sense of the word, which is now being used, both on the left and on the right, to refer to an abomination.

This socialism was as much dialectical as democratic – a description which might be seen by some, I suppose, as longhand for right-wing Labour. I came to think that in seeking a basis for action you have to be alive to contradiction, while also alive to the seductions of compromise and the middle way. I came to think that the golden rule is that there tend to be two golden rules where there are any at all. That the *New Statesman* was both a people's paper and a top person's paper. That the Second World War was, for the British, both a people's war and a top person's war. I came to believe in a socialism which is interested in a mixed economy, and in a fitting together of the golden rules associated with the public and private spheres of communal life and personal fulfilment. By such socialists, Thatcherism was seen, when the time came, as a form of greed, an infatuation with profit and advantage, as the violation of a humane balance between the public and the private.

3. Laughter in the Dark

I STARTED WORK at the *Spectator* in the guise of a working-class youth from Cambridge University who saw himself as some sort of bohemian professional. I shared the cubicled corridor which stuck out at the back of the journal's Gower Street house, like the fuselage of a downed aeroplane, with Bernard Levin and Alan Brien, critics, respectively, of Parliament and of the theatre. Of the three of us, I was the prig and they were the brilliant writers. All three of us knew what critics were expected to get up to, and we got up to it. We judged. On went our wigs and gowns, with Alan's and Bernard's worn with a difference from mine, and without a trace of rue. Both liked to laugh, and Alan liked to lunch, and when the Sixties came in, claimed to do so in restaurants at whose every table could be overheard the firm female-to-male inquiry: 'Have you told her yet?' Back in his cubicle by mid-afternoon he'd settle down to complete, by five-thirty, 800 words on a play by Racine about adulterous passion.

The night I joined the paper, the staff piled into the Escargot in Soho to do honour to the editor Brian Inglis, who ended up being called names, not all of them Bingles. The roars and clinks were those of the carousal scene in a romantic opera, and my offended feelings were those that I'd felt when I swore loyalty to the Scouts and then, later that day, caught the troop leaders stealing apples. Juvenile, pharisaical feelings, they were. I'd already roared and clinked in the Army, and even in Edinburgh, and didn't believe in never doing so. But there I stood at midnight in Soho, conscious of Leavis's deplorings of the London literary world. 'How can you sink so low?' A. Alvarez asked me, in Cornwall Gardens, at the time when I joined the *Spectator*. Alvarez was writing for the *New Statesman*. At these stern words, his young bride gave a laugh. She'd grown used to the high standards of young Fifties literary journalists who wanted to be thought, and sometimes were thought, academically responsible.

Well, I soon rallied. I lacked the temerity, and the ideas, to try to write a book. But I had the temerity to set about organizing a flow of opinion, much of it adverse, about the books that other people had written, and sending it through the pipes and ducts of half a dozen or so of the later pages of the journal. It was quaint of me, I now see, and naive of me, to have had so few qualms about undertaking this invidious plumbing work. I did so without delusions of grandeur, though with a measure of visceral self-importance certainly, and I hoped it might be done in generosity of heart. The literary criticism that arose in this country after the Second World War was as judicial, as fault-findingly ambitious, and as youthfully and generationally vengeful, as any there has ever been, and my own editorial and critical activities were to contribute to that. I went into it all believing, as Francis Jeffrey did, in the correction of taste and the wholesome discipline of derision. But it is also true to say that I was always to feel that there is no editorial pleasure like that of praising what deserves to be praised and publishing what cries out to be published.

Not long ago, in a little magazine called the *London Quarterly*, I published such a piece. It was an account by Murray Carlin of his life amid the political and racial crisis-grounds of Southern Africa. I remembered him from many years before, as a lean, prematurely silver-haired, lynx-eyed Leatherstocking reader of Leavis. And now here he was again, writing as if on oath about what had happened to him. When I met someone else, Antonia Fraser, who felt as I did about what he'd written, I told myself that one such appreciative reader was enough, but that none would have been too. I would still have loved Carlin's piece.

'He combines the worst faults of the academic with the worst faults of the literary journalist.' The speaker was Kingsley Amis, during the days of our friendship. At this point, I think, he was still living and teaching in Swansea, his life shared, as mine was to be, with a wife, a daughter and two sons; presently he would be off to be a don, for a while, at Peterhouse in Cambridge. On this occasion, late in the London evening once more, I was standing with him on the kerb outside a Fleet Street pub. The limiting judgment was delivered with earnest force, with a lift of the old proud head; it might almost have referred to closing-time in the gardens of the West. It referred to a critic whom I admired and who was to become the admiration of many others. Amis was always highly approving of the happy few of whom he approved, but of the rest he was to become more intolerant, phobically and comically intolerant, though seldom uninterestingly so, with the years. His novel *Lucky Jim* appeared in 1954, and he was already well-known when I worked with him on the *Spectator*. To the older literati he was his jokes and sneers and funny faces, a low and vulgar fellow – which helped to endear him to readers of his own age. To his friends he seemed gifted, abrasive, condignly abusive, enjoyable, engrossing. He was the glamorous beauty of his circle, while also its ringleader and ironic centre. For me, as the receiver of his typescripts, he was the complete contributor: punctuation-perfect, presentation-perfect, no chink for subbing to climb in and vent itself. At one time, he was someone you might imagine hefting a pole on the river at Oxford, dressed in the white shirt and grey-flannel trousers of the Forties; then, in the days of his American wardrobe, I'd picture him in a fawn sports-jacket, attacking a mixed grill to the sound of Handelian trumpets, the bubbles rising in his glass of lager, and in Kingsley. Later on, I'd picture him, from photographs, wedded to his typewriter, with his cat patrolling near by. I liked to think of the ads he'd invent, in rebuke of the agencies' new wheezes. There was the no-nonsense one: 'Drink Bowen's beer. Makes you drunk.' And the perverse post-modern one, which moved from coaxing to the hysterical-sublime: 'It's twice as expensive. *And it's not nearly as good.*'

Class came into it, into my feeling for him. I'd have thought it absurd to talk of being proud to be working-class, but I didn't mind crawling with the scholarship-boy lice on the locks of literature. I didn't mind that the example set by Amis, and by the pupils of Leavis, was thought to convey a broad hint of the nemesis threatened by the profligate award of government grants for under-graduate study. The young Kingsley spoke of himself in 1957 as not very decidedly political at all – and yet 'any right-wing sentiment in the mouth of an intellectual (or anywhere else) is likely to annoy me.' This was a time, he believed, when 'intellectuals' had moved to the right, and had come to dislike the welfare state, as Leavis was reckoned to do. Like John Osborne's Jimmy Porter, he felt there was a shortage of protestable causes – he was writing three weeks into the Suez crisis – and it may not have been wholly in irony that he mentioned the need for 'a good, long, steadily-worsening crisis out in the open where everyone can see it'. Efforts to do away with 'the colour bar' and to reform the laws on homosexuality and divorce did not register with him as primarily political causes, attractive though they were to 'romantics'. Never-theless, he is said to have marched against the Suez War, and was to speak in 1958 of 'nationalizing everything in sight'.

The young Kingsley was alert to literature's patrician poses, and patrician writers, in their turn, were alert to his alertness, with Ivy Compton-Burnett, for one, more than willing to let fall a drop of poison on this counter-jumping talent. In relation both to Kingsley and myself, there hovers in retrospect the notion that relative depri-vation can instil an uncertainty masked by shows of confidence. Fear, and hurt, whatever their source, may go with an appearance of strength, and a tendency to repudiate and condemn: Kingsley's son Martin has taken an interest in this principle, and the life and works of Kingsley's disparager, Ivy Compton-Burnett, could be thought to illustrate it. The confident, writes Martin Amis in one of his novels, may be afraid, may be vulnerable. No doubt they may also be confident. I used to fancy that there was a more than period partial resemblance between Kingsley's act and that of the comedian Tony Hancock, who suffered from depressions which ended his life, and whose act was to stage shows of confidence which failed to work. Kingsley's worked, both on and off the stage, and enabled him to make old bones.

'Pain and bitter laugh' is among the significant joke mishearings which occur in Kingsley's fiction, in which a pursuit of pleasure also occurs. It took me years to plumb the extent of his anxiety. He was the dedicated joker, the disciplined drinker, the principled hedonist, whose be-haviour reflected both a frightening aggression and a repertoire of fears – of dying, flying, the dark, of entering rooms, of Communism, eventually experienced as a cata-strophe liable to bring about the end of the world. To more than one of these fears, hearts will return an echo. But some hearts may have been stopped by the discovery in his *Memoirs* of a late piece of light verse, a take-off of 'My Old Dutch', in which he expresses the wish to wallop his second wife in the crotch. This is the kind of wish which one would have expected the Amis of the Fifties to suppress, or to be innocent of. Nor would I then have expected him to worry quite as much as he was later to do about friends dodging their rounds in pubs. 'Standing your round' could be made to sound like courage under fire, or the Charge of the Light Brigade.

Kingsley sometimes appeared to believe that it was all right for him to do things which he wanted to blame others for doing, and he may have been helped along in this direction, when he was young, by reading the works of D. H. Lawrence and of the libertarian psychologist Homer Lane, by the 'do what you want to do' – the DWW – of the generation or two before his own. The expression is to be found in his novel *That Uncertain Feeling*, and the idea is to be found everywhere in his novels, side by side with the idea that you shouldn't do what you want to do. Early and late, he was a critic of rudeness – to women, for example, or waiters. Poets shouldn't suppose that they're allowed to be rude just because they're poets, and so on. You might even say that rudeness is high on the list of Amis-infuriants. And yet in these *Memoirs* of his, and in the cronyish life of Amis by Eric Jacobs, which rests heavily on the *Memoirs*, there is no lack of rudeness from the critic of rudeness. Jacobs tells how Kingsley used to say 'Oh Christ' when bores accosted him at the Garrick Club, where he spent many of his last days, and where a number of the lads may have applauded such habits. Approaching him at the club, where females are now allowed through the door on special occasions, a woman of his acquaintance appears to have caught the deterrent note of his 'Oh Christ'. Jacobs then reveals that Amis was due to be her host at his house that evening, when she would be bound to be – in womanly fashion, one might suppose – late.

Writers can be as rude as the lords they sometimes think they are, and Kingsley grew to be somewhat patrician in this respect, while keeping on with a particular disapproval of arrogance. His memoirs offer an encomium on John Betjeman in the course of which he winces at his audible defaming of a servile waiter who'd forgotten that Betjeman had been knighted. This lapse into contempt on Betjeman's part is attended by an authorial lapse of ampler proportions: the story is told of how Kingsley and Malcolm Muggeridge were once too drunk to have sex with a woman whom the memoir names. A chapter is devoted to exclaiming against the racial prejudice encountered in Nashville, Tennessee, in a gracious-living academic community: but then the first novel Kingsley wrote on returning to England was one which mocks a man for his fashionable dislike of Apartheid, on the understanding that such a dislike would necessarily be suspect — one of those sure signs on which the novelist of manners is entitled to depend.

The *Memoirs* show an ill-manners surprising in a novelist of manners and an uncouthness foreign to the stylist of *Lucky Jim*. What is also surprising is how little their brutalities have been minded. His old admirers hardly noticed. His old detractors had died, most of them, or had swallowed their bile and yielded to his fame. In this hardly-noticing, and in the *Memoirs* themselves, there seemed to lie an ounce or two of the indifference, the hardness of heart, which did something to spoil the postwar bid for freedom.

I remember next to none of exactly this sort of hurtfulness, however, from the days when I was first friendly with Kingsley. There was carnival, carnality, carnage, but not this madness of hostility. His writings were launched on their account of a struggle between bachelor licence and the claims of family life, on their progress from a concern with adultery to a concern with senility. His various marital books were never to abandon the question of the new freedom. Within them all shines the kindly light of his wife Hilly.

During a visit with my own wife to the Amises in Swansea, we took a trip by car out to the Gower Peninsula. I sat in the car with the place-name Mumbles rumbling in my mind, rather in the way that the name Mau-Mau had lodged, on an occasion not long before this, in that of Kingsley's *bête noire*, Swansea's Dylan Thomas, the Rimbaud of Cwmdonkin Drive. It came on to rain in the course of a trip which was like one of those chronicled in the novel about his mismated Welsh Methuselahs, *The Old Devils*. A shower dumped on the heads of the young devils of this excursion, and I made a far from diabolic joke when we crossed the threshold on our return. 'Home and wet,' I quipped. It was a joke of such mildness that a man might easily have been thrown out of the Garrick for making it, a joke that one of William Blake's lambs might have made: but no feral gleam entered the Amis eye. He responded with a laugh of pure kindness. Inside the house a shot rang out from a squalling television set attended, or neglected, by his three blond children. 'Shut up,' barked Kingsley; the time would come when he'd swear never again to read a book which didn't open with a shot, but this was early days. The boy Martin threw a dark glance – not feral either, but definitely watchful – at the visitors.

The adult Kingsley Amis struck some people as a man who could not be told anything – and as a man unlikely to laugh at lame jokes – but his friend Robert Conquest managed to tell him that there was no such person as a lefty who was not also the dupe of a predatory Soviet Communism, no such person as a lefty who was not also a trendy. Both had once been Communists, the adolescent Kingsley a Shelleyan nationalizer. But these two very clever men were later to support each other in the enactment of an at times burlesque simplification of left-wing attitudes, with Kingsley the more dependent of the two, and the more burlesque. Left-wing activists, suggests *The Old Devils*, are fond of blue curaçao with passion-fruit juice. The suggestion falls somewhere between a farcical joke and a statement of fact. I probably hated Soviet Communism as much as Kingsley did, but our friendship was to dissolve in a solution of blue liqueur.

Not that we came to blows, or to angry words. But there were words of his, in the winter of 1963, which indicated that our ways might be parting, and that future jokes had better be pretty God-damned good. By now he was with his second wife, Jane Howard, and he wrote me a short-story-like note, perfectly composed and punctuated, to air a disapproval. Its object was Peter Jenkins, at that time a *Guardian* journalist – politically suspect as such, no doubt, in the eyes of Kingsley and Bob Conquest.

I didn't much care for your friend's behaviour, but I should hate you to think that any of us were rude to him. This is what happened.

As we filed out of the Kilmartins', P. Jenkins, who

I had never seen before, suddenly turned his head. 'Going to Karl's?' – 'Yes.' – 'We'll get a taxi.' Bob then said he had his car, which we all 5 walked along to. I had not taken to P. J. and nor had anyone else, but I am quite sure one of us would have perched on another's lap to make room for him – Bob's car takes only 4 in comfort – if P. J. had merely said something: something like 'Could you possibly find room for me?' However, we all agreed afterwards that he had said nothing, but merely stood waiting for room to be made for him. So we didn't. Bob called, in a not very concerned but certainly not hostile tone: 'Sorry, I'm afraid I can only take four.' Jane, Caroleen and I had said nothing at all. Accordingly I was taken aback to be thanked sarcastically 'for the lift' when after a long circuitous drive (Bob thought you were still living at your old place and took some time to be convinced you weren't) the 4 of us appeared.

My powers as a host were no doubt tested by the reception of these disgruntled guests. Worse than that, though, was the arrival at Limerston Street, on another occasion, of the uninvited Tony Crosland, who could be heard, when I opened the door, explaining, in a weary drawl, how boring he expected his visit to be. Kingsley would have sympathized with me there. He thought Crosland outstandingly rude, never forgot that he'd leant against a mantelpiece and filled a pipe with Kingsley's tobacco without so much as a by-your-leave, and used to plant retaliatory allusions to him in his fiction. But by then I think he'd started not to care very much for my behaviour either. The letter had that in it, perhaps. It was strange for the trouble it took in setting 'the record straight', and for its wish to speak collectively about this misdemeanour, on behalf of 'the 4 of us'.

In 1972 came a retaliatory allusion, in his fiction, to myself. I wouldn't count it as a blow, though it was certainly a distancing. In one of his best stories, 'Dear Illusion', he writes about a sympathetic grand old poet, who explains: 'I write poetry to be able to go on living at all. Well, not quite at all, but to function as a human being.' The poet presently announces, during a dinner in his honour, that he has been a fraud, testifying that he has been no good at writing poetry. A really terrible 'modern' poem of his is quoted in corroboration, and is said to have been published in the *Listener* – which I was then editing.

Kingsley believed, as many do, that imaginative writings are a thing apart from the individual human life from which they proceed, and that biography is a sin for blurring this distinction. His own novels do not bear him out. They exhibit a fidelity to his art. Equally, they exhibit a fidelity to the circumstances of his life, and to the tenor of its confidence and anxiety, which marks him as at least as much of an autobiographer as most novelists are. His later life – as he himself made clear – and his final illness – as recounted by a biographer more interested in the record of his drinks than in the evidence of his books – brought ordeals not unlike those of Waugh's Gilbert Pinfold, spells of delusion which read like a worsening of old worries and antipathies. His books were never to succumb to his worries, and were a way of not doing so. But his opinions were to show the strain. His comedy was like, and was beholden to, Jane Austen's, as he would once have found it possible to accept. In the course of his last days, however, he gave Eric Jacobs the impression that he thought Jane Austen was no good.

The Old Devils is a novel which can undoubtedly be read as a story of his life. It is a stew of allergies and Kingsleyfications. Three at least of its elderly males resemble the author: Charlie, with his fear of the dark and his principled dislike of Dylan Thomas; famous, philandering Alun; and decent Peter. Alun is humiliated by plunging Charlie into a panic attack when he leaves him in the dark in order to philander with Mrs Charlie, and he is then killed off. Of the woman Peter is liked for liking, Peter remarks: 'One of her distinctions from other females had been that she only ran to catch buses and such, not to let the world know about her wild free spirit . . .' There is a flavour of that blue curaçao here. These free-spirit female sprints are far-fetched, and it's hard to decide whether the tease is directed at Peter or at the offendable liberal reader, or at both, or whether it isn't a tease at all and he actually believes it. Of Peter's feelings, 'the two foremost ones were remorse and self-pity. Well as he knew them both, he had never learnt how to deal with them . . .' This is a problem with which the author of Kingsley's novels became familiar.

His novels were, on balance, and if anything, even better late than early. His talent held up because it helped to hold *him* up. He had the temperament and obstinacy to turn his problems into art and to face the discomforts which this entails. These are remorseful novels, constrained, every so often, by a certain awkwardness of self-reproach. In book after book, he can seem to be blaming himself for the behaviour that was to make the Sixties famous. Very important to them were the dynamics of his first marriage, the breakdown of that marriage, and its qualified Late Shakespearean resuscitation when he shared a house with Hilly and her third husband in North London.

In his later behaviour Jacobs sees a reversion to childhood. The gratifications, the tempers, he presumably means. The play-school sessions at the Garrick, as you might say. Then back to Primrose Hill. Well, late Shakespeare has its heath too, and its fractious old fellow who can sometimes seem child-like. But there's a danger of getting lost in analogies here. The case of the late Amis is complex and mysterious. If it encompasses a child, it is a child with a capacity for self-criticism.

His art reached one of its high points with his attention to these questions in his second-last novel, *You Can't Do Both*. It is written in the plain colloquial style progressively favoured in his work, a style which incorporates the note of the hero's, and of Kingsley's, London suburb. It is no less funny, and more poignant, less awkward, than some previous self-blames. Robin Davies is the son of a vague mum and a martinet dad, who absolutely insists that if you're down to go calling with your parents in the evening you just can't go visiting a chum in the afternoon. The thing speaks for itself. You can't do both. Robin takes up with clever, conversational gay Jeremy and with nice Nancy, whom he marries, after she has narrowly escaped an abortion at the hands of a shady foreign doctor in Cardiff. When her parents object to the match, Robin's mother rides to the rescue by shedding her reserve and persuading them to behave like human beings. 'I've nothing to be proud of him for, to say the least, but I'm going to his wedding.' She throws that in to complete the rhetorical *coup de main* of persuasion, and may not mean it. But Robin has suddenly become less likeable than we may have thought. He vows to 'stay true' to his wife, but fails to do so. Nancy steals upon him as he is settling down in a hotel for a spot of adultery, and bashes him in the face. The novel ends with an ultimatum. Again he will be trying to stay true. His wife, and the novel that contains her, seem to be saying what Robin's arbitrary dad had been accustomed to say: 'You can't do both.' The novel gives a sense of the Sixties, when people couldn't do both and did both, and of the preceding post-war years. It is the story of a life, and not just Kingsley's. It is the story of an episode in the history of this country.

In October 1996, a year after Kingsley's death, a memorial service was held at which I was asked to speak. The prospect filled me with 'an odd sort of fear', to make use of some words of Kingsley's, with a subspecies of the emotion which is the subject of this chapter, but the thought of that second-last novel enabled me to take heart. I had remained fond of him, and of his books. He had been kind to me. Despite our falling-out, I was often to go on thinking of him as benign, as the man I'd known in our early days, so that limiting judgments on my part were likely to feel treacherously out of place in any speech I might make. I was able to feel that our friendship had been the victim of what was often to prove a rough and bitter time, among writers and the politically-inclined, and of literature's tending to be, at the best of times, well-stocked with fallings-out. Still, the fact was that we *had* fallen out, and that we'd ceased to be able to bear each other's opinions. Could I get up and call him the Jane Austen of our time if he'd taken, as reported, to going around joking or insisting – which? – that Jane Austen was no good? I also doubted whether he'd have wanted me to speak at his memorial service. It wouldn't have been among his gratifications.

What follows was planned for the service, and most of it was spoken there. My contribution was too bleak, I now suppose – not enough of a celebration, of the celebration it was intended to be. After the service, it was said by a former leftist, of the various contributions, that leftists had hijacked the occasion, had moved to claim Kingsley back. Tears were shed in Covent Garden, on the steps of St Martin's-in-the-Fields, on account of this snatch by the agents of Hell. My own contribution opened with an allusion to a sour remark of Larkin's, and went on to do what it could to be equal to my complicated feelings about the dead lion. Here it comes.

'It is not only possible but easy to find something nice to say about Kingsley at his memorial service, and I'm not going to resist the temptation. But it would be a mistake, and would be doing him a kind of injustice, to attempt to deny that he could be a caution, and that he had hard things to say, not all of them richly deserved, about a large number of people. He was an anxious man who was also a very confident one, and at times an intimidating one. He commanded a force of will which I can feel about me as I tread my way through this preamble, and which had in it the "invigorating coldness" relished by him, when he was young, in the works of Jane Austen.

'The funny faces he used to pull when he was young included an Evelyn Waugh face. Then the wind changed and that face became more frequent. And the day would come when he could be thought of as an angry old right-wing writer. I worked quite closely with him in the days when journalists thought of him as an angry young man, and we saw less of each other when the wind changed and our political views diverged. But I always liked and admired him, and never really recovered from catching up with his arrival on the scene as a writer of resolute taste and great intelligence who was out to make people laugh and to annoy them as well. His elders were duly annoyed. Cyril Connolly said that he could no more bring himself to laugh at his faces than he could at the blinding of Oedipus. A nice try, that, at putting him down, which was one of many such tries, scored and fumbled at the dawn of it all. But there can never have been a time when he failed to fight his corner and to make his case. It wasn't that his literary taste was never wrong, or that it never changed, though his taste changed rather less than his opinions did. What mattered in these early days was partly that it sent so clear and so authoritative a signal. He wanted writers to make sense, a revolutionary new demand, as it almost seemed at the time, and a controversial one at any time, since there will always be those who prefer vision, and other such things. He also managed to make you feel that literature is a democracy. Not everyone longs to do it, or can. But no one should be shown the door. I can't claim that he was in the habit of saying: the more the merrier. But I don't think that he wanted to say about literature, in those days, what he later said about higher education – that more would mean worse.

'He was a good poet, a good critic, and he is with the very best of the comic novelists in the English tradition. When he wrote something – provided it was not exclusively concerned with the consumption of food and drink – you ran to get to it. It was fun. It cheered you up, "cheers" being not just his way of signing off his letters but a statement of intent, and a word of his no less characteristic of him than the words "fear" and "remorse". Given the "striking panorama of horror" with which in certain moods he believed that human life was confronted, cheerfulness badly needed to break in.

'His art and his opinions were marked by a conjunction of intelligence and anxiety, to a degree which only became fully apparent in the later stages of his adult life. His novels began as an expression, and a critique, of the freedoms, the permissiveness, and of the aggressions, of their time, and worked towards a view of that first subject-matter which was to show – with no loss of the early confidence – an element of self-blame. While remaining as funny as ever, his books became in some degree penitential, if one can say so without sounding like a passage from Robert Conquest's spoof article, "Christian Symbolism in *Lucky Jim*", and without glossing over how far from regretful most manifestations of Kingsley ever were and how much he was enjoyed for not seeming regretful at all. At the latter end of this process was to occur one of his most compelling books, his second-last novel, *You Can't Do Both*, which deals, as do many of his books, with the subject of family life – and, in particular, with the question of what it is to "stay true", as the novel puts it, and to do both that and the other thing, with the question of what it is to be unable to do both and to do both.

'There are passages of his criticism in which he has points to make about comedy and hostility, and causes you to think of the confidence which enabled him to control the anxiety that confidence expressed. Two of his most re-warding critical pieces are the early essays on Jane Austen and Ivy Compton-Burnett. In the first of these, he presents well-founded objections to Jane Austen's novel *Mansfield Park*: but he also speaks up for that "invigorating coldness" of hers, a coldness sometimes indistinguishable from hostility, and has you seeing an affinity between Austen and Amis. In the second piece, he concludes, with reference to "the triviality inseparable from fantasy", that Compton-Burnett's work is rescued from this danger by her comic sense and by "a dyad composed of her hatred and her pity". He speaks of her "ability to turn out novels – two or more of which are masterpieces – that conceal under great homogeneity of tone a conglomeration of all but incongruous elements". Some part of this applies to Kingsley's novels too. There is homogeneity there, and incongruity. And there is hatred and pity there. No wonder we like him. No wonder we find him funny.

'For me, as for you, there is so much to think of when I think of Kingsley. I think of the music he listened to, of choral surges on the Maida Vale hi-fi in the days when he lived in that part of the world with Jane Howard – of Zadoc the Priest, and of Fats Domino, who found his thrill on Blueberry Hill. I think of a visit to Hilly and Kingsley in South Wales, of an excursion by the sea on the Gower Peninsula, of returning soaked to the house in Swansea, of making a lame joke about that, and of Kingsley politely laughing at it, one of his most selfless actions. And of having lunch with him years afterwards in London, in Charlotte Street, when I paid his round in order to persuade him to write for a new journal, and he went off and agreed to write instead for James Gold-smith's new journal, which did not survive. I think of the story he published in 1972, seven years before that, in which he invents the most dreadful of all imaginable modern poems and alleges that it eventually appeared in a journal I was editing at the time. And I think of his published words and of their unkind cuts and other features, choking on their nutritious images. Of his witnessing, in 1970, a permissive Church of England, "fighting to be in the forefront of her own demolition". Of his pitting Warwick Deeping against Virginia Woolf, "as regards the ability of each to describe an event in terms that make it clear what actually took place". Of the girl whose boyfriends' cars were supplied by their firms, and who mentioned this "with the sort of lift of the old proud head that he could hardly believe had not accom-panied a limiting judgment on Villiers de l'Isle Adam". Then there are the words of the poem by him which addresses an inexperienced, maritally deficient Jesus Christ, who had suffered on the Cross, but whose acquaintance with human life had not included "love, marriage, children":

> All good, but bringing some
> Risk of remorse and pain
> And fear of an odd sort:
> A sort one should, again,
> Feel, not just hear about,
> To be qualified as
> A human-race expert.
> On local life, we trust
> The resident witness,
> Not the royal tourist.

The poem has the royal shocks which he liked to deliver: "You won't get me," he says, "up on one of those things." And it has some of the words which he most needed to use in the course of his service as a resident witness, and as a cross-bearer himself. These are words which might suggest that, despite his disclaimer, he was both.'

4. Great Turnstile

ANEURIN BEVAN DIED in 1960, and when I moved to the post-Bevanite *New Statesman* the year after, it was unlikely that I would be shunned as a filthy Gaitskellite. As I've said, such a move was not surprising at a time of consensus, when a principled centre ground had held for some while, a centre ground where there was very little talk of a tax-cutting possessive individualism and where Gaitskell's arguments for government control of the commanding heights of the economy were widely respected. The features of this landscape were no longer found as distressing at Great Turnstile as they'd once been.

Consensus is often despised, on both sides of the political fence. Few people would say that they shared Margaret Thatcher's categorical preference for contention, but some who voted for her in 1979 may have been voting against this particular consensus, which had expired fifteen years earlier, and which has recently been spoken of as 'much-derided'. It was by no means as bad as all that. A politics based on a fair measure of inter-party agreement doesn't have to be any less productive than the politics of Northern Ireland.

John Freeman had just become editor of my new paper, in place of Kingsley Martin, whose literary editor had lately been Janet Adam Smith. Janet used to take the trouble of writing to people to tell them forthrightly what was wrong with their articles. Literary editors haven't always taken that, or any, trouble. Janet and I hailed from adjacent slopes of the Pentland Hills: we were Edinburgh reviewers, latterday examples of an auld Scots element in literary journalism.

The *New Statesman* began, ten years before the BBC did, in 1913. It set out to serve, and had continued to serve, the cause of democratic socialism. This had always been plain enough. But it was equally plain that the paper had contained within it an editorial tendency which was eclectic, nostalgic and, at times, for those who stood to the left of the paper, openly reactionary. A good deal of the early paper was written by gentlemen, by public-schoolboys willing to bestow consideration and compassion on lower-income Glaswegians and their like. It was felt that it was the paper's job to discuss and display an excellence capable of raising up the huddled masses. Both halves might do this. Both halves of the pantomime horse were at such times in this sense élitist. At the time of the *New Statesman*'s jubilee in 1963 a historian of the paper, perhaps put out by the changes that had been made at the back, stressed that the back had formerly been versed in the civilization of Classical antiquity and in that of France. For this élite, Glasgow had scarcely possessed a culture worth the name.

At certain times, and to a degree that transcended its division into two spheres of editorial responsibility, the

paper was two papers – as perhaps was also true of the
Spectator of the late Fifties. In both journals an Establishment and an Enlightenment could sometimes be thought
to coincide, and the *New Statesman* could be seen both as
subversive and as quite the opposite. The duality is visible
in its purported dealings with British Intelligence. Kingsley Martin is thought to have been in touch in his early
days with MI6 – such discussions have been common
enough in British journalism – and two of his associates
have been wondered about by insiders as possible Cold
War double agents, in the style commemorated by biographers of the novelist Graham Greene. These possibilities
concur with the division of loyalties, the co-presence of
conservative and iconoclastic, élitist and egalitarian strains,
which was there on the page for all to see. But they
should not prevent one from recognizing that, whatever
its complexities, and whatever the aberrations of individual contributors, this was a patriotic paper. Its patriotism
could be like that of Orwell, or of the Labour leader
Michael Foot, whose alleged KGB connections were made
to vanish into thin air, not long ago, by a threat to sue.
'This England' was derided in a feature of that name,
which consisted of a sottisier of ethnic asininities, sent in
by readers, and in other sections of the paper too. But
that could be considered part of a dialectic, of the duality
of the paper at large.

Likewise, its élitism had generally been subject to
internal challenge. But it was there, and it must have
helped to ensure that there were few sightings in the
paper, for much of his career, of Raymond Williams,
whose conception of a common culture was far from

presenting the working class as culturally-disadvantaged; and it entailed that there should take place, at the front, in 1963, an attack by Paul Johnson on the Beatles, on their dreadful music and dreadful proletarian fans. The article occasioned my only trip downstairs on a mission of protest to the editor's office. The protest was diplomatically fielded, and John Freeman went on to become Harold Wilson's Ambassador to India.

In 1961, a letter to the paper found fault with a reference by one of its writers to the existence of a 'real if often raw culture of working-class life', and proceeded to say, with university students in mind, that 'the boy or girl who has known what working-class life is makes no such claims for it.' The letter came from the poet and academic Donald Davie, who would not hear of such a thing as an actually existing working-class culture. My own view was and is that this thing exists, that it contributes to a national culture, and that it need not be thought incompatible with an interest in the writings of Donald Davie.

His letter belongs to the long history of the battle between classics and commercials, 'serious' music and pop music, literature and the best-seller – a terminology which has assisted those devoted in the matter to notions of hierarchy and authority to prejudge the issues it raises. It was a matter which had at this point become sharply divisive. There were élitists at the back of the paper, where we had no desire to abolish the literary canon; the paper could, in fact, be regarded by many as having in the past been a canonical stronghold, rather more than it had ever been, politically, a revolutionary one. But now there were also people at the back who liked the popular arts, and who thought in terms of a general culture sustained by mutually enlivening subcultures, in terms of a spectrum of taste. Highbrow praise of the Beatles raised its cry – quaint-seeming, no doubt, in retrospect, but the struggle continues in which it was a bid to intercede. Somewhat deterred, the old notions of an élite culture, of outright division, and of seriousness and superiority, survive. For my own part, I wanted the popular arts to be enfolded in the amalgamations, the integration, which was a large part of the point, as I saw it, of weekly journals and of their book sections: but I was never able, either on the *New Statesman* or elsewhere, to take this project as far as I hoped. I had been kissed, after all, had I not, by the star of the small-circulation hard-cover book.

Circulation of the *New Statesman* rose in the Sixties to a peak of around 100,000. Under Kingsley Martin, the paper backed the cause of unilateral nuclear disarmament, and in later modifying this stance, it was held to have lost its Hampstead constituency, among other sections of the *bien-pensant* Left, and in consequence to have lost its way. This is not an opinion which can be confirmed by looking at the circulation figures for the mid-Sixties, but it isn't without substance. It became necessary to make up for lost appeal, or for a putative lost appeal, by discovering a new way, new causes, some new magic. When Wilson became leader of the Labour Party the journal supported him, but then broke with him over his support, as Prime Minister, for the American war effort in Vietnam, which it had initially seen in terms of a containment of international Communism. His predecessor as leader of the Party, Gaitskell, is only very faintly remembered at present, and there may be those who would be puzzled by the suggestion that the betrayer of socialism was distinctly to the left of Tony Blair, if not, indeed, of Harold Wilson. The paper praised him at the time of his death in 1963, while remarking, at the front, that his fault had been to split his party. The most feeling tribute was paid, at the back, by Conor Cruise O'Brien, who took his tone from a tram-driver whom he'd met in an Irish pub at the time of Suez, and who thought well of this foreigner Gaitskell. 'You can't beat an Englishman,' said O'Brien's source. 'When he's straight.'

From the late Fifties onwards, sexual liberation, pop music and the emergence of a youth culture invaded and divided the outlook expressed in weekly papers. A concern with the first of these came later to the front half of the *New Statesman* than it did to the back, at a time when the principal word for copulation was still excluded from dictionaries. Early in the Sixties a think-piece at the front asserted that virginity was a girl's best friend, and leader-writers there were not inclined to wrap in the duffel-coat of liberation the philandering Tory minister John Profumo, who had shared a girlfriend with a Russian spy. Public men saw his conduct as a serious matter, and arranged for his friend Stephen Ward to be the victim of trumped-up charges, which led to his suicide: *New Statesman* book reviewers were right to protest about this.

When the issue of Europe, and Wilson's manoeuvres in relation to Britain's entry, appeared on the agenda, a prophecy was credited in the paper to the British Empire press magnate Beaverbrook, who was quick to disown it. The prophecy was one which tickled the *New Statesman* at the time, and might seem at present to have gained in cogency with the years: British accession would prove to be 'an economic Munich which would be surely followed by an economic Dunkirk'. European unity could be seen by the paper as solely a mercantilist project, and when Gaitskell died he was commended there for having tried to keep Britain out. On Europe, as on the Vietnam War, the paper displayed some of the uncertainty which it had displayed over the diplomatic Munich which happened in 1938. Nuclear disarmament remained high on the agenda, as did John Kennedy, viewed in hope as a kind of tough young left-winger. The political part of the paper was drawn to toughness, on certain subjects. In dealing with race relations, however, it was consensually tender – the consensus here being one that encompassed the liberal press, the Labour Left and the political centre ground, though not, as it turned out, the polity as a whole. I would imagine that many back-half contributors wanted out of the Cold War they'd been experiencing, and into a Europe of common purposes and diminished sovereignties.

Both papers stood for a repeal of the obscenity laws, and for the licensing of Lady Chatterley and Fanny Hill, those ill-assorted sisters. I entered the witness-box during the second of these trials, to be foxed by Mervyn Griffith-Jones, the living breath of banning and subordination, who'd been into back-numbers of the paper to smoke out past tolerances of censorship on the part of its contributors, and who attempted to break the jury's heart by reminding them of the books a man might not want his wife and servants to read. Here was 'This England' in person.

A dispute about Yeats arose on the *New Statesman* when William Empson opposed an essay by O'Brien ascribing to the poet a fascist political outlook and practice. They were agreed, though, in favouring a conspiratorial interpretation of John Kennedy's murder, with Lee Harvey Oswald in the role of dupe: this is a controversy which is still running, and which has come round to representing their view as less romantic than it may have appeared to the tough-minded of that time.

Nineteen sixty-three was an eventful year of departures and of turning tides: Kennedy killed, Gaitskell dead, Wilson elected Labour leader, Macmillan and Profumo gone from office, the spy Philby gone to Russia. It was the year in which Britain was refused entry to the Common Market, and in which, according to Philip Larkin and under protest from Paul Johnson, sexual intercourse began. And it was a year in which I'd like to think that the method we'd developed for the back of the paper worked successfully, and that a union of politics and literature was consummated in the books and arts pages. Conor Cruise O'Brien, expert in both politics and literature, celebrated the paper's jubilee by publishing, at the back, a critique of its vacillations on Appeasement – the diplomatic Munich of 1938. The *New Statesman* used to be known as 'The Staggers', with reference, no doubt, to such vacillations, and to the rumour that its staff had been paid in roubles to stagger about a bit on behalf of a vacillating international

Communism, and, perhaps, to the pantomime shamble
and shuffle of its front and back halves. It is to the credit
of John Freeman and Kingsley Martin, who was editor at
the time and was still on the scene as an editor emeritus,
that O'Brien's Munich piece was carried without demur.
It was accompanied by a piece by Empson on Falstaff and
Auden, who, said the ever-so-slightly Falstaffian Empson,
'regards the old brute as a saint'. This was in April. In
May, shortly after seeing his great light in the sky, and
decades before such arguments became publicly familiar,
Dick Crossman took a line he'd pursued during the war,
in arguing against the destruction of Dresden by British
bombers; and V. S. Pritchett wrote in the same issue
about the 'conversational criticism' carried on by contributors to the old back part of the journal. It was a journal,
he was happy to recall, which had 'always been torn in
half'.

Victor Pritchett was a veteran of the *New Statesman*'s
literary coverage, and a critic whose rapport with the
general reader, at this level of journalism, was beyond
compare. We were leery of one another initially, and he
would allude to my young prig's talks with contributors
as 'Mrs Miller's sewing sessions'. But we grew to be
friends. He once sent me a postcard from abroad, of a
cow, with a request for books to review: 'nothing to
browse on'. He *liked* books, at a time when newcomers in
literary journalism were blamed for disliking them and
for being philistine. Another *New Statesman* totem, J. B.
Priestley, said that, like Leavis, I 'hated literature'. For
Priestley, the sewing sessions were ones that Madame
Defarge might have conducted.

There were two Christmas numbers in 1963. In the first Eric Hobsbawm discussed E. P. Thompson's *Making of the English Working Class*; a magnificent new iconoclast, Brigid Brophy, discussed the new how-to-do-it literature of love-making; Christopher Ricks praised Kingsley Amis's novel, *One Fat Englishman*, and the sliver-thin Viennese Hans Keller praised Tottenham Hotspur. Both Hobsbawm and Keller could be considered bi-part people like O'Brien: Keller wrote about music and about sport, while Hobsbawm was a historian who also wrote about jazz. In the second of these Christmas numbers Brigid Brophy attempted to slay the dragon of Ivy Compton-Burnett. This was a good year for the journal. Its small staff pulled together in their separate ways and pushed forward at the stroke of the cartoonist Vicky, whose 'earpiece' cover drawings used to decorate the top left-hand corner of a concise and elegant format.

Two years after that saw another good spell. In the issue of 14 January 1966 O'Brien gave his opinion of President Kennedy's assassination, and Kingsley Amis detected, as others have not, a fulsome Edmund Wilson, who does at least stop short, conceded Amis, of admiring 'the American post-war writers'. There was Gilbert Ryle on Stuart Hampshire, Robert Taubman on Queenie Leavis, Alan Taylor on Kingsley Martin. Taylor was an old *New Statesman* hand with whom I went on working with pleasure, on this paper and that, for the rest of his spunky life – his love for Lord Beaverbrook our only cloud. Also present, in the severity of his youth and at the outset of an excellent career in literary journalism, was Ian Hamilton, who became a big friend of mine.

The following month Vicky took his life, to the dismay of many people. An underrater of de Gaulle, whom he drew as a Louis XIV museum-piece captioned *L'état c'est moi*; and an underrater of Gaitskell, whom he drew as a prissy little face peering out between Supermac and the matchstick children of the Third World. But an artist and journalist of wonderful abilities.

Three months after that, Malcolm Muggeridge announced his conversion to religion in the front of the paper, where changes had been made when Paul Johnson took over as editor during the previous year. I resigned at the end of 1966. I was to the right of the paper when I went in and to the left of it when I came out. Some of those at the front had once been to the left of left: but now there were pieces from the born-again, once progressive and permissive Muggeridge claiming that socialism and liberalism were responsible for Stalin's mass murders. Two years after my departure, in discussing the events of May '68 in Paris, the paper staggered back to proclaiming Daniel Cohn-Bendit 'this jovial young Robespierre'.

My most vivid memory of my days on the journal is of the sight of Seamus Heaney's typescripts, meekly attended by a stamped and addressed envelope for their return. So far from hating literature, we were as eager as could be to find it, and here was a new writer whom we knew we should publish at the earliest possible moment. One of the poems had him watching his father dig the controversial Northern Irish soil:

> Between my finger and my thumb
> The squat pen rests; snug as a gun.

At the end of the poem he says he'll dig with that pen, instead of his father's spade. He doesn't speak of firing that gun. Apart from early marching songs on behalf of the Catholic community in Northern Ireland, he has never been a warrior poet or a politician poet: but he has been there when guns and bombs were going off. He has known what it was to have his address published, in 1972, in a Paisleyite newspaper, the *Protestant Telegraph*; a man he knows, a close friend, has just been killed by Loyalist paramilitaries. And his poems can't be understood without a sense of the troubles contemporary with them. The poem's otherwise incongruous gun arouses that sense, in premonitory fashion, and in so doing testifies to the union of politics and letters which was in mind both for the *New Statesman* as a whole and for the second half of it, where he was to write in prose about the troubles, gentle bulletins which gave fair warning of the barricades which were going up.

When Heaney was awarded the Nobel Prize for Literature in 1995, A. Alvarez told the *Guardian*: 'He's very, very good but relatively small-scale.' What kind of scale is it that would register as small something that was very, very good? It is the one that critics use, with its low ratings and its shades of disparagement. Alvarez has long held this view of Heaney's work; it must have seemed an appropriate time to come out with it again. And critics have long been accustomed to come out with such views. This one particularly and piquantly resembles the 'critical comment' that used to be deployed – to put people down, as it were, or to keep them out – in the judgmental 1950s.

Criticism has been expected both to make judgments and to avoid them, and as this might suggest, judgment has more than one face. It can mean measurement, assessment. It can mean punishment. It can mean intelligence, discrimination, the weighing of one consideration against another. It can mean both action and contemplation. It can encourage commitment, engagement, the cultivation of a political point of view, and it can inspire a distrust of all that. T. S. Eliot thought that literary journalism should be disinterested, objective, without politics, and that the treasonable clerks who disagreed were carbuncular. The two book sections I've been talking about were not disinterested, any more than Eliot himself was, in his capacity as literary journalist, and one part of what some of us came to be interested in expressing was an opposition to certain features of Eliot's journalism — to the politics, prejudice, and mugwump pretence of impersonality, that we were to discover there.

5. A House for V. S. Naipaul

V. S. NAIPAUL'S NOVEL *A House for Mr Biswas* was published, in London, in 1961, which was the year when I joined the *New Statesman*, where he was working as a reviewer of novels. We became friends, save for an intermission due, I think, to my giving offence by smoking an imperial cigar (actually, a humble Wills Castella) during a conversation with him in the office. I also became a lifelong friend of Mr Biswas. No intermission there.

A year later, far away in the West Indies, next door to Andrew Marvell's 'remote Bermudas', Trinidad and Tobago became an independent nation, and a member of the Commonwealth – of the alliance between the mother country and her former colonies which promoted during the last days of the British Empire. It was a time for new countries – for liberation. But also for restraint. Shortly before this, in Africa, Rwanda had emerged from Belgian control, while in London the Commonwealth Immigrants Act had been passed – a measure designed to limit the admission of those who wished to leave the West Indies and come to Britain with their black and brown faces to fill the jobs that needed to be filled. Had he not already moved to Britain, the measure might have excluded V. S. Naipaul. He had arrived in 1950, an eighteen-year-old from Trinidad, one of a family of high-caste Hindu stock, Brahmins who had moved in the course of the previous century, as indentured labour, from India's Gangetic plain to the Spanish Main, as remote to these wanderers as it had been to Andrew Marvell. Naipaul was soon to become what could then be called in Britain, sometimes with a hint of condescension, a Commonwealth writer. Many years later, many books later, he was knighted. In 1993 he received the first David Cohen Award, bestowed in London for a lifetime's services to 'British literature'.

His many books are a rich accumulation, and an order of events has to be borne in mind for his writings if their idiosyncrasies and opposing qualities are to be understood. A pattern of exile and emigration, departure and return, hostility and sympathy and reconciliation, can be assigned to the big book of their accumulation – to the whole endeavour. The three books which preceded *Biswas*, two novels and a collection of stories, were really lovely pieces of work – and play – which could be interpreted in Europe and America as a celebration of West Indian life, and as an unheard-of elegance and civility from the back of beyond. Here was another comedy of manners which was not remote from that of Jane Austen. It contains a bride of whom it is said that all she needs to keep her 'straight as a arrow is a little blows every now and then': this remark, made by a wise woman in the vicinity, carries a breath of Austen's irony. It also repeats an irony that appears in a story by Naipaul's father, Seepersad: 'It would be a fine world if a man could not beat his own wife!' The West Indian world celebrated in these books by V. S. Naipaul is a fine one in which a man is expected to beat his wife, and in which there is poverty and cruelty.

Naipaul's is, as he says, a 'many-sided background'. His art originates in Trinidad's Hindu community. But it also originates in the world-wide English-speaking culture to which he was led by his schooling – a schooling that equipped him to shine at Oxford, where his abilities as an Anglo-Saxonist were praised by Tolkien – and by his father's example. His life has entailed a move from the periphery to a centre of things in the metropolitan West, a move which has been represented, and which he himself has sometimes chosen to represent, in a politically contro-versial light. He felt that in order to be a writer he had to quit the West Indies for Europe. But it could also be claimed that he was already a writer when he left, and that the West Indies had made him one, as Mantua made Virgil. Perhaps there is another poet with whom he could be compared – Robert Burns, who grew up with thatched cottages, hovels and animals, much as the peasants in Seepersad Naipaul's stories do. But he did not have to travel to Edinburgh in order to become a contributor to the literature of his time. Poetry came with the thatch. Hard times did too, of course, and an early death.

A House for Mr Biswas shares with Naipaul's three previous books some of the ingredients of a festive, commemorative approach. But the comedy has darkened; there are hard times here, and no desire to make light of them, or to make fun of them. Nevertheless, the novel has a buoyancy of spirit which goes well with its act of homage. The novel is a homage to Naipaul's father, who advised him to write this sort of book. 'Be realistic, humorous when this comes in pat, but don't make it deliberately so. If you are at a loss for a theme, take me for it. Begin: "He sat before the little table writing down the animal counterparts of all his wife's family."' Dispatched to his son in London, the advice was that of a writer of excellent tales, scenes from expatriate Hindu life, which were full of promptings for the author of *Biswas*, who took his father for a theme and whose hero owns a repertoire of derision which includes animal counterparts of his wife's family.

Seepersad's autobiographical tale 'They named him Mohun' – a name long ago conferred by cowgirls on the god Krishna – tells of an inauspicious arrival in the world at the 'unseemly' hour of midnight, and of a 'cruelly mingy' father. This name and a version of this bad start are incorporated in V. S. Naipaul's novel, which then proceeds to trace the course of Mr Biswas' life. Before very long he is married, and enveloped in the life of Hanuman House, so called after the eminent Monkey God. Hanuman House is the stronghold of his wife Shama's kin, the dynastic Tulsis, the seat of a micro-politics of the extended family – preferred in the novel to the pre-Independence politics of the island at large, where the Tulsis' originals had a role. Then come his stint as a shopkeeper at The Chase, where he falls foul of the law and of the stick-fighter Mungroo, and his ensuing sojourns, shifts and calamities: his time at Green Vale, where he builds a house which is washed away in a cataclysmic storm; a spell on the estate at Shorthills, where his house is reduced to charcoal; a flit to the Tulsi house in Port of Spain. Also in store are a son and three daughters; his work as a journalist on the *Sentinel*; his purchase of the rickety house on Sikkim Street – a house of his own, over which he has been cheated and which plunges him into endless yet seemingly weightless debt; his illness and premature death. Mohun Biswas might be regarded as a simplified version of Seepersad Naipaul. He would not, perhaps, have been equal to Seepersad's stories; it is a shade difficult to think of him communicating Seepersad's interest in Conrad and Aldous Huxley. There may be a connection here with Naipaul's later division of the world into simple and complex societies. But this simplification is not such as to diminish Mr Biswas. He is interesting, appealing, gifted, funny, fussy, cross, wrong, right, lifelike.

It was at this point in his career that Naipaul began to diversify, to publish travel books and histories. Both his fiction and his non-fiction were to prove, by and large, strongly autobiographical in tendency, though the distressed romantic solitary who performed some of the earlier journeys was, in time, to efface himself, to make way for informants, skilfully and patiently interviewed and assessed. The middle part of his writing life incorporates a series of descriptions of 'Third World' countries – some of which, like his own Caribbean background, have been ranked by him with what he terms 'the Conradian dark places of the earth'. This ranking suggests that the earth has yet to say goodbye to the colonial dereliction pictured at its worst in Conrad's story 'The Outpost of

Progress' and in *Heart of Darkness* – where Marlow strikingly suggests that the dark places of the earth had once included London, and might do so again.

Short as were most of his stays in these dark places, they inspired searching and informative accounts – accounts, however, which have exposed him to criticism. Opponents of his work are more inclined to be offended by his non-fiction than by his fiction, and their objections are in part expressive of a difference of political outlook. The novel *Guerrillas* – both factual and fictional, as so much of his writing is – would seem to have confronted some of these opponents with an inadmissible scepticism about political action, and a jaundiced view of Third World leaders and revolutionaries, rather than a powerful and plausible work of the imagination. There are opponents who must be inclined to class him with those British writers of the Fifties who were subsequently discovered to have turned to the right. His writings were experienced as left-wing in the Fifties, by readers sympathetic to the 'emergent countries', the former colonies, of the day, and could be experienced as something different in the Seventies and Eighties – by readers nostalgic for empire and disposed to learn that such countries were now boring or afflicted, backwaters or hell-holes. We may say that the times had changed. May we say that his writings had changed too?

In a postscript to one of the books of his middle period, *The Loss of El Dorado* (1969), a chronicle of exploitation and revolution, of adventurers and their victims, of the installation in Trinidad of a British Empire of blacks, plantations and instruments of torture, he lets fall the remark: 'To be a victim is also to be absurd.' Did he mean by this what the Scottish Whig Francis Jeffrey meant when he said in the nineteenth century what the poet Juvenal had said long before – that poverty makes men ridiculous? Naipaul is playing with opposites here – cruelty and humour, slavery and absurdity. Bringing them together, watching them spring apart. And it can be said that, in one way or another, this often happens in his books. The difficulty of being quite certain, initially, of this particular remark is a difficulty which recurs in his writings, some of which can seem both cruel and kind.

The remark can, in fact, be fathomed as compassionate, and seen to belong to writings which are charged with compassion, and with a feeling for poverty. Naipaul can none the less be held to have surrendered his hostages to fortune by speaking as he sometimes does of the 'small lives' led in 'small houses' at the ends of the earth, by speaking of the dark places of the earth, of its areas of darkness, where no one knows what is going on, where there is not much hope, where liberations and revolutions fail and are fraudulent, where an old order gives way to a new one that is worse.

On such occasions we come face to face with the Naipaul hauteur and scepticism, which are not always what they seem, which can be found to accompany, and to mediate, a compassionate concern. They have helped to surround him with an aura, and an apocrypha of funny-intimidating stories. But there is nothing apocryphal about his inclination to say that there are societies which are doomed, places which are blanks – sans history, sans politics, the people there given over to a mimicry of the

metropolis. The novelist Paul Theroux, who was with
Naipaul in a disrupted Uganda, rather as one might once
have been said to have been with Kitchener at Khartoum,
has recalled his companion's joking use of the pet name
'Infy', for inferior, and he is unlikely to have made that
up or got it wrong. Black people can attract black jokes
in Naipaul, and the absurdities attributed to them, it has
been supposed, are those that a West Indian Brahmin
might perceive. The same sort of observer has been
recognized in this writer's special distaste for the unclean
or impure ('tainted' is one of the most alarming words in
Naipaul's vocabulary), and in his taste for a pessimistic
cultivation of uncertainty, of Conradian mystery. He is
known for his detachment, for his distrust of simplifying
political causes, and there are moods of his which can
bring to mind an approximation to the fatalism or
quietism, the submission to karma, whose manifestations
are criticized in the second of his three India books, where
a stasis reckoned to have overtaken the Gandhian tradition
is discussed.

There would seem to be a good deal in the subconti-
nent to which his writings return an echo. The 'darkness'
that was India, when Naipaul was a boy, was never to be
entirely dispelled by his travels in the region, but there is
no mistaking the fascination which the country has held
for him. Within the darkness of India lay a further
darkness that had to do with difference of caste, with the
hierarchy of caste. The author of *An Area of Darkness*, the
first of his India books, refers, in the second, to a novel
about the Brahmin experience of the modern world, by
U. R. Anantamurti, in which a spiritual leader, a collector

of impurities, refers to inferiors as 'men of darkness', and these two somewhat different uses of the word might be thought – if only by opponents of his work – to call to one another. There is a limit, though, to the ethnicity that can be ascribed to his work. His detachment is not just an Eastern detachment. Apparent there too is the devotee of a romantic isolation, someone who is neither a Hindu nor a Trinidadian. Nor, for that matter, an Englishman.

He has spent his later years in the English peace and quiet of Wiltshire. For much of the time he occupied a cottage on the estate of a becalmed and unequivocally isolated eccentric, glimpsed but never spoken to by his tenant. A strange conjunction of recluses took place in this *solitude à deux* – with the estate a far cry from 'places like Trinidad, where the word "estate", when I first got to know it, especially if it was a sugar estate, didn't hold any idea of grandeur or style, carrying connotations instead only of size and sameness, and many small lives and small houses at the edges.' In 1990, a woman with an Indian name wrote to the *London Review of Books* from an address in Wiltshire to say this:

Naipaul is a good example of an Indian who has become a brown Englishman as a result of his youthful exposure to a typical colonial education, transmitted out of context to uncritical and passive clients, victims of unrecognized and much-prized Imperial propaganda. Many recipients of such an education internalized Imperial, British values underpinned by belief in the inherent superiority of European civilization. Such cultural hybrids, whose mental landscapes were permanently colonized by the English language and English literary culture, would almost inevitably feel themselves to be misfits in their indigenous culture, distanced and alienated by a superimposed sensibility.

'Hybrids' could almost be felt to have the force of 'halfbreeds' here. Malathy Sitaram's hard words – those, surely, of a seasoned and responsive student of English literature, as well as a resident of Wiltshire – look like the preamble to a diatribe of 1992 by Rob Nixon, entitled *London Calling*. Nixon, originally South African, accuses Naipaul of inhabiting, in his non-fiction, a fictitious solitude which both transmits and dissembles a commitment to hegemonic Western values, to the metropolitan preconceptions of London and New York, where his success as a writer was first secured. A year or two before that, a similar argument had been pursued in a book by Selwyn Cudjoe, a writer of West Indian background who approves of Naipaul's early work while believing that he has chosen 'to accept the ideology of the colonizer', and deploring 'the misanthrope that he has become'.

There are those for whom Naipaul stands revealed, in certain of his dimensions, as politically incorrect – hopelessly incorrect, one might say, remembering a story that used to be told of him by West Indian friends. Asked on the telephone if he was coloured, by an English landlady to whom he was applying in his youth for a room, he was said to have replied: 'Hopelessly.' This is not a story which shows him sorrowing or apologizing; the reply is a patrician joke, which may (if uttered) have meant, among other things, that there wasn't much hope for the landlady. In one sense, for all his honours, he has moved from knowing about rebuff to knowing about censure. He is a retiring man who can't be said to have led a sheltered life.

The case against him deserves to be acknowledged, even (or especially) by readers who believe that his work is unlikely to be badly damaged by it. It tends to leave out, however, much of what he puts into his books. Above all, it leaves out the compassion they have in them. 'Hate oppression; fear the oppressed,' runs a dictum from his novel *The Mimic Men*, and Naipaul does both. The case against him can come close to indicating that there is something wrong not only with European civilization but with all moves from the periphery to the centre. As Malathy Sitaram, Rob Nixon and Selwyn Cudjoe may themselves have found, there can be good reasons for making such moves, disturbing though they often are for those who make them, and harmful though they may be in aggregate for the places left behind. And it is also true that Naipaul's writings have done something for the periphery. Biswas listens to the human sounds 'thrown up at the starlit sky from a place that was nowhere, a dot on the map of the island, which was a dot on the map of the world'. Naipaul's books have done something for these dots. They have contributed to the somewheres they describe, as they have to the English literature which made his books possible.

In doing the second of these things, they pay tribute to the literary culture which enabled his father, starting out in the midst of Trinidad's Hindi-speaking Little

India, to write his excellent English stories, and which, whatever its defects and for all its services to the British Empire, has been a source of happiness and strength for human beings throughout the world. Naipaul's mystic masseur, in the novel of that name, a man who is a bit like Mr Biswas while also a hustler who will one day be honoured by the Queen of England, sends away, in darkest Trinidad, for his Everyman's Library books ('Night and day he reading'), and then, forty years on, Naipaul's *Mr Biswas* was to appear as an Everyman: this, too, is a tribute to the culture in question. There is something here to be set against the ingesting of metropolitan preconceptions.

It is also the case that there are dark places of the earth which are as dark as he says they are and as few other writers have been prepared to find out for themselves. There is much that has still to be told, and much that will never be told, about latterday social and political failure in out-of-the-way parts of the world, and about the looting and carnage which have happened to the emergent countries of the Sixties, and to many more of the world's vulnerable countries. Vulnerability has many faces: it is the disappeared of Argentina, a country visited and discussed by Naipaul, and it is the mass-murdered of Rwanda, who have gone on being mass-murdered over the years, and who can be allotted a presence, under other names, in his African fictions. On the subject of deprivation, and of the oppressed, and of their capacity to become oppressors, severity has had its home truths to tell.

None of this is to deny, however, that it was reasonable to object to *Guerrillas*, for example, with its fake revolutionaries, for appearing to say, in 1975, that there was nothing to be done with the emergent country where the fake revolution is enacted. What were other countries doing with themselves? It was as if the West had let him down by shrinking to the condition of one of his peripheries, one of his emergent countries, by coming up with its own somnambulistic states of emergency and of economic arrest, its racial tensions and brutalities, its enigmas, its own barely understandable crises glimpsed out of the corner of an eye. In 1975 it seemed to me as if there might be a trouble for Naipaul in the West's appearing to have become an area of darkness, and it has since grown clearer still that European civilization is no longer what it was taken to be, by some of those on the periphery, in the Fifties. But it is also true that, on his arrival in the West, Naipaul lost no time in spotting its deficiencies, and in becoming aware of the deficiencies of his own youthful admiration for it.

Since first occasioning these reproaches, he has been seen to relent. Not that he has expressly conceded to the arguments against him. Nor has he altogether abandoned the acerbity of approach to be found in the writings of the middle period that dates from *The Middle Passage*, his first travel book, whose title is taken from the name for the Negro slave's Atlantic transit into bondage. Nor would it be right to stigmatize the writings of the middle period as lacking in compassion: *The Loss of El Dorado* is a deeply compassionate book. But he is thought to have changed some of his ways in the course of the Seventies. Mythic and ethnocentric – Indian, arguably, in its attitude to Africa and to the wanderings of its hero – the novel of

1979, *A Bend in the River*, is neither phobic nor gratuitously severe in its dealings with individual Africans, or indeed with the regime of the black 'big man' in power by the bend in the river – the same river that flows through Conrad's *Heart of Darkness*. In *A Turn in the South* (1989) the Americans he meets are treated in a kindly manner, and the emergence of the country's blacks from their history of servitude and segregation is movingly commemorated, with marked sympathy for their consoling religions. This has not protected him from the charge of neglecting areas of darkness in the country his Americans inhabit – most of them at a pastoral remove from those areas. An unexpired prejudice in favour of the West has been suspected.

He has certainly changed his mind about his ancestral India in the course of his visits to that country. The third of his books on the subject, *India: A Million Mutinies Now* (1990), is a departure from the highly authorial, comic, complaining, taint-fearing manner of his enjoyable *An Area of Darkness*, and from the bleakness of the prognosis embodied in *India: A Wounded Civilization*, which was written at the time of Mrs Gandhi's State of Emergency. The interview technique progressively employed in his non-fiction delivers here a multitudinous testimony – drawn mostly, to be sure, from the comparatively prosperous – and the distress caused him in the earlier accounts by India's millions of victims, by Indian suffering, and by the sheer volume of Indian inconvenience, cedes to a sympathy with his informants. A woman tells him that 'male ego is the most hideous thing in our present society', and Naipaul's book makes clear what it is that has caused her to speak as she does. He now thinks that an ancient self has been restored in India, that Indians have attained a new freedom and self-consciousness in the course of the past century, which he hopes will withstand the rage and fanaticism that continue to threaten the country. A sanguine Naipaul makes an appearance in this book, in which he speaks no longer of 'the intellectual second-rateness' of India, and shows no signs of believing, as he had once seemed to do, that Indians – R. K. Narayan apart – are temperamentally unsuited to writing novels.

Two notable later works illustrate both change and persistence. Each of them is both a novel and a memoir, each a sequence of lightly fictionalized retrospects of his own life. *The Enigma of Arrival*, published in 1987, celebrates his Wiltshire years: a romantic solitary reflects on his work, his walks, on his few neighbours – simple people made subtly interesting – in a river valley near Salisbury and Stonehenge. His landlord is glimpsed. There is a devotion to plants and landscape, and quite a lot of lingering: but the book keeps going, and thrives, by virtue of a kind of Wordsworthian fidelity to an experience of country life, an exotic country life by which he has come to be possessed. The old hauteur has not gone: there is the hint that servants may be 'neutered' by their occupation, and a neighbour is incongruously beautiful – her looks 'extraordinary in a woman of her station'. But the scene is sufficiently far from the anxieties of poverty and race as to seem, for much of the time, pastoral. Here – though with relatively little in the way of idyll or ornament – is his shepherd's calendar.

A Way in the World (1994) opens with memories of his youth in Port of Spain, with his stint as a clerk at the Red House, an administrative centre, a registry. He has just left school and is about to go off to Oxford. The time is 1949, a time of hope for the scholarship boy and for the island, where a politics of liberation is gaining ground: the boy is able to feel that 'the world is beginning to change'. There is a passage about his upbringing which is bound to appeal to the reader of *Biswas*. He walks with his father through the town centre, with its complement of homeless Indians.

> These people were without money, job, without anything like a family, without the English language; without any kind of representation. They were utterly destitute. They were people who had been, as in a fairy story, lifted up from the peasantry of India and set down thousands of miles away – weeks and weeks of sailing – in Trinidad. In the colonial setting of Trinidad, where rights were limited, you could have done anything with these people; and they were tormented by the people of the town.

Not long afterwards he mentions an admiring book about the island and its new politics, a good book, deemed at the time to be an encouraging display of attention from a British visitor, which is lacking in that 'sense of the absurd', that 'idea of comedy', native to the people known to the young Naipaul. Their 'true position', moreover, is misrepresented by the visitor. 'The social depth he gave to ordinary people didn't make sense.' It may be thought that with this we are back on the Naipaulian periphery, though the Indians seen in the square have scarcely been dismissed or demeaned by the summary of their plight, a summary that reminds one of how tenderly Naipaul can write of his nobodies and nothings. The scene could nevertheless well appear to be as dark as one of the small countries depicted at an earlier point in Naipaul's career, as dark as a peripheral scene from his middle years; and the impression may for some readers seem to be confirmed when they notice that the book is built to accommodate the activities of three successive sham liberators – more or less ineffectual revolutionaries, at any rate – two of whom are based, one presumes, on real West Indians. The third is the nineteenth-century freedom-fighter and colonial drifter, Bolivar's confederate Francisco Miranda, who had figured earlier in *The Loss of El Dorado*. All three are associated with absurdity and disaster – though Bolivar's revolution is widely thought to have succeeded, with the emergence of various countries from what was left of the Spanish Empire. Despite such persistences, however, a change can be detected in the book.

This is a more benign West Indies than the one to be met with in Naipaul's middle period. His revolutionaries go uncondemned, and the isolation which surrounds them can call to mind the moods of authorial isolation which have come and gone in the products of his writing life. They have more of his sympathy than the condemned man, the phantasmagoric rebel Jimmy Ahmed, receives in *Guerrillas*, though in that novel, too, a question of fellow-feeling could be thought to arise. This is a book about the West Indies which is at all points a book about

Naipaul. Contrary to his practice in several of the later books, he inserts himself here, inserts his own history, in the history of the Caribbean first told – without him, so to speak – in *The Loss of El Dorado*.

Such is the environment, the before and after, of what many consider to be V. S. Naipaul's best book, the one about Mohun Biswas, whose creation came ten years after that time of hope in the late Forties, and was to coincide with the creation of an independent Trinidad. When the novel made its first impact, it was natural for the hopeful, as for most readers, to notice a connection between the two creations. The acquisition of a house for Mr Biswas could be interpreted as the advent of a free country. The novel could be thought to express the defeat of an old by a new order, and the Tulsis to resemble the British Empire, with the senior female, 'the old queen', a not so distant relative of that other old queen, Victoria. Naipaul's books up to his novel of 1967, *The Mimic Men* – in which the new nations of the day are severely regarded – could then be thought to define the transition from colonialism to a problematical independence. When *Biswas* is read now, these many years later, the triumphal connection may seem less pronounced: some sense of it, however, is bound to survive. What is undoubtedly the case is that the objections which have been raised to the metropolitan bias in his work can find very little lodgement in this novel of 1961. Mention is made of 'nondescript' people, of nonentities. But none of the people in the book is other than a human being.

The chief human being is Mr Biswas himself, the novel's dominant image that of its hero stretched out in vest and pants on his Slumberking mattress, crooning his exotic song, 'In the snowy and the blowy . . .', his calves swinging like hammocks, in contrast with the tough legs of the Tulsis, his wife Shama's extended family. He wants, in his injudicious and stumbling fashion, to be shot of the Tulsis, and to live, with his nuclear family, a life of his own. At the start of the book, which previews the end of the story, we hear that Shama has ceased to run to her mother for help, which would at one time have been her first thought. Late in the book we hear that Biswas has longed for her to depend on him. His house is frail, and heavily mortgaged, and his victory coincides with an early death. But something has been accomplished, against the odds.

In his study of Naipaul's earlier work, Landeg White has written impressively about the conclusion of the novel: 'Achievement and failure are aspects of a single experience.' This seems like a good description of the political independence that has come to the new countries of the twentieth century. Landeg White goes on: 'The truth lies in the paradox, and the house is the image of that paradox.' The paradoxical in Naipaul is as much a matter of his own complexities as it is of those that can be assigned to his dominant themes, and to the emergent country he describes and redescribes, and it is a feature of some of his most compelling passages. Opposites coincide there. Extremes meet. Achievement and failure can be found in one another's arms, and so can sympathy and contempt, scorn and pity.

In *A House for Mr Biswas* Naipaul exhibits a judicious feeling for his hero, and is wholly unsentimental about him. His hero's humour can be as barbed as the behaviour of any of the satraps and memsahibs of Hanuman House, which resounds with quarrels and exclusions. Halfway through the novel Shama remembers the 'old warmth' she had felt there – a tribute of a kind, which has to be respected, and which reminds the reader that Seth, Mrs Tulsi's prime minister, has had much to be said for him. But Hanuman House was never an Eden. Naipaul was to remain adamant about the cruelties that belong to extended families. In his amends-making *Million Mutinies* book about India, one of his informants is a modern-minded Indian, a publicity woman and a Tamil Brahmin whom he calls Kala – an invented name, presumably, and an intriguing near-approach to the name of the personage whom Naipaul elsewhere, and earlier, calls 'the coal-black aboriginal goddess, surviving in Hinduism as the emblem of female destructiveness', and whom he links with the Naxalite revolutionary outrages of recent years. Kala informs him of the harsh treatment received by her mother when she went to live with her husband's family, whose females were at once a superior sort of social worker and a set of slave-drivers, and she thereby elicits from him one of his rare personal interventions in this book:

Cruelty, yes: it was in the nature of Indian family life. The clan that gave protection and identity, and saved people from the void, was itself a little state, and could be a hard place, full of politics, full of hatreds and changing alliances and moral denunciations. It was the kind of family life I had known for much of my childhood: an early introduction to the ways of the world, and to the nature of cruelty. It had given me, as I suspected it had given Kala, a taste for the other kind of life, the solitary or less crowded life, where one had space around oneself.

Perhaps this does make the extended family sound a bit like the British Empire. And it certainly makes it sound forbidding. It makes the solitude he has wished for seem sympathetic, and other than fictitious. But Naipaul goes on to qualify his account by saying of the treatment received by Kala's mother: 'Such a disciplining of a child bride would have been considered virtuous; the cruelty, however willed, however voluptuous, would have been seen as no more than the cruelty of life itself.'

Naipaul is frank about cruelty; it is a word which he often feels he has to use. And his own writings can be hurtful at times. To fasten on this matter – and on the objections which have been levelled at his views, and which politicize his 'misanthropy' – is one way of dealing with the business of understanding what he has achieved. His books, so far as they are painful, can make one want to say that they testify to the cruelty of life itself and to a shared suffering. But his readers must also have reflected on the part played there by a wounded willingness to wound. Some of them may have told themselves that it is wounded of him to speak of a wounded civilization, given that all civilizations may be seen as such, and to have made so much of the dependency of small countries, given that every civilization has made use of others, mimicked them, and that this is part of what civilization means. According to another Scottish Whig, Francis Horner, a friend of Francis Jeffrey and a contemporary of Burns, imitativeness is 'the mainspring of improvement'.

Naipaul's jokes are a wonderful compacting of what he has to say in his novels and non-novels. In saying their several things at once, they enable his opposites to coincide, which means that some of these jokes can give pain. But the jokes in *Biswas* give remarkably little of that – considering its sore subjects. The Tulsi son Owad, one of the two household gods identified by the deviser of nicknames and animal counterparts – this god is mocked, and despised, but there is no revenge, worth speaking of as such, against Tulsidom. *Biswas* has the hurtfulness that runs in families, but it also has, in abundance, the affectionate candour evident in the tease inflicted by Shama on her husband when, engaged on her accounts, she shoos him away with 'Leave me alone, Mr John Lubbard.' The name is that of a romantic hero in one of the stories which Biswas has been writing to console himself and at which she has been taking a peep. The comedy in the book – which is never 'deliberate', which 'comes in pat', as his father prescribed – is the secret of its achievement.

One of its most potent scenes, the scene with the oyster man, is among its funniest. There is an outbreak of spitting and scuffling – Mohun Agonistes, at grips with other Hanuman House males. He tells the clan: 'I not eating any of the bad food from this house.' Off he goes, descending into the courtyard, where he catches the note of laughter, at his expense. He approaches the alternative food supply of an oyster stall, tended by a frantic proprietor and his female drudge:

The oyster man was talking drunkenly, in a mixture of Hindi and English. 'My son is a helluva man. I feel that something is seriously wrong with him. One day he put a tin can on the fence and come running inside the house. "The gun, Pa," he said. "Quick, give me the gun." I give him the gun. He run to the window and shoot. The tin can fall. "Pa," he say. "Look. I shoot work. I shoot ambition. They dead."' The flambeau dramatized the oyster man's features, filling hollows with shadow, putting a shine on his temples, above his eyebrows, along his nose, along his cheek-bones. Suddenly, he flung down his knife and pulled out a stick from below his stall. He waved the stick in front of Mr Biswas. 'Anybody!' he said. 'Tell anybody to come!'

The woman didn't notice. She went on opening oysters, laying them in her scratched, red palms, prising the ugly shells open, cutting the living oysters from their moorings to the pure, just-exposed inside shell.

'Tell anybody,' the man said. 'Anybody at all.'

'Stop!' Mr Biswas said.

The chapter is nearly at an end, but there is still time for Mohun's distress and disgrace to be followed by the likeness of a piece of good fortune. He is expelled from Hanuman House and departs to mind a shop in the sticks. Shama goes with him, pregnant. They are like Adam and Eve, with the world before them. But in the sticks there lies in wait the stick-fighter Mungroo, and the shop belongs to the Tulsis, who know what they are doing. It is not the sort of shop in which ambition is rewarded.

6. Mozart and Aeroplanes

BRIGID BROPHY IS one of a number of British writers who died in or around 1995. Another of these, Kingsley Amis, fell out with her, while a third, Donald Davie, fell out with certain features of the modern world, of the people's century, as it has come to be called. All three were fighters, and many of their more strenuous battles were fought in the Sixties. Brophy was a Londoner of Irish extraction, a novelist, essayist and feminist, a sexual and animal liberationist, and a half-believer in the proposition that there are only two classes – highbrows and lowbrows. Amis, also a Londoner, moved from left to right in the course of his life, having begun as a sort of democrat and an opponent of highbrows. The poet Davie was of Nonconformist stock. His was a Northern sternness. He liked hymns. He was, as was Brophy, a lover of the eighteenth century. For him, as for Amis, the advent of Thatcherite conservatism in the Eighties had the air of a liberation.

I worked with all three, as their editor on weekly papers, and in writing about my dealings with Brigid in that capacity, I find my mind wandering to these two contemporaries of hers. Different from her, as from each other, but no less polemical. Two of the three funny. Davie, in his sternness, was an English moralist and a moralizer of his minstrelsy, at once a Modernist and a traditionalist in artistic matters, and a devoted and accomplished highbrow poet. Amis was a man of the people, the people highbrows disliked, even after his turn to the right at the start of the Sixties and the gathering haughtiness associated with that.

The year 1963 dawned with a warning from the *New Statesman*. An article in the first half of the paper, mentioned earlier, suggested that the country was confused about whether or not sexual intercourse should take place outside marriage, and decided that 'her virginity will remain a girl's best friend.' An accompanying cartoon made clear how confused people could be – a brutish rocker was shown sitting in one of the coffee-bars of the day, and was captioned as saying, in richly demotic vein, to a girlfriend in tears: 'Yeah, I know it's mine, but I ain't marryin' no bird wot ain't a virgin.' In years to come, a fellow like that would not perhaps have known that it was his. Despite such editorial warnings, and there were plenty of others in the newspapers of the time, Philip Larkin felt able to produce a poem, in another of these years to come, which remarked that

> Sexual intercourse began
> In nineteen sixty-three
> (Which was rather late for me) –
> Between the end of the *Chatterley* ban
> And the Beatles' first LP.

Sexual intercourse outside marriage, that is. The marital kind had been struggling on for centuries.

Two months after the journal's advice about virginity, one of its star contributors, Malcolm Muggeridge, then on his turn towards religion, erupted with a lava flow of brilliant sarcasm to the effect that, 'on our side of the Iron Curtain', an indefatigable sexual intercourse *within* marriage was being relentlessly urged in handbooks of self-improvement. This had been too much for Malcolm. 'In the light of these careful conjugal instructions, the mass self-inflicted castrations which took place in the first years of the Christian Era, so elegantly described by Gibbon, become comprehensible at last. One feels, like Origen, that it might, after all, be more prudent to disarm the tempter.' The review refers to a letter from 'Mother of Two', in praise of *erotica domestica*, which had appeared in the journal: 'One would like to make the acquaintance of "Father of Two" and silently shake his hand.' After the review came out, 'Father of Five' wrote to say he'd supposed that 'making love (which covers everything from cuddling to copulation) every morning, evening and at odd times during the day' was normal practice.

Such was the comic give-and-take attached to a sexual revolution which was affirmed and condemned and denied, which happened in 1963, or had started to happen long before, or which hadn't happened at all. The condemnations and warnings at the front of the *New Statesman* could be followed by affirmations at the back, where I was in the middle of my time as literary editor. A back-half contributor noted for his affirmations on the subject was William Empson. Feeling that he'd been treated by Rosamund Tuve 'as a pagan stumbling towards' the divine light of Christianity, he wrote about George Herbert's poetry, in January 1963, to say: 'Clearer now about what the light illuminates, I am keen to stumble away from it.' And part of what he was stumbling away from was Christianity's element of sex hatred. Brigid Brophy also affirmed. Her début in the paper occurred soon after Empson's Herbert discussion, which shared an issue with Paul Johnson's defence of virginity.

That first piece of hers, entitled 'Good and Bad Breast', assailed the writings both of the psychoanalyst Melanie Klein and of an admirer of Klein, the Hampstead painter and aesthete Adrian Stokes, himself much admired, a Bloomsbury survivor, the golden youth of an enchanted past and now a golden gnomic sage, a very subtle character, with a keen eye for the cultural weather, as disclosed in the weeklies and in the *Observer*. A psychological parthenogenesis was said in the review to be predicated by the Kleinian account of an early stage of child development: an effacement of the father, in other words, had allowed Klein to concentrate on the idea of a life-determining infant experience of the mother's two different breasts. And Melanie Klein was likened to a kindly district nurse. As for Adrian Stokes, he was seen to have quoted a saying of Turner, 'Indistinctness is my forte', and to invite the retort: 'I think it must be Mr Stokes's, too.'

Indistinctness was never Brigid's forte, and the piece was distinctly offensive and audacious. She was then and remained a Freudian, and she was writing at a time when the movement's internal fissure between the Anna Freudians and the Kleinians was festering, not least in Hampstead, where some of the combatants lived, including more than one formidable Kleinian. Brophy indicated in her review that Klein had slipped into her book the notion of a profundity on her part greater than that of Freud the father. The Kleinian heights of Hampstead had been stormed from the riverine lowlands of Brigid's South Kensington, with the publication of such a review, and a friend of mine wrote to the paper to exclaim: 'How singularly inappropriate was the sickening vulgarity of her opening paragraph!' The sexual revolution had clearly not proceeded so far as to make 'ribaldry' correct, or to license 'jokey, philistine' references to breasts, in every corner of the land, a land where virginity could still be thought a girl's best friend. Sophisticated newspapers could still speak of extra-marital sexual activity as abhorrent. What fans of chastity their leader-writers could be! Empson and Brophy emerged from a time of repression whose rigours were, lots of them, still in place, and were by no means to vanish on all sides, as if by magic, after, if there was one, the revolution. Both of them were disgracefully sent down from ancient universities for the infringement of a national decorum in respect of sexual conduct.

This was nevertheless a time when there certainly was a more than usual degree of uncertainty, and of hypocrisy, as to what this decorum might consist in. In Brophy's novel *Flesh* of 1962, Marcus, about to marry, 'confesses' he is a virgin. '"Yes, I know you are," Nancy said. "That doesn't matter."' Many unmarried people are not, apparently, but Nancy doesn't mind that Marcus is pure. The uncertain Marcus then finds that his bride has a talent: 'It was for sexual intercourse.' Post-marital sexual intercourse has revealed this talent: but Nancy, no prude and no hypocrite, would seem to have been at it with others before the banns were called. The Sixties were getting into their swing, and in three years' time the front half of the *New Statesman* would get round to acknowledging the arrival of a new decorum. There came a point when what had once been generally viewed as bohemian or Hampstead or Bloomsbury behaviour appeared to have spread quite widely up and down the British Isles – a change as palpable as the change from heavy to light, from iron bar to microchip and space module, in the material and industrial culture.

Norman Mailer has been heard to say that the sexual revolution was set going by John Kennedy, with his looks and lovely wife. But it can more plausibly be said to have been set going, if not long before, by the Second World War, when those who were dying for sex were at risk of dying for their country, and embargoes were lifted or suspended. This is a somewhat vexed question, and the consequences of the revolution are as difficult to be sure of as its origins are. But it's plain enough that the printed word of the last forty years has changed in accordance with its imprimatur. There can now be books which are a tissue of what would once have been all but unanimously considered obscenity, with the vocabulary of the national press comparatively mealy-mouthed.

At the very beginning of the Sixties, having set up house near South Kensington, I was presently to learn that Brigid lived in the vicinity with her husband, the art historian Michael Levey, and her daughter, who went to the same school as my children, and with her fearsome, but I believe cowardly, fluffy Chinatown dragon of a white cat, which looked like her familiar, in the manner of a certain story by Colette (and in the manner of a cat of Kingsley Amis's, which could make Amis look like a witch). Her looks were a fascination. She was catlike, I suppose, and like a caster of spells. She had a round-faced, slightly sleepy-looking vigilant glamour. She could seem like some powdered eighteenth-century person, an inhabitant of her favourite century; that round face would have looked right, you felt, supervising a crinoline and surmounted by a wig – Madame de Brophy, queen of her salon, but too much the author and independent mind to have one. Her writings take a semi-clandestine interest in her appearance, to which she might be deemed to be awarding an intriguingly bad review when she describes one of her autobiographically-redolent heroines – Anna of *The Snow Ball* (1964):

> The face would yield sensuous pleasure: but the sensualist must undertake an ascetic self-discipline first. He must harden himself to tolerate a tragic face whose tragedy was couched in half-formed baby features which, individually smudged and then squeezed up close together, had finally slipped or been twisted sideways in relation to the face, making it the face of an immortal baroque baby pettishly carrying into middle age the impress of being newly, and distortingly, born.

Brigid's mother, to whom she seems to have been closer than to her father, the novelist John Brophy, is awarded Anna's smudges in a filial essay which belongs to the same year:

> She has a pretty little figure and the legs of a pin-up, dresses well and has a flair for scent and for hats – which she buys for about 10s each in department stores in Paris and wears not quite so much provocatively as evocatively: behind an eye-veil her shapeless small nose and curry-coloured irises turn into delicate smudges, and she achieves, like some French period films, a ravishing pastiche of Impressionism. It was at her most Impressionist, at once crisp and melting, that she came, one high summer day, to visit me when I was up at Oxford.

Her idiosyncrasies and contrasts were a further fascination. Like the heroine of her charming 'Movement' novel, as I think of it, *The King of a Rainy Country* (1956), she came across as truthful, direct and yet demure, as having stepped out in all confidence from the closet of a considerable shyness. This heroine is solicited by a brash American tourist, who calls her 'a serious girl' and guesses that she reads a lot. Doesn't she? 'Yes,' she replies. Has she read the Kinsey Report – that leading manual of the Sixties? 'No,' she replies. This has the note of the girlhood of Brigid Brophy. Among her idiosyncrasies was her sometimes faintly weird worship of aeroplanes – Concorde in particular. Her sympathetic professor in *Hackenfeller's Ape* 'admired aeronautics ... the only achievement of his own century which he would compare with Mozart's music'. Another idiosyncrasy was her preference for the old spelling 'shew' for 'show': I can see it now, as it appeared on one of her postcards, in her scriptorial Italianate hand. She and Kingsley Amis were about the only two English writers of the time who could be imagined compiling a manual of English usage, and after a series of earlier adjudications on the subject, Amis wrote one shortly before his death.

Her contrasts were inescapable. She had a touch of the boarding-school about her — a school where she might have played the part of the sly or naughty girl who is also the serious and confident girl who becomes head prefect, the 'captain of chambers' about whom eighteenth-century girls, according to their contemporary Louisa Stuart, were apt to fall into flusters. She was an aesthete, an artist, who was meanwhile a controversialist and a righter of wrongs. She truly was a righter of wrongs. This lover of Firbank's novels — but also, granted, of Shaw's plays — stood up for women's rights, and for authors' rights, for a scorning of superstitions, and for the prevention of cruelty to animals. She was very magnificently 'for' these various things, and she even managed to do something about them — apart, that is, from writing novels about them. Two of her novels, *Hackenfeller's Ape* and *In Transit*, are especially disposed to enjoin attitudes — towards animal liberation and human bisexuality, respectively — without ceasing to be novels. The second, set in an airport, is admittedly quite strange: androgyny is a pyrotechnic word-play here, and the human nature of the narrator is to be in transit, to be seen at moments as a pun, as a two-in-one, Anglo-Irishly and otherwise.

She was never, though, predictably right-thinking. Her next piece for the paper added insult to injury from the point of view of Hampstead – or of what was left of Bloomsbury, to whose old goals she was in some respects attuned. Brigid, in her distinctness, was impatient here with Virginia Woolf's 'devastating' vagueness – Woolf thought that champagne bottles were opened with cork-screws – and with the 'absence of characters and incidents' in her fiction. Nor was she drawn to whatever can be glimpsed of a revolutionary spectacle in the hermaphrod-itic *Orlando*.

This review was flanked by two other fault-finding reviews, one by Robert Taubman of Dan Jacobson's confessions of a liberal (published in the *New Statesman* and thereafter in a book of essays), and a castigation by Donald Davie of Stephen Spender's *The Struggle of the Modern*, in which the author of the book – who also died in 1995 – was mocked for not knowing what any graduate student knew: that Hopkins's reference in his poetry to 'shook foil' had to do, not with tin foil, but with the weapon of a fencer. Two months later came a not unbeady letter from Stephen Spender pointing out that a 'dis-tinguished colleague' had pointed out that Hopkins had said in a letter that he'd intended the sense of gold leaf or tinsel. Donald Davie was a man who was not easily corrected. He rejoined: 'The quotation from Hopkins's letter reveals what his intentions were; it leaves open the question of how far they were fulfilled in the poem. The poem in isolation can be read in more ways than one.'

Later he wrote again to say that colleagues had pointed out, and that he now accepted, that his review had been 'unclear and uncharitable'.

These were pugnacious and at times uncharitable pages, in which dog ate dog and sister sister, and journalists and academics were prone to mutual sectarian disdain. Brophy was well able to shake a foil in this setting, and she had to endure Frank Kermode's strictures on her *Mozart the Dramatist*. I could hardly complain that, thanks to my notoriety as a pupil of Leavis's, and to my responsibility for such items as Brigid's initial interventions in the paper, I became a displeasure to friends of its former Bloomsbury stars and literary editors.

She was not, in fact, the kind of judicial critic whose era or hour this was, so much as a combative and affirmative one whose journalism went with her fiction and was no interference with her 'serious writing', as she was careful to explain: 'As a matter of fact, my journalism *is* serious writing.' There were a couple of occasions during the Sixties when her foil could be thought to have missed its mark. The first was her review of a novel by Ivy Compton-Burnett, whom you'd have expected her to like but who was declared to be 'not exactly an artist' – more 'the inventor of a wholly original species of puzzle'. Here again she found a lack of character and incident. Compton-Burnett's novels could be called a continuation, and a severe stylization, of those of Jane Austen, Brigid's favourite novelist. But the affinity did not soften Brigid's disapproval. It's true that it's often a puzzle to grasp who is speaking in the novels of Compton-Burnett; and that the sameness there exceeds the sameness to be found in Jane Austen; it must certainly have seemed excessive to a novelist as various as Brophy. But I don't myself see any lack of plots or people in 'Ivy's trash', as her novels were known to the friend she lived with, and it was a surprise to me that Brigid, herself a comic writer, and a funny one, was unable to see the other woman's jokes.

I remember a nursery scene in *A God and his Gifts*, published in the year of liberty 1963, the last of Compton-Burnett's far-from-libertarian novels to appear during her lifetime. A small boy, growing into his heritage at a country seat, is upset by a small girl who is visiting him, and who takes the pencil with which he is drawing pictures: 'Her host broke down.' Such a good sentence. It reminds me of another nursery scene – the occasion when Ivy, responsive but probably unsmiling, peered into my son's pram. Brigid smiled sometimes, and chuckled: but not, in those days anyway, at the work of pencil-stealing, androgyne Ivy Compton-Burnett. Leavis's journal *Scrutiny* could hardly have been expected to exert itself on behalf of Compton-Burnett's work, though there was every reason why it should have. But Leavis's pornographer Kingsley Amis saw the point of her, though she herself was to fail to see the point of *him*, and was to think him, in Bloomsbury style, vulgar and squalid. Amis's essay on her novels is a triumph of the judicial approach at its best – cogent, appreciative, tolerant of limitation. And his essay on Jane Austen is equally valuable. No one would rush to commend its tolerance; but the reservations it expresses, to a degree that few critics have ever dared, are entitled to respect.

The following year, 1964, brought the second of these two occasions – an angry attack on Kingsley Amis. 'At rewriting much the same novel under different titles and with different names for the characters he is beaten only by Miss Compton-Burnett' – whose prototype, however, was reckoned to be greatly superior. The principal character in the Amis novels is Lucky Jim over and over again, Brophy said, and Lucky Jim is a case of arrested development, likened to Richmal Crompton's delinquent schoolboy, William, of the William books. Which leaves this author looking like some Kingsley Crompton-Burnett (later knighted). She claimed that it's philistine of Amis – not, in context, funny of him – to have Lucky Jim refer to her favourite composer's music as 'filthy Mozart', and that there's no fun in having Amis say of his character Patrick Standish – whose name is the same in different books and who is accused here of committing rape in one of them – that, 'turning off at the electricity showroom, he was lucky enough to send the greater part of a puddle over a sod in ragged clothes who was doing his level best to blow his nose into the gutter'. This is, yes, meant to be funny – though it would be a mistake to suppose that lucky Patrick is meant to be absolutely exempt from blame for drenching his ragged sod. Brigid, Bloomsbury's black beast initially, was Bloomsbury enough to refuse a smile to Amis's comic abrasiveness.

Relations between the two were among the cold spells which occurred in the course of the loving Sixties. Amis's friend Robert Conquest crafted a limerick at Brophy's expense, to which Amis claimed to have contributed a line about a 'Krafft-Ebing Trophy'; and the pair of them no doubt managed, elsewhere, to light on a rhyme for her Christian name as well. Meanwhile there was also the cold war that prevailed between Bloomsbury and its upstart enemies, with Brophy intermediate, in some respects, between the two. My personal character was to receive a very bad review in an entry for 1961 in one of the diaries of Frances Partridge, a keeper of the Bloomsbury flame. They are the diaries of an 'elderly highbrow', as she puts it, who admires the writings of Adrian Stokes. Published not long ago, having been left to marinate for thirty years, the entry tells how she had seen through me at one of those dinner parties that were still being held in the Sixties. I can't remember talking to her on any occasion, but I do have uneasy memories of the person she describes – who is someone who would have difficulty in re-membering anybody: an 'auto-intoxicated, young and ambitious Scot; doesn't want to hear anything from anyone else but just to do his own turn ad lib . . . it was like a night out with stockbrokers'. Not just a Scot. A stockbroker too. I should have been shot.

In 1971, in the *Listener*, which I'd gone off in my kilt to edit, one of Brigid's refusals to be predictable, and a further offence to Bloomsbury, took place when she reviewed E. M. Forster's long-awaited gay novel. *Maurice* was read by her as a novelette, with Maurice unsound on blood sports: Forster had learnt from Edward Carpenter about the innocence of homosexuality, but not about the necessity of vegetarianism. The review concluded:

The actual begetter of Forster's book was not Carpenter but his 'comrade' George Merrill, who, Forster records, 'touched my backside – gently and just above the buttocks'. The sensation, the Note says, 'was unusual' and 'seemed to go straight through the small of my back into my ideas, without involving my thoughts', at which moment, Forster suggests, he perhaps conceived *Maurice* . . . Had Merrill known he was engendering a book, he might have had the forethought to give Forster a solid pinch.

In that pinch there is a touch of Gore Vidal, whom Brigid hailed as a fellow spirit in a *Listener* piece of 1969. She explained that both disliked the work of Henry Miller; pornography was thought by both – as by Amis and by the principal author of that limerick – to be 'harmless and often serviceable'. As for religion – 'God, no'; as for the 'universality of human bisexuality' – God, yes. But they were, in time, to prove at odds over Freud. Elsewhere she called psychoanalysis 'the greatest benefactor of civilization since the wheel'; Vidal would have preferred the wheel. Both people were dandies with a taste and a gift for public life and for good causes. They also had cats in common – and in common with Kingsley Amis – together with a consciousness of the Kinsey Report. Brophy, we may infer, had failed in her girlhood to read it. Vidal figured in it – among the data.

'Suddenly the situation of women is a revolutionary situation,' she wrote in 1970 – in an opening piece in the *Listener*. For her, the sexual revolution and the self-emancipation of women were aspects of one another, and of her plea that others, men, women and animal others, shouldn't avoidably be hurt, a plea she must have experienced both as sanction for, and as a constraint on, the revolutionary liberties of her adult life. It was in this spirit that she wrote about the shortcomings of monogamy, and it was in this spirit that she was apt to celebrate the pleasures of the flesh – as, for instance, in her approving review of a sensible Swedish sex manual, which said that the size of penises didn't matter, and that, as Brigid relayed the point, 'the woman's chances of orgasm' have 'little to do with the man's potency'.

There was also this lyrical account, in her novel *Flesh*, of Marcus's first taste of Nancy:

Where she led him was a strange world that was not new to him, since he had always known it existed, subterraneanly: a grotto, with whose confines and geographical dispositions he at once made himself quite familiar, as with the world of inside his own mouth: but a magic grotto, limitless, infinitely receding and enticing, because every sensation he experienced there carried on its back an endless multiplication of overtones, with the result that the sensation, though more than complete, was never finished, and every experience conducted him to the next; a world where he pleasurably lost himself in a confusion of the senses not in the least malapropos but as appropriate and precise as poetry – a world where one really did see sounds and hear scents, where doves might well have roared and given suck, where perfectly defined, delightful local tactile sensations dissolved into apperceptions of light or darkness, of colour, of thickness, of temperature.

What could be wrong with that, even at a time when the rod of the Lord Chamberlain was still being used to strike out words like 'bum' from play scripts? The point was that this grotto had been closed for centuries to English literature. Such bravura pioneer accounts may well seem old-fashioned and belletristic now to British readers who have become accustomed to watch, on national television, programmes in which women wearing rubber gloves teach each other in close-up how to masturbate – in the interests, allegedly, of standing by their men. The manual has long since come into its own, and may even have got out of hand; talk of women's 'chances of orgasm' must now look archaic to the young, who are also reported to be wary of the apperceptions that come with fine writing. But such accounts were wholly justified and could be a great pleasure in themselves. Among them are the couplings that transpire in the late Terry Southern's burlesques.

The high point of Brigid's argumentative performance at this time, and of her defence of pleasure, was her review in November 1963 of John Cleland's erotic novel *Fanny Hill*, a celebration of sex which has its resemblances to another man's girl book – Terry Southern's ironic novel *Candy*. The reissue of Cleland's *Fanny*, a work immediately preceded and doubtless influenced by Richardson's *Clarissa*, was challenged in court, where journalists and savants were interrogated by a prosecution worried about the corruption of wives and servants. The review opens dauntingly – 'To my mind, the two most fascinating subjects in the universe are sex and the eighteenth century' – but is soon shrewd and vivacious. The chances of orgasm in Cleland's novel are first-rate, both for men and for women. Brigid hears, in the eighteenth century, in the arias of its operas and in the letters embodied in its novels, the voice of women newly articulate and intent on their pleasure. *Fanny Hill* is by a man pretending to be a woman: it bears witness to an intensity of desire that this consideration is overridden here. Brigid's eighteenth century was in part an imagination of the twentieth century, and an expression of her hopes for it. It incorporates an element of fantasy, and she was, in general, a champion of fantasy. One of my chief memories of the Brigid Brophy of those days was of someone who wanted to convey that partnered sexual activity is subject to structure, and that this structure is also apparent in daydream, and in art, with its flights and rests, its peaks, the five acts of its plays. This was an area in which she could be at her most persuasive, as she could also be in making her case against killing, torturing and eating animals. In such areas she could convert people.

Fanny Hill, she wrote, 'sketches an ideally benevolent society, albeit in a brothel. Jealousy is drowned in a diffused bisexuality.' As her august 'albeit' shews, its all happening in a brothel raises a question. While never naive, the review breathes an idealistic optimism. But she would have been well aware that few brothels can ever have been like the one she's extolling here, that most of them have been rather more like the one in *Clarissa*, and she was aware that Cleland was writing for money, as Dr Johnson advised writers to do. She knew, I'm sure, that the sexual revolution was never going to square with the picture presented in the idylls and manuals that helped to bring it on, that it would be debased and exploited, that new varieties of suffering would result from the collective dream of sexual happiness which was uttered in the Sixties. Perhaps the revolution is over now. Perhaps it never happened, for all the laws that were passed in relation to homosexuality and state censorship of literature. But it's at least as likely that it did happen, and it is certain that it should have done.

Brigid was a public-spirited dandy, a politically-engaged rococo artist, a rational and progressive Decadent. She was demure-severe, courteous-contentious, funny-serious, Shavian, Wildean, Firbankian, Colettish. During her later years she gave herself to a good work on behalf of literature – the Public Lending Right project. This, too, came to pass as a matter of law. Authors are now given sums of money in proportion to the rate at which their books are borrowed from public libraries. There are those who think that the scheme excessively rewards best-selling authors, and it has come at a time when libraries have been financially stinted by successive governments, and have steered towards policies inimical to literature and, indeed, to the printed word. But the scheme has rectified an anomaly, as trade-unionists used to say.

I have been dwelling on the years when much of Brigid Brophy's best writing, imaginative and polemical, was published. There then came the moment, all too long before her death, when she learned that she would presently be able to write no more. This was in 1984. She sent me a letter, a work of consummate distinctness, to let me know what she had learned. I quote from it with some compunction. I do so because I believe she would have thought of it as, in its own way, a public statement.

I dare to hope that you will one day, perhaps not in the immediate or instant future, ask me to do something, though I should have to ask you for even more than usual indulgence about dates and choosyness on my part.

It turns out that I have multiple sclerosis. I am a permanent and more or less total cripple, at least in relation to walking. Even with the wheelchair the NHS lends me, which is not deeply practical for our flat, doing anything is desperately slow and laborious and takes immense planning in advance.

7. Public-Service Journalism

THE CRITIC F. R. LEAVIS liked to make out that, with few exceptions and in a number of ways – including the aestheticism of Francophile Bloomsbury – the periodicals of his own time lacked judgment. It would be no less plausible to claim that periodical journalists have always sought to exercise it, mindful, many of them, of Matthew Arnold, and of Francis Jeffrey of the *Edinburgh Review*, for both of whom judgment was the name of the game. There were times on the *New Statesman*, over the years, when politics might have appeared to be treated as the sphere where judgment had to be applied, with the back of the paper seen as the sphere of uplift and recreation; in my own days there, the second half of the second half was still, for a while, headed 'Arts and Entertainment'. But that was a relic of the past, and of a past which the relic might lead one to misconceive. Judgment was an inaugural and essential concern of the paper as a whole, as of all such papers.

The judgments passed by the first Edinburgh Reviewers were intended to achieve what the judgments passed by Scotland's Lords of Session and Judiciary were intended to achieve: the preservation of law and order. Ambivalent with regard to political change, at once reformist and conservative, the journal could meanwhile convey that, in the field of imaginative literature, there were understandings which it was no longer lawful to question. It seemed only right that certain Edinburgh Reviewers should turn into law lords, and in one egregious case, that of the most reviewer-like of all those prototypic Scotch reviewers, Henry Brougham, into the Lord Chancellor of England.

It was said of a certain novel in the *New Statesman* of the Sixties that its writer appeared 'as pleased to be shot of it as we are'. Spoken like a reviewer, like those generations of reviewer who have been in the habit of speaking, *ex cathedra*, about 'we' and 'one', as in the expression: 'One is forced to the conclusion that . . .' The writer of a book is haled before such reviewers like some prisoner at the bar of public opinion, and the guilty are rarely absolved. One is forced to the conclusion that Ivy Compton-Burnett will never do.

This exaggerated journalistic stress on judgment, at the expense of other necessary functions, such as entertainment and instruction, frivolity and discovery, was more obtrusive in the papers I have worked for than in some others of the time. But it has always been widespread and well-known. It has been inseparable from conceptions of law and order, from a conventional wisdom of class subordination and superiority, and from the rise of the professions in the modern world, with their talk of qualifications and expertise, suspension and disbarment. Judgment isn't what it was, but it is still in session. Reviewers, so often themselves ill-qualified, so often wrong, have continued to pass sentence. Current literary theory claims to eschew judgment, without really doing so: theory might be thought to embody a specialized version of it which refrains from going where judgment is most needed and most difficult to exercise – in the direction of new writing and the unfamiliar. It is a new treason of the clerk, of the intellectual journalist, to pretend that judgment can be eschewed or overthrown, and to do this at a point when a problem of the past has got worse with the arrival of more of those damned times complained of by Matthew Arnold, when knowledge has come to new heights and has added to our uncertainties. I am referring once again to the idea of a unified field of knowledge, and to the business of connection, of integration, where judgment has to work hard.

Hans Keller asked *New Statesman* readers of the Sixties: 'What is the good of destructive public criticism?' I am suggesting that this is a subversive question which is worth asking. But I have not been suggesting that judgment should cease. Let me put it this way: if literary journalists should beware of giving their lives to passing sentence, they should also beware of giving them to papers where judgment is little more than an awareness of celebrity and controversy.

Keller himself provided part of the answer to his question by uttering, on several fronts, valuable public criticism which was at once destructive and affirmative. He did so in the *New Statesman* and in the *Listener*, to which I went as editor in 1967.

This journal was owned by a state institution, by the British Broadcasting Corporation, where public-service broadcasting was now exposed to the challenge of Commercial Television. We reviewed the BBC's policies and performance, both affirmatively and destructively, as the BBC was itself engaged in doing at this time. On the subject of broadcasting, as on many other subjects, we attempted to exercise judgment. But there were subjects on which the expression of an editorial view by the staff of the journal, as by the rest of the staff of the BBC in their programme-making capacity, was restricted by ground rules derived from the Corporation's Charter.

The first words I published on becoming editor could hardly have been more offensive to many of the elderly readers of a paper which, at that point, 3 August 1967, the day after my thirty-sixth birthday, had many elderly readers. The paper was actuarially-disadvantaged. This was not a bough to be lightly shaken. The words, written in California by the English poet Thom Gunn, were these: 'Two of the Rolling Stones have just escaped being made exemplary victims to archaic laws on drugs, even as fourteen years ago certain other artists were made exemplary victims to archaic laws on homosexuality.'

Gunn's subject was 'The New Music'. The article, which began on the cover page of the paper, and which had the look of a leader or a pronouncement, went on to speak in praise of pop lyrics and the skirling sounds of the Beatles. And it was followed by a piece on black power. The piece was headed 'Love, Love, Love' and the heading was incorporated, on the cover, in a montage of selected contents, together with page numbers. This sat beneath the new sanserif logo of a journal which had been abruptly redesigned and might well have been felt to throb with the warning that there would be more of this shocking stuff in the issues that lay ahead. And so there was. In the next issue Jonathan Miller explained why he had signed a petition in favour of the legalization of cannabis, while remarking that he himself was not a hippy and had very little time for 'all those flowers, beads and cowbells! And the aggressive loving gentleness!'

The plan was to come out loud and clear and fighting on behalf of the changes we meant to make. We were trying to take the bull by the horns. We wanted the paper to catch up with the initiatives and unrests of what had proved to be, for some, an offensive decade, and for others an exciting one. Under Hugh Greene, who took over as Director-General in 1960, the BBC had set itself to appeal to youth and to the mass audience, and I was keen that the *Listener* should respond to this as best it could, without doing violence to its reputation as an intellectual weekly.

I said in that first issue that we would now be giving as much space to television as to radio, and that this would reduce the journal's dependence on broadcast scripts – on the prepared scripts traditionally important to BBC Radio. We would be dealing, much more than before, with the less premeditated art of television talk. As a result, there would be more in the way of specially-written, original material, based on television programmes and contributed by their writers and producers, and indeed by their viewers. We began on the invidious task of reviewing ITV as well as BBC programmes, and we hoped that we might become a communications journal. The media were to be our message – to use the language of Marshall McLuhan, but to mean something different by it: the evangelical McLuhan, who was to be taken up and then put down by the intelligentsia of the time, meant that the new medium, television, was its own message. I also said in the first issue that the *Listener* had always had loyal readers, a claim that was immediately and sorely tested. The bull we'd hoped to take by the horns charged from England's rectories and came cathedral-close to goring us.

We received so many protests and cancelled subscriptions that my secretary hid them to spare my feelings. One morning I came upon what seemed like the snowy slopes of a high mountain. Not long afterwards, at the Ritz Hotel, I was introduced to the poet Auden, who stonily informed me: 'You're the man who's ruined the *Listener*.' 'That's a matter of opinion,' I weakly said. 'Yes, it is,' replied Auden: 'It's *my* opinion.'

It remains my own opinion that the changes made sense, once we had played ourselves in. But I accept that the first issue was probably a mistake. It looked too much like a dead set at love and youth, at the new street and student leftism, at what Jonathan Miller's piece disapprovingly referred to as the new 'anarchic pharmacological millennium'. There on the cover was Allen Ginsberg, beaded, bearded, hyper-bohemian, hyper-American, plethorically outré and objectionable, for whose poetry I had, myself, no taste; he was being flourished as a sign of the times. But perhaps it's worth examining that inaugural issue for a moment or two more, in order to assess it from the point of view of the bias which the BBC was enjoined to avoid and of the balance which it was enjoined to ensure.

The text of a politically anodyne television interview with the left-wing actress Vanessa Redgrave was carried, and so was a radio talk by Isaac Deutscher on *Das Kapital*. Frank Kermode, Christopher Ricks and D. J. Enright were there – Labour sympathizers, I think, who were none of them given to saying so when they wrote reviews. A review by Enoch Powell found 'depressing' the sense that Harold Macmillan had failed to evolve from the one-nation Tory radicalism of his early days in politics. John Vincent extolled the 'Napoleonic' Maurice Cowling; each was on his way to fame as a Peterhouse rightist and Thatcherite mentor. Then there was a poem by Kingsley Amis, who was on his turn to the right. All in all, I don't see why Auden, who had also turned to the right, and who may possibly have believed it wrong to talk of freeing homosexual conduct from legal sanctions, would have had to have viewed this number of the paper as ruinous. It was not grossly unbalanced. There was no crying need to resort to the argument, then being developed by the BBC, that balance should be assessed over time and in relation to an aggregate of programmes.

Those who complained on such occasions were inclined, in objecting to writers as left-wing, to judge them by reputation, and were inclined to treat conservative sympathies as natural and as politically neutral; the truth was that neither the left-wing nor the right-wing writers in that first issue wrote there in a way that could sensibly be called partisan. But it was also true that many of the objectors were bothered, not by political bias, but by what they saw as a parade of, as a fashionable submission to, alternative lifestyles.

An era of complaint had begun, both in the world of broadcasting and well beyond it. Complaint gained greatly in volume when the Sixties began, and Greene came to the BBC. To go on about the BBC's programmes – while tending to pass over those of ITV – became a lifestyle in its own right. The more popular the programmes – and they became very popular in the Sixties, and better too – the greater the volume of complaint, and the readier the BBC's Board of Governors to field the outcries and to complain themselves. Quasi-judicial commissions of inquiry were formed, and a television programme devoted to the whining 'Why oh why' of complaint still goes out at a peak time. Complaint, though, like judgment, may no longer be what it was. It has certainly not disappeared, but there's an air of exhaustion, and of resignation. Permissiveness has for some time, and for the time being, been permitted.

Balance, bias, impartiality, fairness – these had been, and continued to be, key terms for the assessment of the BBC's programmes and of the articles printed in the *Listener*. They were terms which were frequently employed at a time when the BBC had come under the duress of competition from a broadcasting conglomerate financed by advertising, when the brute force of monopoly which its founding father John Reith had seen as essential to the success of the BBC had been snatched from it. It had become necessary for the BBC to renew itself, to re-invent its role, and to review what it meant by public-service broadcasting. Commercial Television had to mean something by it also, for all its interest in profit and for all the talk of freedom which had accompanied its inception. But there was intense pressure on the BBC to do well in the ratings battle which ensued, and in which ITV was thought to enjoy the advantage of a more unbridled devotion to popularity and a less compelling obligation to offer, as public-service broadcasters were expected to do, instruction as well as entertainment. Under Greene, the BBC did do well in the ratings. In terms of programme quality, moreover, this was the best BBC there has ever been. But its success was deplored by a growing number of critics and nostalgics as the decade progressed.

The imperative that the BBC be impartial was stated in a White Paper of 1946, and a Labour Postmaster-General stated in the late Sixties that its Board of Governors was 'expected to ensure that programmes are balanced'. In a two-part article which said goodbye to Greene and saluted his achievement, I wrote that 'the doctrine of impartiality has been revised to mean that while, as before, an overall political balance must be preserved, particular programmes may at times argue a case, provided that in so doing they avoid the nerve of party-political controversy'. My hope was that this was also thought to apply to the *Listener*. On this doctrine Greene had placed the construction that 'what we want' is 'fairness to all'. In the course of the broadcast conversation of March 1968 from which this desideratum is drawn he suggested that his convictions were just as strong as those of the BBC's self-righteous founding father, legendary for his state of conviction, and went on to offer a tacit description of the ethos of Reith's BBC. 'I personally very much disapprove,' said Greene, 'of the idea of adopting an attitude derived from the traditional values of a particular class to determine what we do in broadcasting.'

It is easier now than it was in the Fifties to think of balance, impartiality, freedom from bias, as one of the BBC's necessary fictions. All utterance, to my mind, is biased. All mind is biased, and this is part of what meaning means. Reith's BBC, to strike a less dogmatic note, was no less biased than Greene's, and Reithian impartiality – in the name of which broadcast discussion of the Beveridge Report, which created the welfare state, was forbidden on the grounds that the matter was political – was a vehicle for the values of the class to which Reith aspired and attained, and which embodied, he believed, the conscience of his country. Working-class speech was largely suppressed on the air. It was seen as biased, and in any case disreputable. Given this history of dubious and contentious terms, it's understandable that broadcasters chose to move to the more manageable and less equivocal word 'fairness'.

Greene retired from the BBC in 1969. It could be said that he had done what he had it in him to do. But it could also be said that he was forced out by complaining and conspiratorial Labour ministers, among others. One Labour minister, Richard Crossman, recorded in his diary: 'So Harold has coolly switched Hill to the BBC to discipline it and bring it to book and, above all, to deal with Hugh Greene.' Harold Wilson had appointed the ITV Chairman, Lord Hill, formerly the BBC's Radio Doctor and a Tory politician, to chair the BBC's Board of Governors, and Greene was to lose his relish, thereafter, for the job of Director-General, a job which had conferred, as in Reith's own long day as Director-General, a very great deal of executive freedom. It now seemed more than likely that this freedom would be abridged. Reith detested Greene and lent a hand, from his retirement perch in Lollards Tower, Lambeth Palace, in the disciplining of his successor, while feeling that, with Greene 'up for another divorce', as Reith put it, the conspirators would have to walk delicately – in view, presumably, of Reith's reputation as a puritan with a histrionic distaste for divorce. Reith was a hypocrite in matters of sexual morality, and there was an element of hypocrisy, too, in his willingness to subvert a Director-General's dealings with the Board of Governors, given what is known about his own convictions, and practice, in the role of Director-General. A Director-General's freedom of action is, to be sure, another necessary fiction. He is and should be subject to discipline, and the Governors have a statutory duty to perform in this respect. A third necessary fiction can, perhaps, also be adduced, as directly relevant here – namely, the BBC's freedom from government intervention. It's certainly possible to feel, looking back over the Corporation's seventy-year history, that its independence has been, as its impartiality has been, both a fiction and a truth.

If the history of the BBC has any single hero, it is Greene, not Reith. Shy and aloof, a bald, beetling, beaming, blinking Wodehousian figure, with the air of a dormouse awakened from his sleep, Hugh Greene was a dynamic, decisive and persevering leader, while also an effective delegator. His well-disposed biographer, Michael Tracey, writes of him that 'it is almost impossible to find someone for whom he really cared, other than, at certain moments, for his wives.' And an anonymous close colleague is quoted by Tracey as saying: 'I'm not really sure that Hugh actually believes in anything.' I would have thought myself that he did believe in certain things, including his conception of the BBC: he once said on the subject that you can't be impartial about 'the basic moral values – truthfulness, justice, freedom, compassion, tolerance': the values of the Sixties, as it might be thought, or at any rate, the values that some Sixties people liked to invoke. He held that the BBC should 'concern itself with the whole of life in Britain, with the popular and the unpopular', and that 'people must turn to the BBC to find out what they want, whatever it is'. But then many of them aren't going to want the unpopular. There was a difficulty here, which took effect as a day-to-day constraint. It is a hard task to run such an organization, and to do so as an editor and inspirer, rather than as a manager and a value-for-money man. But Hugh Greene pulled it off.

He put a stop to old habits of grovelling and condescension, to the long-distilled institutional cant of the place. He gave it a more adult outlook, while seeking an audience amongst the young, and encouraging producers to take account of the 'poor and disadvantaged', as Tracey phrases it. He also encouraged them to be journalists. 'There is no news tonight,' BBC Radio newsreaders are said to have announced, in those early days to which some people were to look back in fondness when newsgathering expanded under Greene: tonight and every night and all day too, there would now be news. In the article published in the spring of 1969, at the time of his retirement, I wrote:

> Sir Hugh has brought about in broadcasting a wider appeal and a more interesting subject-matter. He has shown that the avoidance of risk is a doubtful virtue, and is likely, in E. M. Forster's words, 'to confirm thousands in our congenital habit of avoiding unwelcome truth'. He has shown that a freedom from considerations of profit need not be stultified by a servitude to political opinion. He has given a new energy to the concept of public-service broadcasting by encouraging livelier and more affirmative programmes, and by showing, as he put it himself, that 'one can be enterprising without loss of public confidence.' Nor has he lost the confidence of politicians . . .

About these last claims I was wrong, and so perhaps was he, at times. There were politicians who had moved against him, and there were members of the public, and of the Board of Governors, who were bitterly opposed to him.

Greene's successor as Director-General said that the Corporation would reflect a 'consensus' classification of 'prevailing' values. This was a touch on the tiller which was meant to take the ship away from the course steered by Greene. But there are ironies here. Greene's revolution was to shape the consensus addressed in time to come by the BBC, which was to find itself operating in a permissive society, and having to keep up with it. The world as seen by those Governors who had banned outspoken programmes in the Sixties stands at some distance from the world in which BBC2 has been running an effervescent magazine programme entitled *Gaytime*. *Gaytime* is what the consensus now contains. Perhaps one might go on to suggest that competition, in the field of broadcasting, was invented by politicians, and that competition and politicians have between them done harm to the BBC, but that it was good for the BBC to have a rival. The exploding new technology of the present time, however, may mean that this rivalry will become archaic, and that we may be entering a world in which public-service broadcasting will cease to be perceived as a commitment which should be defended.

In February 1970, the year after Greene's departure from the BBC, an editorial piece appeared in the journal which dealt with the controversy which had arisen, both inside and outside the Corporation, over the changes projected in its policy document 'Broadcasting in the Seventies'. These changes were in the field of radio and were consequential on the realignments of the Greene directorate. They were also affected by the maraudings of pirate radio, and by the prospect of a lawful commercial radio. The old exacting highbrow Third Programme was to go, and its material was to be distributed between Radios 3 and 4. Radio 1 was to be all pop music, Radio 2 all sweet music. The old principle of mixed programming, never exactly inviolate, was to be further eroded, in favour of generic wavelengths – or streaming, to lift a term from the educational debates of the period. It could also be said, however, that the Third Programme had been generic enough to have incurred the description of a cultural ghetto, and the 134 BBC employees who wrote a letter of protest to the *Times* took the line that mixed programming was preferable to generic wavelengths, but that an enclave of difficult programmes should be retained for their own protection. The changes were Greenian in the sense of participatory, democratic, attentive to audience demand. The protesters, some of whom felt they had insufficiently participated in the changes, were many of them Reithian in their suspicion of the element of participation involved in too great a dependence on audience research. Anyway, the question was: would difficult programmes – unpopular programmes – die out under the new arrangements?

The challenge to the plans for radio was impassioned, and none the less impressive for the uncertainties it could perhaps be thought to contain. It expressed the fear that competition with Commercial Television would lead to neglect of the BBC's Chartered obligation to instruct as well as amuse, and to a spiralling down into vulgarity. A letter to the *Listener* from King's College, Cambridge, whose twenty-eight signatories included E. M. Forster and Bernard Williams, objected to the plan to turn Radio 3 into a 'music tap', for all the classical seriousness of its music, and said that 'flexibility and surprise – the two great virtues of the Third Programme idea – should be fostered, not stifled.' In the issue before that, incidentally, Robin Blackburn of the New Left had talked to Joan Bakewell about 'revolution in our time' and been asked to promise her that 'when the revolution comes and you lead it, you will tolerate and listen to an articulate opposition'. Blackburn replied that there would be no leaders: 'The new style of revolutionary politics is people doing things for themselves.' The articulate opposition to 'Broadcasting in the Seventies' was an example of people trying to do things for themselves – and failing. The changes went ahead.

The playwright Alan Bennett wrote to the paper about my piece on the changes. He said he hadn't always been able to follow it, but managed to convey the gist of it very well. 'Wait and see?' he wrote. 'Not likely.' I'd suggested that the changes didn't have to be considered irreversible, and I still feel that the restructuring didn't have to mean the stifling of flexibility and surprise. Nor has it done this. But I would have to accept that the intellectual content of BBC programmes suffered a dilution from which they have yet to recover.

The long last volume of Asa Briggs's long history of the BBC discusses at length the controversies which arose at this time over the future of broadcasting and over its coverage of dissent and civil disobedience. Much of the book reads, in fact, like a chronicle of complaint. But the importance of these controversies is underrated. The contributions made to the debates on broadcasting by such experienced and thoughtful periodical writers as Raymond Williams, Stuart Hood and Hans Keller are barely mentioned, though plenty of space is awarded to the amateur views of tabloid commentators. There is, furthermore, a bias against Greene, who merits practically no warm words at all in a volume which employs an enormous number of words and is often approving of senior BBC officials. 'He liked raffish people,' writes Asa Briggs, in Reithian accents. Oliver Whitley 'was to act in a sense as Greene's conscience', Briggs says elsewhere. Oliver Whitley was indeed Cromwellianly conscientious, a decent man and a loyal servant of the BBC and of public-service broadcasting, who was also able, when he needed to be, to stand out against Reith's arrogance. But Greene had a perfectly good conscience of his own, though differently-textured, no doubt, from that of Briggs, who here accedes to the strategy, noted earlier, of attempting to evacuate Greene's inner life.

The emphasis on complaint in the book seems excessive, but it's true that there was a large amount of expostulation for Asa Briggs to write about, and for the Governors to react to and exploit. At one point they banned the repeat of a BBC Television 'Wednesday Play', *Up the Junction*, based on stories by Nell Dunn first published in the *New Statesman*. Her racy working-class girls were too much, allegedly, for the public, millions of whom had nevertheless watched the play, and too much for the Governors, very few of whom were or had ever been working-class girls. Greene's most controversial programmes tended to deliver high audience figures, which did a good deal to defuse this institutional deference to complaint; his scandalous satire shows, *That Was the Week that Was* and so on, were very popular, though they never rated very highly with me. At another point I was summoned to Lord Hill's office to discuss whether a poem we'd published by Ted Hughes was as blasphemous as a reader was alleging. It was as if I was up before the Radio Doctor with a bad back or mysterious pain. Both of us certainly had some trouble in following the future Poet Laureate's poem. But the complaint was not upheld.

The issue of the so-called trivialization of the BBC needs to be separated from that of its accessibility to iconoclastic or, for that matter, socialist opinions, though the two issues could sometimes fly together with the force of magnetism. Likewise the *Listener* could be criticized both for being vulgar and for being left-wing in a pretentiously intellectual fashion. Those who found the paper hard to follow were often able to grasp that it was fashionably subversive, and I wouldn't claim that there can never have been the slightest reason for them to think so, however many of them may also have thought that Thom Gunn was a rock star. This raises a problem of perennial concern about which I am anxious not to speak merely defensively. I'm referring to the problem of how a state-owned broadcasting service or a state-owned journal, neither of them subject to direct government control, can manage to be interesting while remaining politically impartial.

My years on the paper taught me that the public-service principle in journalism and the arts is beautiful and vulnerable. It became clear that public-service broadcasting can only thrive, can only survive, in a society whose politicians see the point of it, see it as an estate of the realm, and are willing, as far as possible, to let it alone. Many influential British politicians, however, have been inclined to treat it solely in terms of political advantage, and Labour leaders, it should be said, have been as coercive as all but a very few Tories: I remember the staring-eyed hostility to Greene's self-confident BBC which was expressed in a conversation of the time by Tony Benn, who was to argue, when in office, together with Crossman, that the Corporation should take advertising. The BBC is still widely regarded as the best broadcasting service there is, but politicians have moved to diminish it. They have portrayed it as suffering from giganticism, waste, vulgarity, revolution. They have tried to cut it down to size – a size commensurate with the meanest of mean conceptions of what the medium can encompass.

In order to run a publicly-funded magazine properly, you have to pay attention both to the need to be politically impartial and to the partiality of governments and oppositions. Was it proper for the *Listener* to look to the left and make use of the talent assembled there in the mid part of the century, without ensuring, as an inflexible priority, that there was a balance, over time, in respect of politically-sensitive material? This is what Robert Conquest thought was happening on the paper under my editorship, and he thought it was improper. He would not have been mollified had I told him, even more earnestly than I think I did, that I was *eager* to print material by right-wing writers, and that I felt I was capable of recognizing the merits of such writers. I had no trouble at all with those of E. S. Turner, a master of his art with a liking for the British Army, a journalist noticeably 'incorrect' by the standards popularly ascribed to left-wing zealots; he can hardly over many years have written as many sentences that were other than shapely, interesting and humane. Robert Conquest is one of the leading historians of Soviet Russia, and had long been one of the Western world's leading anti-Communists. In 1968 he wrote me a forthright letter: 'I can only say that, as a matter of principle, I do feel that the organ of a public corporation should not be so one-sided politically, should not be a *journal d'opinion*. I think that this basic principle should be overriding.' I had got 'into a false position'; there had been 'a lapse of discretion'.

Bob Conquest went on to dissociate his strictures from an attack which was being made on the *Listener* by a trade union of sorts called the Periodical Proprietors' Association, an attack buttressed by legal threats and backed editorially by the *Times*. These proprietors invoked the principle which condemns restraint of trade; the changes at the paper were an interference with private profit. The attack was in the end to come to nothing, and the organization was subsequently to change its name – proprietors were bad news for a while in the Sixties. In March 1968, Crossman, then a Cabinet Minister, remarked in his diary that the *Listener* had occasioned 'the fury of the *Spectator* and the *New Statesman* because they think it's unfair for a subsidized BBC weekly to compete directly for their readers'. Unfair to private enterprise – not an attitude entirely compatible with the *New Statesman*'s enthusiasm for a National Health Service.

'Fury' was a state which the *Listener* of these years was capable of arousing on other occasions too. My understanding of Conquest's letter was enhanced by a letter to him from Kingsley Amis which I found quoted in Eric Jacobs's life of Amis: 'I nearly shat myself in fury on hearing that the Pistener had put up that bastard Che Guevara as Man of the Year.' The two anti-Communists loved to exchange their bits of bad news, hamming them up to comic effect, with Bob the less inflamed, the more inflaming, of the two. It is clear that Kingsley had lost his regard for me, or for my presumed politics, and that Bob may never have had much of that to lose. But it is also clear that Kingsley might have been spared the threat of the disaster that almost overcame him if he had read the opening article in question. It was an article on the death of Guevara by a Latin American specialist, Peter Calvert, which formed part of material about to be broadcast in the Third Programme, and was accompanied by a picture of the photogenic revolutionary and of his smouldering cigar. It was entitled 'Man of the Year?', and the question mark was intended to be teasing. The piece was honorific only in so far as it suggested (with palpable truth) that Guevara's memory might live on in Latin America in the manner of a heroic legend. The following month the paper opened with a piece by Robert Conquest entitled 'Coping with Communism', and the face of Oswald Mosley was on the cover later that year, to signal an interview with him inside. I like to think that these developments may have had a calming effect on Kingsley's bowels.

Conquest's rebuke caused me to examine my conscience and to take more care. But I was sure that I had, in fact, no desire to grind an ideological axe or to be partisan, while also sure that some regard should be shown for the principle of editorial self-expression, in the matter of choosing to publish what seems good to the editor in question, and of seeking to reflect the excitements of the time. I felt that there was no such thing as a journal which was not a journal of opinion, and that what matters, where the journal is publicly accountable, is that it be fair. Buttoned-up, self-consciously impartial and impersonal journals, moreover, may well be no fairer than the ones that come out with things. It is not unknown for editorship by committee, and by recourse to referees, to be both unfair and dull.

Objections to the paper were gradually to subside after that initial circulation loss, and we were holding steady at 40,000 – which was the figure for the paper in the late Thirties – in the course of my last two years. But that first loss proved damaging, at a time when the weeklies had come under pressure from the revamped quality Sundays, with their colour-supplements, and we wouldn't have minded carrying many more advertisements than we were ever able to obtain. The *Listener* was no pantomime horse in the sense that the *New Statesman* had been; there was no stagger or lurch, no discordant front half and back. I suppose you could say that I had changed my dissenting back-half ways, that I was now a gamekeeper instead of a poacher. At all events, we were the one paper, with plenty of give-and-take between Derwent May's province as literary editor and the rest of it, and with the staff writer D. A. N. Jones operating both at the back and the front; and we had for a while our binding element, our Vicky, in Mark Boxer, whose String-Along strip, with the antics of its Camden Town broadcasters, served our ambition to be a media journal. The strip was programme-related, we might have been able to plead. We were not committing a restraint of trade.

As a journal both of record and of opinion, the *Listener* was crowded with events and with other people's preoccupations, some of which became our own. We specialized in student protest, alias the complaining young, and in flower power, as the decade slouched towards the events of May '68 in Paris. To offset, perhaps, some expression of scepticism with regard to the paranormal, and for its own interesting sake, and for the hell of it, we published a piece by a believer in flying saucers and ley-lines – the Wizard of Notting Hill, John Michell. The Soviet invasion of Czechoslovakia, breakaway Biafra, the outbreak of the Northern Ireland troubles, EEC entry, the progress of the Vietnam War, Heath's defeat of Wilson in 1970, the miners' strike of the time and the three-day week – we did what we could, in our impartiality, with all that. We also did what we could with what was known for a while, in progressively unsuitable style, as Women's Lib. 'Suddenly the situation of women is a revolutionary situation,' wrote Brigid Brophy in the piece, pointedly entitled 'Everybody's Lib', which made the front page of an issue of 1970. This was a revolution to which we offered our assistance, without wondering whether such statements had to be balanced by some act of misogyny.

The astronauts' journey to the New Found Land of the Moon was celebrated in the paper with the publication of a new-found poem by Tennyson on a trip to the same destination, a poem Conor Cruise O'Brien did not like.

> 'Tis nothing but one ashy calx,
> One cinder all from pole to pole.

That was the Moon, that was, Tennyson's Moon, and not his poem, which was really rather good. It registers an adventurer's disappointment with what he finds when he flies there, a disappointment which gives way to a thrilling interplanetary glimpse: but it's mostly a praise of planet Earth, many of whose inhabitants were beset, in 1969, with enough commotions for an escape into space to seem inviting. The journal had in the past been an outstanding publisher of poems by living writers, and we were ambitious to keep up with our predecessors in that respect. In one particular year, 1973, we carried 'The Old Fools' by Philip Larkin, 'A Disused Shed in County Wexford' by Derek Mahon and 'Grauballe Man' by Seamus Heaney.

Nineteen seventy was a good year for judgment and argument, so far as the journal was concerned. There were these discussions concerning feminism and the future of the BBC. The climax of the football World Cup was discussed by BBC Music Division's Hans Keller, superbly admiring of the Brazilian mastery of the game. The question of how far Wagner is to blame for Nazism was debated, with Keller, a former prisoner of the Gestapo, arguing for a dissociation. Ian Hamilton and Clive James wrote respectively about television and radio.

Two related mistakes of mine could be felt to show the slips and strains that can occur in the context of public-service journalism. One was a piece by my friend Robin McEwen, an Africa hand and constitutional lawyer, which welcomed General Amin on his accession to power in Uganda, while granting that he was no doubt capable of ruthlessness should the need arise. The second was a critique of Allende's South American socialist state by a golden-haired Chile hand, a friend of the Prince of Wales, as I was later to learn. Such, at times, was our desire for right-wing writers. The mistakes illustrate the interaction between political and journalistic motives and appraisals that can occur in editorial decision-making. The regretful view of these pieces which I now hold is at least as much political as it is journalistic or literary, while the decision to publish them was political too, though in a different sense. The decision reflected the wish to give space to an oppositional account of Allende's Chile, soon to be swept away in a military coup which resulted in his death, and to offer a knowledgeable account of Uganda's new strong man. And we were aware that we would be publishing other people's accounts of these countries in later issues. Both pieces, however, lent a little involuntary aid to military dictatorship. It wouldn't do to try to persuade myself that I was betrayed by the public-service principle, with its homage to the balanced view, though the consideration did enter into the decisions that were made on these occasions.

Quite a few of the occasions I remember best belong to the correspondence columns. There was, for example, the old physicist Herbert Dingle's indomitable refusal to believe in the theory of relativity – one of the great non-serviams. An anonymous letter from within the BBC consisted of a spry parody of a Late Medieval pre-incarnation of the seventeenth-century chronicler John Aubrey. The letter complained about an 'apprentice scrivener' who'd been writing in the *Listener*, and it imparted a veiled bureaucratic threat. Does the editor, 'in encouraging the enemies of the Queen's Broadcastynge to publish their attacks within the Recorde of the Queen's

Broadcastynge, serve well the Illumination of the Realm'? Should the Queen's Broadcastynge allow this? In other words, we'd been attempting to maintain circulation by publishing criticism, by a probationary producer, of the Arts Features Department of BBC Television.

In 1967 we published a letter from the Cambridge academic Graham Hough which declared that those editors of the journal *Encounter* who had not known that it was covertly financed by the CIA *should* have known, since this had long been widely suspected. *Encounter* was a journal of opinion which did not quarrel with its paymasters, but which got into trouble for concealing them. Hough went on to say that 'the policies of the CIA and the American politico-military-economic machine that employs them are a programme for the suppression of freedom, for dictatorship and war.' It would have been impossible for us to have published this sentence in any manner that might have suggested editorial endorsement. But we claimed the right to publish articles like the one carried a fortnight before which digested an interview with the veteran American socialist and journalist I. F. Stone, who would have had no difficulty at all in grasping what Hough was getting at. As it turned out, Stone was revealed there as holding a balanced view of the Cold War protagonists, Russia and America. Of Russia he was reported to have said previously: 'This is not a good society and it is not led by honest men.' Of the American military commitment in Vietnam he said in the interview: 'We feel that this is a dreadful war, that it's a crime, and that nothing else matters except bringing it to a close.' Robert Conquest felt that the commitment was justified, and he wrote a letter to the paper conveying that it was in order for a Communist like Eric Hobsbawm to object to it, since Communists didn't pretend to believe in democracy, but that it was wrong for liberals to do so. Defenders of the commitment did less than they should have done to count the cost of intervention or to acknowledge the risks that were being run. It was as if they could not understand how unwise, never mind how wrong or right or democratic, the Americans were to intervene, and to take on one of the best and bravest armies of all time, a phantom troglodyte force which started up literally out of the ground to see them off. These and other aspects of the war were intensively discussed in the *Listener*, and from several points of view, including Hobsbawm's.

The journal was helped to address the subject by the fact that the subject figured relatively little in Parliamentary contention, and that the Prime Minister, Harold Wilson, had finessed it, so far as Labour was concerned, by going along with the Americans while keeping out of the war. In 1965, for domestic 'presentational reasons', as he put it, he wanted to be seen to have discussions about the war with President Johnson. 'If you want to help us some in Vietnam,' responded the President, 'send us some men and send us some folks to deal with these guerrillas. And announce to the press that you are going to help us.' No folks were sent. But if the *Listener* enjoyed the freedom afforded by a measure of inter-party accord, it was significant that our strongest piece on the subject came from an American, Anthony Lewis of the *New York Times*, who'd been interviewed about it on the BBC, and who was able to say what many readers might have found harder to take from a British writer. In the issue of 29 June 1972 he charged that British Prime Ministers of both parties, Edward Heath and before him Harold Wilson, had shown an 'uncritical' complicity with the 'hubris' of the American war effort in Vietnam. Heath had praised President Nixon's 'unparalleled restraint', and Lewis commented:

> To anyone who has lately been in Vietnam, North or South, the notion that President Nixon is showing 'restraint' is staggering in its unreality. The United States now has based in and around Vietnam the greatest air and sea armada in world history. It is bombing and shelling both halves of that country with unparalleled intensity. The tonnage of explosives used by American forces in Indo-China over the last seven years is already more than twice the total expended in World War Two.

Lewis also said that Vietnam was a small country, a peasant society, and that 'even if one has no sympathy whatever for the Vietnamese revolution and its contemporary Communist leaders, one should see the need for great-power restraint'. This is a statement which leaps out at you from the bound volumes of back-numbers.

It's instructive to glance across, in 1997, at the heading on the opposite page, which refers to 'the Provos' cease-fire'. The by now familiar ground of a Northern Ireland cease-fire that fails to happen was admirably covered, in 1972, by Keith Kyle and by the BBC correspondent Martin Bell, whose pieces for the paper, in every sense finely composed, on the deepening crises in Ulster and Vietnam, and on the Middle East war of the time, were sufficient in themselves to justify its existence. Bell wrote as a believer in old-world impartiality, and could make it seem like that old but often inoperative thing, human decency.

In recent times, he has explained that his approach has been radicalized, or at any rate radically changed, by his experience of the horrors of the Bosnian conflict, and of the inadequacy of the British Government's response to the conflict: 'I was brought up in the old and honourable tradition of balanced, dispassionate, objective journalism. I would now call it bystander journalism.' He went on to say: 'What I believe in now is what I prefer to call the journalism of attachment.' I think of this as an important event in the history of British journalism, both public and proprietorial, but it is one we should be careful not to misconstrue. It does not mean that Martin Bell has lost his sense of decency, or fairness, or that decency and fairness are incompatible with 'attachment'. He had earned the right to express himself as he did, with an eye on the approach of the former British Foreign Secretary, Malcolm Rifkind, who proclaimed a detachment from any principle other than that of national self-interest, who thinks, with Lord Palmerston, that 'the furtherance of British interests ought to be the sole object of a British Foreign Secretary.' Rifkind can certainly be exempted from the charge of yielding, on this front, to the cant of impartiality.

By the end of Greene's reign the BBC had started to take advice, as it still does, from management consultants and time-and-motion experts. The radio show *Round the Horne* predicted that Alistair Cooke's *Letter from America* would become a postcard. The *Listener* did not suffer any early ill-effects, but in 1973 a former advertising strategist for the *Sunday Times* Colour-Supplement was asked to report on it, and his firm's report was, from my point of view, a cinder and an ashy calx. It gave off a dislike of intellectual weeklies and said of the paper that 'there is basically very little market here.' It said that the proportion of material unrelated to broadcasting had risen, though I don't believe it had, and that the articles had become 'more erudite, less middlebrow, less informatory and explanatory, and more provocative'. 'The shift towards a more "permissive" and "anti-establishment" tone,' said the compilers of the report, 'while being in line with similar trends in intellectual circles and in other magazines, and while probably reflecting changes in broadcast material in general, has possibly run ahead of changes in "intelligent-layman" thinking.' At the same time, apparently, and not altogether consistently, there were former readers of the journal who, 'hot for certainties', felt that it had been giving them a 'dusty answer'. It was made to seem that we'd been displaying both too many certainties and too few.

No action was proposed in the light of the report, but I don't doubt that there were BBC Governors and executives who felt, as I did myself at this point, that my time as a public-service journalist was up. Twenty years later the BBC killed the *Listener*. The journal was a place where broadcasting and literature, in the widest sense of the word, could live together, and now this place has been destroyed. Narrow notions of marketability and mass appeal have destroyed it. The cost of the *Listener*, let me add, when set against the profits generated by the BBC's hugely-selling almanac of programmes, the *Radio Times*, could be considered minute.

8. Conor Cruise O'Brien

OUT OF AFRICA, in November 1964, came a thought, relayed to me by Christopher Ricks, who had first talked it over with William Empson in the course of a stroll through Blenheim Park. Then Empson had written to Ricks from Nigeria, in preference to Nkrumah's Ghana, where people's letters were opened and read, Empson believed, and where the adventurous Irishman Conor Cruise O'Brien was Vice-Chancellor of the University. O'Brien was finding relations with the Ghanaian Government very sticky; Nkrumah wanted 'a propaganda university only', wrote Ricks in his relaying letter. And he suggested that O'Brien might be interested in an invitation to edit the *New Statesman* if John Freeman were to leave in order to serve in Harold Wilson's new Labour government.

It struck me as a good idea. But it was also a hopeless one, and I was in any case a hopeless intermediary. I was on the paper all right, as literary editor, but did not take part in the kinds of deliberation where the succession would be decided. Nor were the paper's privy councillors likely to be ready for O'Brien, approved of for his actions in the Congo on behalf of the United Nations, but known to them, too, as a contributor to the paper who had a year before contributed an article to its Jubilee number which criticized its record on Appeasement: not for the only time in his life he had behaved as the candid friend who gets called an enemy, had behaved in a manner construable as perverse, adverse, contrary. Gifted journalists can come to grief in editorial chairs, as Dick Crossman was to discover at Great Turnstile, and it may be that that chair would have proved electric for O'Brien also. Despite the sound of raised and lowered voices that could be heard from the precincts of the *Observer* when he became its editor-in-chief, however, it seemed to me, as a reader, that he did well there. Living on a houseboat on the Thames at Chelsea, as if in distrust of Albion's shores, he behaved like some writing editor of the periodical past, like a weekly journalist of the old opinion-forming school, rather than the president of a Sunday paper. His editorship of the *New Statesman*, though, wasn't to be, and Empson, that outlandish kingmaker, was soon to be seen, by John Freeman's successor, as an undesirably abstruse contributor to the journal.

When I began working with O'Brien it was on the *Spectator* of the later Fifties. He was a member of the Irish diplomatic service, and the author of two impressive books. He was as impressive as his books, handsome and awesome. In person, there was something 'not amused' about this often highly comic writer; a Yeatsian cold eye could occasionally be spied, a feature more unsettling, I'd imagine, than the 'humourless twinkle' he ascribed to the Scandinavian gaze of Secretary-General Hammarskjöld of the United Nations. I remember him early on, at a drunken party, speaking in tongues – even in his cups, formidable and contained, even as there flowed from him speeches in Russian and in French. We were in England at the time – and God knows what foreigner-dreading Kingsley Amis, who is likely to have been at the party, must have made of the tower of Babel in the corner. The vanity which has been attributed to O'Brien was no more naggingly evident to me then than was my own, which did admittedly give me trouble on occasion; in part, it was that of the altruist and crusader whose interventions were an aspect of what caused him to become known in Dublin as 'the Cruiser'.

For several years we worked successfully together, and when our association ended he expressed a willingness for it to continue. But we never married, though there came a time when we appeared to have become divorced. When, in the Eighties, he visited University College London to give his Northcliffe Lectures on Edmund Burke, lectures I'd helped to organize, he came and went with the stealth appropriate to the arrival and departure of a secret agent at a drop. I may have displeased him at some point, and he would certainly not have been happy with the discussions of Israeli government policy which were published in the *London Review* in the course of the decade. But it may simply have been that after our early collaboration, and, in particular, our accord at the time of his candour on the subject of the CIA-funded magazine *Encounter*, I went from his head. He was a man who always had plenty to think about.

His first book, *Maria Cross* (1954), was written under the pseudonym Donat O'Donnell, to spare the feelings of the chamberlains responsible for the proprieties of the Irish Foreign Service. It is a collection of essays on the imaginative world of the modern Catholic writer – exasperated spirits, most of them, stranded in a hostile environment. There's a fine chapter on the fine novels of Mauriac, half-forgotten now in Britain, which views him as a writer who delights in his own torment and who will last for 'as long as humanity continues to enjoy torment-ing itself'. The book was written, O'Brien invites one to think, in a 'middle-aged' Ireland, 'the least romantic and the least revolutionary of countries'. Before long, romance was to come with a vengeance to the north of the island. O'Brien was romantic enough in this first book to try to understand the fantastic extremes of an unusual austerity of outlook: 'That "curiosity" which for Bernanos repre-sented the devil might be defined as the criticism of love by the conscious intellect.'

O'Brien's mother was Catholic, and his father agnos-tic: this might be thought prophetic of a writer both responsive to the Catholic sensibility and opposed to priestliness and to clerical despotism. He was also to become a writer who is opposed to revolution, to enforced programmatic change. Jacobin sympathies are reproved in his work as a historian. But if some revolutions are condemned, others are not. He was to sympathize with the Sandinistas in Nicaragua and with the programmes pursued by the radical clergy which arose in Latin America.

Three years after *Maria Cross* came his study of Parnell and his party. Ironically, perhaps, in view of a later involvement with the writings of Lewis Namier, this could be considered a Namierite work, by virtue of its stress on quantification, on the political rank-and-file and on Parliamentary and electoral manoeuvre. Handsome Charles Stewart Parnell emerges as a master of this material, before it abruptly destroyed him, with the exposure of his adulterous partnership with Kitty O'Shea; and O'Brien emerges as a master of Parnell's political supremacy. He admires Parnell, however coolly and critically, and there are those who might think that he identifies with him. But he does not exert himself to portray, in any psychological depth, an individual human being. So faint is the breath of scandal, and indeed of private life, so thoroughly absent from the book are Parnell's interesting sisters, that it can almost read like a disdain directed at other forms of biography. He has in general been very good at brief lives, but the leading figures in his books – with the exception of his own autobiographical presence in more than one of them – are a less vivid portraiture than his thumbnail sketches. Nevertheless, this book is an exquisite account of Parnell's politics, of what it means to say of his politician's inconsistency or ambivalence that for some he was a revolutionary, and for 'a more discerning few' a 'far-seeing conservative. Both avatars were necessary to him.' Parnell was both a separatist and a Home Ruler. And he was a high-handed man who might have made a dictator in the mode that was about to endear itself to European electorates. Yeats would have found it in him to praise Parnell in that capacity – having supplied a preamble in the poem where Parnell assures a stone-breaker, no doubt correctly, that when Ireland is free he will still be breaking stone.

O'Brien's essays and reviews were soon thought to contain some of his best work. I carried a number of the pieces that were later collected in *Writers and Politics*, which came out in 1965, and it was mildly educational to observe how long it took many, though not all, members of the academic community to notice that an important new critic had turned up on the other side of the fence that marked academics off from the world of letters and that of public affairs; I would doubt whether Leavis ever got round to reading a word of O'Brien. In this collection he is willing to describe himself as a socialist and as a liberal, while speaking severely of liberal indifference and hypocrisy in relation to the Third World. He sees himself as 'chipping away' at Western mendacity, and might have been seen, though not by every single American who read him, as a critic of America who had no illusions about Soviet Russia. 'In conditions of plenty, of corporate might and community weakness, brains are diverted from education into advertising,' he writes in Galbraithian vein, with America in mind. The adman of the Western world is conceived of as a kind of playboy: the suggestion is that he 'is behind a parapet firmly watching other people drown'.

The collection has in it, reprinted from the *New Statesman*, his essay 'Journal de Combat' of 1963, on the magazine *Encounter*. Funded at its inception by the CIA in Washington, and watched over by the Congress for Cultural Freedom, *Encounter* was to stand up for Western values and, less avowably, for American interests. The Communists specialized in secrecy, not least in the area of cultural persuasion. They had their fronts, their dupes, their covert subsidies. The Congress for Cultural Freedom had elected to fight fire with fire. They too were going to keep secrets.

His article issued what amounted to an early warning, about constraints due to the journal's devotion to American interests; more was to happen before the state connection was admitted. He took the journal seriously, while assessing it from the familiar point of view of Julien Benda's notion of a *trahison des clercs*, of the declared or undeclared ideological bias which can poison intellectual discussion.

'These two Russian Jews decided to save Western civilization,' wrote a friend of theirs, Edward Shils, in praise of Michael Josselson and Melvin Lasky. And the Congress for Cultural Freedom was born. It was born in the late Forties and died in 1967. A CIA agent 'became an editor of *Encounter*', wrote a CIA spokesman, of the magazine sponsored by the Congress in 1953 and sited in London. Thirteen years later its cover was finally blown, and it folded in 1990. *Encounter* spoke up in heterogeneous style for America, freedom, neutralism, Europeanism, Atlanticism. It was designed to appeal, and did for a while appeal, to 'the non-Communist Left' (I wrote for it myself, very badly, on Beckett's limitations and other matters, in its early days). It wanted, at times, an end to ideology, to Cold War demonizing, to a division of the world into light and dark, and it also wanted to make an ideology of the free market. The purport of its pieces

could hardly be called covert. There can in a sense be no
such thing as a secret magazine: *Encounter* said what it
had to say, and you could find out what that was by
reading it. And yet there was an intention to deceive its
readers, and some of its editors. It had practised what
Edmund Burke was the first to call 'an economy of truth'.
One that can't have harmed many people. But it was a
mistake to throw a veil over its funding and its founding,
and a big mistake for a journal sworn to openness and
freedom to do so. One of its insiders, Raymond Aron, felt
sorry for a colleague who'd had to bear the 'burden' of the
original lie. Other *clercs* made light of the load. In 1985,
'the British philosopher Roger Scruton' was sorry that the
CIA had become so intimidated that it was refusing to
engage in 'its most honourable occupation – the support
of those publications which tell the truth about the
modern world'. Covert funding, he urged, should be
restored.

I am raking over these embers – with the assistance of
Peter Coleman's too often hagiographic Australian version
of Congress activities, *The Liberal Conspiracy*, which supplies instances of CIA interference with editorial decisions
on the paper – in order to refer to O'Brien's part in the
challenge that was to confront *Encounter* and its free-spirit
cover story. Coleman is comparatively unmoved by the
British actors in his drama, and by the London end of it,
and his book says nothing about O'Brien's *New Statesman*
piece of 1963, which did a great deal to inaugurate the
challenge. O'Brien was not then concerned with the
funding question, but with the claim that there could be
a *trahison des clercs* on behalf of the CIA as well as the

KGB: 'Benda's point was that writers were not to cheat, for any side.' The trouble with the *Encounter* of those days was that where some truth is 'uncomfortable for the Soviet Union it is promulgated; where it is uncomfortable for the United States it is mitigated'. Few journals can ever have been so discomfited. Dog ate dog as seldom before or since.

Three years after that, in 1966, O'Brien did mention the matter of the magazine's CIA funding, in a lecture delivered and printed in America: he said that *Encounter* was published 'in the interests – and as it now appears at the expense – of the power structure in Washington'. In August of that year he was subjected to 'ridicule', as Coleman puts it, in *Encounter*: an unsigned diary piece, the work of a ridiculous and subsequently discredited fisher in Cold War waters, Goronwy Rees, accused him of bungling bloodily about in the Congo, shortly before this, on behalf of the United Nations, while posing as 'a Machiavelli of Peace' – a description of O'Brien's which had been employed with reference, not to himself, but to Hammarskjöld. Rees claimed to detect 'elements of high comedy in the transformation of the Machiavelli of Peace into the Joe McCarthy of politico-cultural criticism, hunting for CIA agents beneath the beds of Stephen Spender, Irving Kristol, Melvin Lasky and Frank Kermode'.

In a life of O'Brien, festively-titled *Conor*, which appeared in 1994, Donald Harman Akenson recalls that the *New Statesman* offered to publish a self-defence by O'Brien, but was deterred by a threat of legal action, and that Conor was at first reluctant to sue *Encounter*, scenting a trap. A darkness had fallen. Old friends gossiped and advised; one of them was thought to have been sighted carrying an attaché-case filled with derogatory material for use against him in court. I don't remember the conversation between Frank Kermode and myself which may, Akenson suggests, have mediated the threat. But I do remember seeking to support Conor throughout. In due course, after the cancellation of that *New Statesman* article, he decided to sue, having made up his mind that the Rees piece was so plainly defamatory that if he didn't sue it would be taken as a sign that its statements were well-founded, and he took pains in preparing his case against the magazine. He wrote me a letter on Christmas Eve in which he discussed my helping him by testifying on his behalf, and his helping me, since I had just resigned from the *New Statesman* and was making plans for another shot at editing. He said he would write for me if I managed to get going again, and he did when I went to the *Listener*. 'I have long thought,' he remarked in the letter, 'of founding a resigners' club to be called Islam (which, as you certainly know, but as I take the liberty of reminding you, is Arabic for Resignation).' This was the closest to one another that we fellow 'Islamists' ever came. In the end, a settlement was reached with the magazine, which tendered an apology in a Dublin court. *Encounter*'s American editor, Mel Lasky, I should add, had written me a supportive note when Islam occurred at the *New Statesman*. Mel, for one, was aware that I was a member of the non-Communist Left.

The stances for which O'Brien has been best-known have related to the fortunes of nations or peoples with a history of intrusion, of intruding and of being intruded upon, a colonial or, as he took to saying of recent developments, a neo-colonial history. The concern with his own country has been chronic, while the other two principal stances have belonged to successive phases of his career. The concern with American might and with the Third World, evident in his critique of *Encounter*, was also evident in the episode that preceded it – his season of active service in the Congo. With regard both to the magazine and to the discharge of his duty as United Nations Representative in the Conradian tropical remoteness of Katanga, it seems to me that the abuse aimed at him at the time for his interventionism in the Congo must now appear, to most people, no less partisan, no more disinterested, than it did to his friends during the events which reached their crisis when Hammarskjöld's plane hit the ground at Ndola – sabotaged, as Conor has continued to believe. The Katangan secession was to last for a further two years.

'Who is Conor O'Brien?' asked the British Prime Minister Harold Macmillan in 1961, and O'Brien proceeds to answer the question, which begins its opening chapter, in his book *To Katanga and Back*, a notably personal account of what it was to attempt to do the contradictory biddings available from the United Nations in relation to the breakaway of the mineral-rich Katanga province from the newly-emergent Congo state. Belgian interests had rallied to install a puppet prime minister and to hold on to what they could of the 'splendid piece of cake' which civilizing Leopold II had discovered in the Congo. Here were a neo-colonialism militant, and conspiratorial, ministerial murders in Elisabethville, gen-ocidal sweeps in the bush. O'Brien was targeted by UN member states sympathetic to the Belgian appetite for a share in the region, and was deserted by some of his UN superiors. Macmillan's colleagues may be imagined responding to his question with the portrait of a subversive Irish hothead reminiscent of the O'Brien – the Anglophobe rapparee or pirate – who figures, as a resident of Cuba, in Conrad's and Ford Madox Ford's preposterous novel *Romance*. The 'great end' which the United Nations O'Brien was struggling to serve in the field was the preservation of a united Congo – an end which was only imperfectly and equivocally acknowledged and endorsed by the UN Security Council and Secretariat. Having struggled for a time, he resigned.

Nkrumah then invited him to go to Ghana to be his Vice-Chancellor. He has naturally been blamed subsequently for enlisting in a despotism, but there were no indications at the time that he deserved to be seen as failing in his duty to resist Nkrumah when resistance was called for. 'Islam' was practised, as in the Congo, when his position became untenable. He moved back to the quiet of his eighteenth-century white house on Howth Summit near Dublin. It was to prove, however, quite unlike the farm retired to by Cincinnatus, though on moonlit nights, looking out on a gleaming expanse of Irish Sea, you might think you were in Positano. He became a Labour Party politician, and was Minister of Posts for a time. Meanwhile, a terrorist war of attrition had broken out in the North and was to claim his attention from that day to this.

Enter, in later years, Conor Cruise O'Zion. This was another persona awarded to him by opponents, but a more authentic one than the Irish Nationalist pirate chief apparent to Tory politicians. 'Conor Cruise O'Zion' was the aggressive heading placed by me on top of a discussion in the *London Review*, by David Gilmour, of his history of Zionism, entitled *The Siege* and published in 1986. The heading gave offence – to a Jewish historian in New York, for example, who felt that it stood in the same relation to the history and survival of the Jews as the journalism of Julius Streicher. It expressed a difference of opinion with O'Brien over the interpretation of Israeli government policy with regard to the Palestinians, displaced by Israel from their homeland.

The Siege is a brilliant narrative. Here is a turn of events around 1936, when a faintly perfidious Albion

> could not concede Arab demands backed by the murderous violence of bands of roaming *fellahin*. But might Britain not, freely and honourably, accept the advice of its proved friends in the Arab world? Surely it might; even though in practice the advice of the princes would coincide exactly with the demands of the *fellahin*. What mattered was the look of the thing, and the princes undoubtedly looked well, in an indigenous sort of way.

It is also a vigorous defence of Zionism, from Theodor Herzl – who saw himself as 'the Parnell of the Jews' – to the point of publication. That point lay four years after the Sabra and Chatila massacres in Lebanon, where the

Maronite Christian milita ordered in by senior Israeli commanders, one of whom is now in the Netanyahu Cabinet, murdered hundreds of civilians, including women and children, in these Palestinian refugee camps. Prime Minister Begin denied everything at first, then stated: '*Goyim* kill *goyim*, and they immediately come to hang the Jews.' Later he was to accept the adverse findings of an Israeli commission of inquiry. O'Brien notes that such massacres have been customary in Lebanon's civil wars, and pictures Begin as a pious and patriotic 'victim of the war he had started', who felt betrayed by his Defence Minister Ariel Sharon. He was soon to retire. 'It was as sad an end as might well be conceived to a long career, which had been entirely devoted to the selfless service of Israel.'

In a discussion of the crucial Arab-Israeli conflict of 1948 O'Brien speaks of the departure of half a million Arabs from Israeli-held territory. Which of them were driven out, and which of them fled? The distinction has been debated by casuists. O'Brien puts it like this: 'it appears that some – perhaps a majority – fled, while some were driven out.' The language seems unduly diplomatic. He goes on to say that Arabs had 'fled' earlier on – 'mainly in panic caused by the news of the Irgun's massacre at Deir Yassin'. You might almost have supposed that they had been driven out.

The slaughter at Sabra and Chatila left a deep and lasting impression on the journalistic coverage in Britain of successive Middle Eastern crises. But it can also be seen as in some degree customary, and as part of a complex regional history of right and wrong, atrocity and counter-atrocity. For my own part, I have long felt for those many Israelis who have done what they could to contend with the self-destructive harshness and intransigence of Israeli government policy, and with a siege mentality which can run to an approval of the murder and intimidation of Israelis trying for coexistence with the Palestinians; and I have sympathized with the case made on behalf of the Palestinian cause by Ian Gilmour and his son David and by Edward Said, names rarely if ever mentioned in Conor's book. Neither I nor the writers I have named can truthfully be called anti-semitic. In writing about the Middle East, as in his exertions in Africa, O'Brien had to bear in mind Security Council Resolutions. Resolution 242 is paraphrased by him here as 'eventual recognition of Israel', and what we were arguing for in the *London Review*, during the Eighties, was its implementation – recognition of Israel by the Arab states, together with a move towards peace whereby Israeli-occupied territory was ceded for settlement by a separate, and perhaps sovereign, Palestinian community.

In 1986, O'Brien did not believe in 'territory for peace'. Israel's position was 'more precarious – with its large and growing Arab population – than would be the case if the "territory for peace" option were really there'. But it wasn't really there. Nor did he believe in 'bold steps'. The siege must go on. He thought it questionable to assume 'that there are *any* results at all likely in any general election in Israel, ever, that would lead to . . . Israel's withdrawal from all or almost all of the West Bank, and the creation of some kind of Palestinian political entity there.' Since then, steps have been taken.

There *has* been movement. Some kind of Palestinian political entity is being attempted on the West Bank. An abrasive Israeli leadership has kept a tight grip on the new Palestinian enclaves, where a return to intifada is in the air and a hedged-in President Arafat has become a censor, and a torturer of his people, with Hanan Ashrawi unlikely to replace him. But the situation looks – though not to Edward Said – a little less hopeless than it did to many in 1986, when the circle of wagons seemed to O'Brien set to stay intact for ever.

Many years ago I dined with an Irish friend of his, a sensitive literary civil servant, who told me quietly that he didn't like Jews. It was clear that he was not what I would have thought to call an anti-semite; it was as if he had lived his life beyond the pale where anti-semitic sentiments, of the sort I knew about, were expressed, repressed and reprehended. And it may be that the sophisticated O'Brien's zeal for Zion and affection for Jews shares that provenance, that innocence, and is somehow the stronger for it. Sharing his sense that Jews are likeable, I've occasionally been intrigued by this feature of his commitment – by its seeming disinterested, seeming to stand outside the ambit of Anglo-American and European sentiment on the subject, while conscious of home truths and domestic applications that can be discovered in the Middle East.

He has ways of seeing Ireland in Israel. At one stage in the book he asserts that no British government could force the Israelis into a state with an Arab majority, 'any more than any British government could force Ulster Protestants into a Catholic-majority state'. One might feel that if it's possible to say that Ulster's Protestants resemble the Israelis, it is also possible to say that Ulster's Catholics resemble the Palestinians in having been denied opportunities for a legitimate redress of their injustices, but that there's a difference of degree in this last respect which makes it difficult to equate the IRA with the PLO. Both Ulster Protestants and Israelis were planted where they now are, but can both be considered incomers to a land with which they have ancient connections. Neither will surrender. No surrender – and with regard to the difficulties faced by both peoples he has talked as if there could be no solution. There's a certain fatalism in O'Brien. In the Nineties the former interventionist was firmly declaring that UN military intervention in the Bosnian conflict would do no good: but it did do some good when it finally arrived. There are, at present, no mass exterminations. A pause, if not a peace, has broken out.

He has been an enemy of IRA terrorism, both as a minister and as an ex-minister. Then, in 1996, at the age of seventy-eight, he appeared in the North as a Northern politician. 'The Cruiser' has acquired 'Unionist credentials', sang the British press. He now belongs to a sub-group of that uneasy alignment whose leaders include the Rev. Ian Paisley, loud mouth and hard head, the reviler of Catholics who was in at the start of this thirty years' war. 'I feel very much at home with the United Kingdom Unionists,' said Conor, as he passed the spot in Belfast where, eighty-five years before, the Solemn League and Covenant pledging resistance to Home Rule for Ireland was signed by the Southern Irish Ulster patriot, Sir Edward Carson. Earlier in the life of this United

Kingdom Unionist recruit there had been a time when Unionists attempted with foot or fist to remove his teeth at a rally in the North; I remember his remarking with enjoyment that, according to his dentist, only a certain resilience in the gums had saved them. 'The Orange population of Ulster,' wrote George Dangerfield in 1935, in *The Strange Death of Liberal England*, is 'not lovable'. And now here was a man from the South come up to have a try – the most striking arrival of the kind since Carson, who delivered one of his warlike speeches at Blenheim, where Ricks and Empson were to stroll, talking of O'Brien.

On this recent occasion in Belfast a woman standing by was heard to inform her friend that nobody likes a turncoat. She may have remembered that the youthful O'Brien had been against partition. He has also been charged, as have many politicians and many other human beings, with inconsistency, and with contrariness, with a need to go against the view expected of him or against the general opinion: and by the novelist Mary McCarthy, in the heat of controversy, he was once charged with being 'a tricky Irishman'. But while certainly subject to change and development, and unlikely to be averse to stratagem and to the art of the possible, he seems to me as straight as any Gaitskell. For scrupulous people in Ireland, North and South, it can never have been easy to escape the pressure of divided loyalties, and the unscrupulous have not allowed them to forget it. 'Turncoat' is a word which has often been used and abused in that part of the world, as has 'betrayal', that magic word of the British Left. But neither of these words fits O'Brien.

'Betraying sisters,' writes Seamus Heaney in a poem, of girls tarred and feathered by the 'tribal' IRA for going out with British soldiers. O'Brien has objected to this use of the adjective 'betraying'. So used, it was, he conveyed, an IRA adjective. Only the IRA, or a certain sort of innocent bystander, would apply it to O'Brien.

His stand against the IRA's killing game has been valuable and courageous. Both Ireland and Britain would be the poorer, and the more vulnerable, had he not pursued his indictment of the armalite politics of Sinn Fein (in a sense, no politics at all), his indictment of the Republican tradition, with its cult of murder and martyrdom, its notion – attributed the other day to Seamus Deane – that 'fairness' and 'objectivity' are alien words, weasel words perhaps, best left to the English. The indictment has had to deal with the fact that Sinn Fein has in Gerry Adams a leader of exceptional ability, and with a tendency within sections of the British media to sentimentalize the revolutionary IRA. When O'Brien was ministerially responsible for Irish television, they were banned from the screen. In Britain, some television producers have been a little in love with them, and have complained about having to have the IRA's words spoken on the air by actors. Their actions speak for themselves. They have spread misery and disorder by murdering, for the most part, passers-by, by inventing for the six counties a colonial power that has to be forced out, and by denying the hostility towards Northern Catholics of Northern Protestants in their millions.

Where his position can be criticized, I think, is in relation to what comes of his occasionally appearing to suggest that there can be no solution beyond that of an indefinitely prolonged military containment. Are we to say what Andrew Marvell said in his ambivalently triumphal ode on Cromwell's return from Ireland, which, in the Seventies, I thought of as the best poem – in the sense of the most revealing – which had been written about modern Ulster?

> The same arts that did gain
> A power must it maintain.

What such a criticism must mean, for the negotiations which have been nightmarishly starting and stalling over the past few months, is that they can't afford to exclude, unconditionally, representatives of physical-force Republicanism: if it would be painful to have them in, it would be hopeless to leave them out.

O'Brien has sometimes appeared to look away from what has been suffered, in their state of subordination, by the Catholics of the North. Perhaps he has insufficiently sentimentalized the life from which Republican activism proceeds and for which Adams speaks. His tough arguments offer too little to Northern Catholics by way of legitimate redress, and can even at times appear to deny the validity of their defiant way of life. This way of life is revealed in a recent novel, a fictionalizing of family annals, by Seamus Deane, a professor of history, a schoolfellow of Seamus Heaney's, and a man of Catholic background who is said never to have known a Protestant who wasn't a policeman until he left Derry to go to university in Belfast.

Reading in the Dark is about the generations of a household crucified on the idea of betrayal. It has a true and a false informer, and the execution – within the family, in more than one sense of that word – of the wrong one. It is, from some points of view, a romantic work. It has mad scenes from Shakespeare, a dungeon and an ancient castle, and a household that yields more mysteries than the castle of Udolpho. But it may be that it also has in it the secret of an oppressed community, as besieged as Israel is. The characters in the novel are not figments, or fantasies, or bigots, or zealots, or murderers. They are magnificent people, and there can be no justification for asking their descendants to go on with, or go back to, the way of life described in the novel. As for their relocation in the South, that seems more unlikely than ever. For seventy years Ulster's Catholics have refused to leave the native place which has supplied them with their ordeal. They too have refused to surrender.

The police sergeant in the novel who handles the family informer is the Catholic servant of a Protestant state, and he is named Burke, a name that appears to have belonged to a real-life original. Conor Cruise O'Brien's Burke is the political thinker studied in his book *The Great Melody*, of 1992. Both Burkes embody the complex fate of being Irish. Did Edmund Burke betray his people by joining the Hanoverian élite in London? How inconsistent was he, and what was the measure of his inconsistency?

Not many politicians of consequence have been free from the reproach. Parnell, with his contrasting avatars, was not free from it, and Burke's inconsistency is a time-honoured issue which O'Brien, with avatars of his own, is eager to address in his book. Burke's friend Samuel Johnson thought him enviable for being 'constantly the same', and Coleridge thought likewise: 'No man was ever more like himself.' Hazlitt, who may have had less than the others of the eighteenth-century suspicion of human changefulness, thought differently: 'his qualities contradict even themselves.' In later times Burke's contradictions have been stressed – by the antagonistic Lewis Namier, for instance. O'Brien won't have this view of Burke, and preoccupies himself with Namier's disparagement of him. He grants that a change of front took place in respect of the colonial exploitation practised by the East India Company: early in his career Burke took a Whig line in deploring the Crown's interference with the Company's profits. Thereafter he sees a seamless continuity: no break, or breach of principle, as between his denunciations of the French Revolution and his previous campaigns on behalf of the American colonists and against the looting of India.

Burke's mother was Catholic, his father a probably reluctant convert to the state religion. And when he became an English politician he worked hard for free trade with Ireland and for Catholic emancipation there. In all Burke's defining political commitments O'Brien sees a concern with Ireland, and with the oppression suffered by its Catholics at the hands of his adoptive tribe, the Protestant élite whose might and excellence are commended and corrected in his writings and speeches – a prime theme for the *verbum ardens* relished by his contemporaries. But Ireland was a concern which he also had to dissemble. He had on occasion to make himself 'sound more Protestant than he actually felt'. And he could make himself sound like the *laudator* of Protestant lordship which he was later blamed for being. George III came to appreciate him and to patronize him, remarking that he had 'supported the cause of the Gentlemen', the cause, as Burke expressed it, of those natural aristocrats who, 'bred in a place of estimation', had seen 'nothing low or sordid' from their infancy.

All this may be thought to have placed Burke in a quandary and to expose him to the charge of inconsistency. But it does not make him a turncoat. O'Brien's book argues cogently to this effect – without, perhaps, fully imagining what it might mean to think otherwise. Burke's feelings about Ireland and its relationship with his political masters may be presumed to have run deep: O'Brien talks of these feelings in a language uncharacteristic of him, in terms of psychic depths, and he thinks of them as attested to in Burke's silences on occasions when he may or must have wanted to speak about Ireland. 'Whatever you say say nothing' – there's a poem of Heaney's of the Seventies which plays with that Irish saying. And Edmund Burke of the burning words sometimes says nothing. Heaney's poem was written in a revolutionary, and counter-revolutionary, Northern Ireland, in which 'little platoons' were mustering:

> The phrase is Cruise O'Brien's via that great
> Backlash, Burke . . .

O'Brien's book induces a consciousness both of Burke's silences and of those of Namier, who was apt to be silent, or terse, about the inner or personal lives of his politicians. According to O'Brien, Namier's strategy for the disparagement of Burke pursued in his books is seldom to mention him. But it is clear to O'Brien that for Namier Burke was a servant of the aristocracy, a snob, a rhetorician, a politician who never attained high office, and an outsider in relation to the Parliamentary rank-and-file whom Namier specialized in itemizing and inspecting: he was not of that number, or of any number, though he knew all about party.

Beyond the confines of his books, as it happens, Namier was less silent about Burke, and in this respect a silence of O'Brien's can be noticed. In 1958, during my time at the *Spectator* – which was also O'Brien's time there as a contributor – Namier reviewed a volume of Burke's correspondence, and expatiated, by Namierite standards, on 'the character of Burke'. Burke is described as contra-dictory, egotistical, paranoid ('a streak of persecution mania'), and a 'poor observer'. There are moments in the review when a high-born Jewish refugee, with a high regard for the natural aristocracy of England, might seem to be engaged in putting down an unstable Irish upstart. Burke was emotional, rootless: 'a solitary, rootless man who preached party', and a party politician with 'a minority mind'.

America, India and regicide France elicit the 'great melody' of Burke's principal eloquence. The expression makes a fulsome title for Conor's book, and is drawn from a poem by Yeats in which several speakers discuss 'Whiggery':

> American colonies, Ireland, France and India
> Harried, and Burke's great melody against it.

Burke is supposed in the poem to have hated Whigs (though he was a Whig for a while himself), and one of its interlocutors calls Whiggery 'a levelling, rancorous, rational sort of mind'. The 'it' in the second of these two lines could be thought to refer to the harrying that begins the line (with France's revolutionaries needing to be seen as attacking her in the manner of levellers), or to Yeatsian Whiggery in general, or, as O'Brien has it, to abuse of power, or to any two of them if not to all three. O'Brien's reading was challenged by Seamus Deane – who plumps for Whiggery – in a review of the book of which it could be said that this was the mildest of Deane's objections to *The Great Melody*.

Deane's discordant review speaks of O'Brien's 'amateurism', of tabloid journalism, of his 'paranoia', and of 'this disturbed attempt to rewrite the story of Burke as a version of the story of Conor Cruise O'Brien – Irish, not British, heroically consistent in his principles and not a venal hack, sympathetic to the Irish Catholic cause, opposed to the Protestant ascendancy . . .' The book is a 'disguised autobiography'. Deane appears to find O'Brien's principles insupportable, and to be suggesting that the book is designed to cover up both a support for the Protestant cause and a proven inconsistency.

Others, too, have found in the book an element of identification with its subject. Excellent books can contain that element; Namier's writings contain it. And it's in any case not bizarre that O'Brien should have responded to a something in common between himself and Burke, and that he should at times have expressed his own feelings about Ireland and its terrorists in examining Burke's feelings about Ireland and France and their revolutionaries. It's possible to say in all simplicity that the two of them resemble one another in major and in minor ways. His long book is made longer still by attaching an appendix which contains a review by him of a book by Isaiah Berlin, followed by an exchange of friendly letters between them about Burke and other matters. One of O'Brien's letters observes that one of Berlin's had set 'joy bells' ringing in his household. This is insufficiently unlike Burke's flattery of élites, his reverence for the insulted loveliness of Marie-Antoinette, 'glittering like the morning-star'. The age of chivalry is not gone.

My admiration of Burke and of his biographer is capable of a bit of unpleasantness, as here. I'm not sure that I can help it. Burke's chivalrous approach to Marie-Antoinette, and to the social role of the French nobility, gets on my nerves. And my admiration of O'Brien was to be made anxious by disagreements, regrets, and a perhaps misplaced sense of rejection. But it is as lively as ever.

It is human to resemble the people you undertake to defend. And it's also human to be vexed or troubled by displays and presumptions of inconsistency, while making too much of them at times. O'Brien has defended both those who are thought to have been oppressed and those who are thought to have been oppressive. But he has been no more inconsistent than he believes Burke was, and in the following-out of his thoughts and the concerting of his various avocations, he has done what writers have always found it very difficult to do. His career, in other words, has been nothing short of glorious in applying an exceptional literary talent to a defence of the public interest and a succession of good causes. Twentieth-century critics aren't often like this, are they? They have wanted to be judges, scientists. They have been professionals and recluses. Hardly ever have they fought for an enlargement of human happiness. In discussing his exposure to intractable, defeating political difficulty, I have spoken, perhaps presumptuously, of a certain hopelessness occasionally perceptible in his writings. It is also true that his effort has been to hold out hope.

I haven't mentioned all of his books, and am barely able to keep up with the ones he is still writing. *Ancestral Voices* – a powerful account of religious and political interaction in modern Ireland and of the involvement in that process of the O'Brien dynasty – was published in 1994. The 'parlous mental and moral condition' of Irish Nationalism, for most of this century, is seen in relation to a kind of strategic pun – in relation to the comparison between the Easter rising of 1916 and that of Christ which has helped to engender a line of suicidal martyrs and armed-strugglers, a sacrificial and homicidal succession. The following year came his reflections on the new millennium. He writes here contra Islam, against those Islamists who are religious fundamentalists and

jihadists, and he 'abhors' the present Pope. He deplores
the 'decline in deference' which he sees about him, and he
foresees the fall of the British monarchy by the end of the
next century. He grapples with his subject 'in a Burkean
spirit', and condemns the Millennium Commission in
Britain for its indifference to tradition, and for the
trendiness and shallowness of its inaugural plans. Burke,
thou shouldst be living at this hour? Well, he is, between
the covers of this book of O'Brien's. It abhors and
applauds the Enlightenment. There's a bad Enlightenment, which helped to produce the French Revolution.
And there's a good one, an earlier one, whose spirit
survives and is discernible in the otherwise deficient
United States, with its hypocritical show of 'restoring
democracy' in Haiti.

This is a divided book which is at times a jeremiad.
A species of 'mental degenerate' is discovered to be in
charge of politics and communications. After it came
O'Brien's reflections, no less consciously outrageous, on
the Pol Pot French Revolutionariness – or bloody millen-
arianism – of the Thomas Jefferson of the early 1790s. Of
these many books of his there are some which have been
found intemperate or ill-judged. But none can fairly be
found to lack the public spirit I have been praising.

His writings give the impression that political opinions are compatible with, and may even be necessary to,
the pursuit of literature. But he also believes in disinterestedness. The fact that his positions have resisted
classification as either right or left has more to do with
that than with changes of mind or coat. And the same
can be said of the fact that his sympathy with many

manifestations of Catholicism has not prevented him from condemning, on humanitarian grounds, the gospel preached by the Pope, or from going up to Ulster and embracing an association of a kind with the Rev. Ian Paisley.

The American neo-conservatives of the Eighties professed to believe in disinterestedness, and he has written well about that, in suggesting that it's easier to profess than to practise: 'Mr Podheretz, the literary critic, discovers, in his disinterested way, that the best of Camus is to be found in the work by Camus which happens to be most to the political taste of Mr Podhoretz, the neo-conservative ideologue.' In Britain, the New Right of the Eighties and after have not been given to talking about disinterestedness. They have made no parade of impartiality. Instead, they have made a parade of what is known to them as 'bloodiness'. Up in the air has hung the hard nose of the right-wing thinker, whose favourite words are 'bloodiness' and its cognates. And what a free run of it they've had.

These are the ideologues who came to print on the back of Margaret Thatcher's victories and filled the silence left by the abdication at that point of their socialist or social-democratic counterparts. Among these ideologues is the philosopher mentioned earlier who has called for honourable spies to support truth-telling journals, and who wants to make it clear that he looks down on 'the lower orders'. Comparison between the people in question and the conference-attending *Encounter* intellectuals of the Fifties indicates that this new New Right has consisted of a lower order of thinker, though some of the best of them can claim countenance from one of the most rewarding of the conservative thinkers of recent times, Michael Oake-shott, who wrote for *Encounter* in the Fifties. At their worst, they are Michael Portillo, John Major's bellicose Minister of Defence. Portillo, son of a refugee, belonged to a government tough on asylum-seekers and indifferent to the reasons for their search. He leapt to the helm, or towards it, with a political philosophy – deniable, perhaps, in the fullness of time – of brutal inanity. Portillistas could be heard to speak of 'the truly minimal state', of a sovereign state inhabited by sovereign individuals who wish to minimize it. Bloodiness means not minding about the contradictions apparent in such a programme. And it also means not minding about a withering away of the unions and of welfare and of aid to starving countries.

All this ran on until recent times, and the Labour government-in-waiting was rather too attentive to it. It has had very little to do with any return to favour of the cause of the gentlemen, as sponsored by George III. But gentlemen need not despair. The category will persist, along with that of the deserving rich.

9. That Night in Ireland

WITH AN IRISH grandfather, two Irish-patriot middle names (Fergus Connor) and a half-Jewish wife, I may well have felt more exposed than most people living in the South of England to the subject-matter of Conor Cruise O'Brien's books. When I was young, however, I knew little of what it was to be Irish, and of what it was for there to be these two tribes of Catholic and Protestant and for them not to get on. I knew as a boy about Yeats and the 'terrible beauty' of the rising of Easter 1916, but was more at home with the lake isle of Innisfree than with the streets of Belfast, or with Irish independence and the Ulster redoubt. Was my maternal grandfather a Catholic or a Protestant? I have never found out. He came over from Ireland and married a Protestant, so he himself may have been one. But then again the name Connor smacks of the Pope, and he may have been exogamous, like me. He was a miner, a trade-unionist, a fiddler, and I somehow can't imagine him in a church. Was my friend the footballer Danny Blanchflower a Protestant, and is the footballer George Best one of those too? I think so, but earlier in life I didn't know and mysteriously didn't care. And when I first became friends with the poet Seamus

Heaney in the early Sixties, I had no idea what the name Seamus was taken to mean in Ireland.

The Seamus of those days was for a brief while a Beatle, a long-hair; he looked like a second Best, a bardic one, when he was featured, with photographs, in *Vogue*, by his sister-in-law Polly Devlin. The period resemblance between the two lads may have affected my ability to tell the difference between categories of Irish person. But all that was to change, utterly. I had started to be able to tell the difference some time before Ulster's B-Special constabulary moved in with their batons on Catholics and civil-rights marchers. Seamus wrote a ballad in their defence, 'Craig's Dragoons', to the air of 'Dolly's Brae' and in the form of a Loyalist vaunt: 'We've gerrymandered Derry but Croppy won't lie down . . .' The 'neighbourly murders' of which he speaks in a later poem then began in earnest, and in another poem of that later time he would refer to 'my wronged people'. Later still, he was to borrow a stanza form from Scotland's Robert Burns to decline classification as a British poet:

> No glass of ours was ever raised
> To toast The Queen.

An early reticence on his part and this initial ignorance on mine were soon to vanish from our conversations. I remember an early occasion when my small children squatted with us in my sitting-room, punctuating our exchanges, and I asked him if he was a believing Catholic, feeling that the answer might well be no. There would come a time when we went temple-haunting, when he took me to the Early Christian sites at Glendalough, and the trip may be said to have completed his answer to my question. I think that he is – as many English-speaking poets of the twentieth century have been – a religious believer. But I doubt whether we should raise our glass to him as a Catholic poet. I could be wrong. Wrong again.

In the Seventies, I stayed with him in Belfast and a ceilidh was held in his house. David Hammond sang, Tommy Gunn played the fiddle, Sean McAloon the elbow-pipes. The poems were like songs and the songs like poems, and there were lines that were like a running stream.

> Would God that I and my darling
> Were a thousand long leagues to the west.

That sort of thing. The house was filled with airs that hurt not, and it seemed like holy ground, though far from clerical ground, or holy-war ground. When I grew up in Scotland, I had a Gaelic-speaking Hebridean teacher and friend in Hector MacIver, who would have loved that night in Ireland; but I had tended to think of ceilidhs as folkweave material, pinned with an ornamental dirk or Cairngorm brooch, tossed about in eightsome reels danced by Sunday-night Celts. What happened in Belfast was not like that. This was their life. Here was a bilingual occasion which made me feel Irish – Irish Irish, that is – while also making me, no doubt, its sentimental mono-glot over-interpreter. I sat at the back thinking of the seductive West that casts its spell in Joyce's story 'The

Dead', during the aftermath of the old-world musical soirée in Dublin, where the 'Irish Irelander' Nationalist, Miss Ivors, speaks up for an outlook shared with Conor Cruise O'Brien's mother; and there was a note as of the gatherings of secret Catholics in Elizabethan St Albans, with their recusant hymns, their sweet sad longing for the Jerusalem of Rome.

During that same visit I sat in a car with Seamus at the side of a Belfast street. We'd pulled over to let through an Orange march. There was a last light in the sky which left the foreground in darkness. Out of the dark swung lambeg drums and shrilling fifes and a long line of Glengarried George Bests. It was as if we were down in a hedge or a ditch squinting up at the masters of the causeway. That they should all look so Celtic seemed to mock my ignorance of Belfast's faces; I was to meet my own face in the streets of Dublin, and to learn that tribal affinity within these islands can be tricky. Its tricks can be played on the ear for words and music. I find myself responding to the music that has gone with the vile paraded threat of the Protestant marching season in the same guilty way that I do to the Carsonian lines by Kipling which, anticipating a line of Hitler's, blessed the intransigence of Protestant Ulster:

> One Law, one Land, one Throne.
> If England drive us forth,
> We shall not fall alone.

The difference between this Orange music and the music of the night before was the difference between war and peace. Meanwhile Catholic intransigence was also on the march, with its own martial music.

The eirenic quality of my evening of Gaelic airs was that of Seamus himself, their Prospero, but kinder than Prospero. I was eating a choc ice in my Chelsea kitchen one nine o'clock at night in the autumn of 1995 when he came calling, having just won his Nobel Prize. My wife and I were by ourselves. The children who'd squatted on the floor when he and I talked about religion were grown up and gone from the house. He stood on the doorstep silver-haired and sturdy, farmer-like, looking a little bit as if the prize he'd won had been won at some market day. I'd never cared one way or the other about the Nobel Prize, but I cared about Seamus's winning it, and his wife Marie's winning it too, as it seemed to me, and I felt it was just like him to take the trouble to seek out at this point someone who'd worked with him over these many years as a publisher of his poems. I walked back with him to his hotel, dressed, accidentally, in antic style, having thrown a long black trailing raincoat over a pair of shorts and a pair of trainers. Two long white legs flashed past pubs and Luigi's delicatessen. I looked like Seamus's zany, Farmer Seamus's village idiot. Swingers said hello to me. They may have thought I was flaunting myself, or making a statement. I now see that my flasher's garments were my joy-bells – rather more embarrassing to read about, I admit, than Conor Cruise's are, in his book about Burke.

I'd be more disposed to say that anyone would have noticed how good Heaney's poems were when they first came to me on the *New Statesman* were it not that an intelligent critic to whom I showed them advised against publication, suggesting that I should ask this man to send in some more of his work later on. But others had noticed his work well before I did, and he had received support from Philip Hobsbaum, whose writers' workshop met for a time in Belfast. When Seamus arrived on the scene, Eliot's supremacy had achieved monumental proportions, and the further monument of an accredited stylistic obscurity, established as long ago as the Romantic period (Byron spoke of obscurity as Coleridge's 'welcome guest'), and lately impugned by the antiromantic iconoclasts of the Movement, had to be taken into account. Auden, for one, when he was young, set himself to *practise* obscurity, which had begun to operate as an aid to publication; and Eliot's example – widely influential and yet finally less productive than was originally expected – was to assist these operations.

I would have thought, however, that Heaney owed nothing decisive to the poetry of Eliot. Nor did he owe much to the Movement school, whose sarcasms concerning obscurity and an advertised profundity were apt to ignore the challenge to their outlook constituted by Eliot's example. Some surviving Movementeers, like Larkin, were less apt to do the same for Seamus, who was open to blame for being ethnic, romantic and profound. Nevertheless, his early poems were in full accord with the Movement dictum that poems should make sense, and when a disparagement of Seamus eventually mustered elsewhere in Britain it wore the face of those offended, not by his being romantic and deep, but by his being, like Larkin, genteel and tame.

His marvellous eye and ear were there from the start, feasting on the countryside where he grew up. They made sense of it, while sounding its depths. Obscurity wasn't his style. But it was his subject, his passion. Here was a nostalgia for muds, mulches, digs, descents, dark interiors. Seamus owed a great deal, at the outset, to the 'parish truth' and multilingual 'art speech' of Robert Burns, whose poetry was 'particularly congenial to natives of Ulster', and he wrote in such terms about the debt in an essay of 1997, where the wee mouse addressed by the ploughman poet looms large. Like Burns, he began with actual farmers, with a known rural place, his own place. Like Burns, he soon became aware of other places, other subjects, other poetries; he became aware of this monumental art of the cryptic and the self-conscious, of the edifice of the difficult poem, and aware, too, of the eloquence required of those who teach (it seems only the other day that I responded to a request for a testimonial on his behalf from the Mother Superior of a training college) and who address large audiences of poetry fans, of academic worthies and of Swedish ones, something he does with unbeatable charm and ease.

The transparency of his early obscurity – to be awkward about it – was never, for all such exposure, to leave him for long. Without being what you'd call a plain-stylist, he has always been less reclusive than most of the talked-of poets of his time. In his collection *The Spirit Level* of 1996, there's a poem entitled 'Two Lorries' which took me back to his beginnings. He is back on the farm, and off it too, for of the lorries in the poem one is driven by the coalman who sweet-talks his mother, and the other, freighted with explosive, blows up the bus station at Magherafelt where the boy Seamus used to meet her. A lump of coal is made erotic, savoury, in the poem, and is turned into silk, an alchemy I remember from my days on the hearth in Scotland reading a book, while also reading the blaze beyond it, my legs in their shorts a 'fireside tartan'.

> This time the lode
> Our coal came from was silk-black, so the ashes
> Will be the silkiest white. The Magherafelt
> (Via Toomebridge) bus goes by. The half-stripped lorry
> With its emptied, folded coal-bags moves my mother:
> The tasty ways of a leather-aproned coalman!

No likely reader of the poem would be uncertain of what it means, for all its play with past tenses. But no one would want to go calling it simple and direct, sure enough.

His soils and excavations, his doors into the dark, were to yield, with the years, the bodies of the sacrificial victim and of the warrior bog-queen, from a past tense common to Ireland and to Jutland. A *Listener* page was lit by the corpse of the Grauballe Man:

> As if he had been poured
> in tar, he lies
> on a pillow of turf
> and seems to weep
>
> the black river of himself.

There are many ways for a poet to be political, and Seamus is political in more ways than the one detectable by some in the grave poems, whose warrior queen is seen at times as a soil soaked in sacrificial blood, as a land which eats its people, swallows their love and terror. I was blamed in Ireland, long ago, for urging him to be political, to write about the troubles, not to be a hermit, and it's true that we discussed such matters. The IRA discussed them with him also, according to one of his poems, urging him to serve the cause. It now seems clear that he has no more been a hermit than he has been a partisan. What are the politics, if any, of his poetry?

There's a clue of a kind in some words of his on a postcard he sent me, which carried a picture of a Modigliani nude: she was 'more delicious', he said, 'than any "bog-queen", in the end'. It was a sentiment that seemed to fit with the music heard at his Gaelic soirée. The victims in his poems may have been experienced as martyrs of the sort congenial to the Republican tradition; a submission to violence and sacrifice may have been found there by some. But to impute a tribal connivance in modern murders would itself be a violence. Kipling called in verse for armed men to ward off an invasion of the North. Marvell's 'Cromwell Ode' hails its Caesar with, at moments, an uncertain sound. Seamus has more in common with Marvell than with Kipling here, if that can be suggested without appearing to deny that in what he writes the Catholic people of the North are pictured in their totality, in all their colours.

Farm poetry keeps on coming. It may be that such poems have appeared hopeful, at a time when verse has been seen as a failing form. Ancient antecedents, new versions of pastoral, may have promised a stay against confusion, and against obscurity, the obscurity which can sometimes seem like a retreat, like a response to failure. The poetry of Robert Frost, whose phrase this was, 'a stay against confusion', excited such hopes, and did more than fulfil them. He was a gentleman farmer, a photographer's farmer too, a nuzzler of horses' heads in meadows. His apple-picking poem is the poem of an apple-picker, spent after a hard day's work. Then again, it is the sigh of a romantic tiredness of life. But it may be thought to take quite as much from its rural setting as it does from the Odes of Keats.

The poetry of R. S. Thomas, who is now eighty-two years old and cantankerous, must be of special interest to anyone who wonders about the persistence of pastoral. I set down his poem 'On the Farm', with reverence, in an anthology I published in 1968, *Writing in England Today: The Last Fifteen Years*, in which an attempt was made to project the Movement contribution, mingled with work done by opposites and adversaries. How Thomas must have hated that in-house Penguin title. He hates the English. They smell. They pollute. Raging westward out of their deplorable cities, they are the holiday-home Anglo-Saxon oppressor. He is a Welsh nationalist pacifist Anglican vicar who has spent his life ministering to and offending his parishioners in various Welsh seclusions, retiring with the years further and further from the English contagion, vanishing up his own lane into the most picturesque of cottages, enclosed in its dell on the Llyn Peninsula. He still lives in the vicinity, at the very tip of Wales, with a view of the Irish Sea. On a clear day he can see Conor Cruise O'Brien.

Seamus Heaney was present in that Penguin anthology, with a poem no less rural than Thomas's, the one in which he watches his father digging; and he was later, as I have said, to decline classification as British, to omit himself for this purpose from an anthology of poems from over the water, no more wanting to be thought British than Thomas, while writing in the 'thin' English language he despises, has wanted to be thought English. Thomas is as severe and as religious as Eliot, who turned down some of his early poems at Faber, and was turned down in turn, for his pains, when Thomas got round to compiling his *Penguin Book of Religious Verse*. He is more curmudgeonly than Larkin, whose spite is often comical and self-mocking. He is the Welsh dragon, in his little grey home in the West. He is an enraged Merlin, and an equivocal one, whose hatred of the English ruling class did not stop him from sending his son to ruling-class schools in England. But in the Fifties and Sixties he wrote a number of very good poems.

His poetry is stark. It speaks – autobiographically, it seems – of his mother's 'infected milk'. It finds its humanity in the mineral hardness, in the uncouthness and courage, of its hill-farmers. This starkness can be very appealing. Thomas's farmers are in part a fiction of the self. He is watching his Cambrians, relishing them, as a poet might a peasant, as Wordsworth did his Cumbrians: he thinks them strange, different, at times inhuman, while also participating in what they are, loving and owning their grimness.

You would have thought that, as in the case of Eliot, there was much here to irritate Movement people, who can have included very few who thought, as Thomas seems to do, that the country is more natural than the city, and more poetic. But Thomas's poems were highly regarded in that quarter, though it is true that, to judge by his epistolary malice-mode, Philip Larkin may not have cared for him personally. He figures in Larkin's letters, at any rate, as 'Arse Thomas', which must mean something. I doubt very much whether there are any references to Tits Eliot in Larkin's letters. Eliot was not a threat, not a rival. Thomas can come on as if he were a threat to practically everyone who has ever lived except Owen Glendower. This has not dissuaded academics, English as well as Welsh, from descanting sympathetically on the poet's opinions. But it may have prevented some readers from going all the way with him into the hermitage occupied by his austere, exact poetry, plainly intelligible, for the most part, even in its transports and abysses.

The poetry of R. S. Thomas, then, is a planet on which there are no soft landings. Over the years his work has moved from a preoccupation with the hill-farmers of Wales towards a greater exposure to the cold light of eternity. 'The higher one ascends,' however, 'the poorer the visibility becomes.' No estimate of what Thomas has done can escape the questions raised by his severity, or, as some might express it, by the pleasures of acerbity apparent in his verse, and in his rugged, cross-bearing opinions. Why, they might even ask, their patience failing them, is he so cross? He himself seems to have believed that his mother's milk had much to answer for.

He is a Welsh nationalist who is far from indulgent towards Wales. It is a place to be buried, where it is 'lovely to lie'. The reading matter of its inhabitants is 'trash', their hillsides are a desert of spruce. The Welsh are preferred, though, to the intruding, carpetbagging English, who have corrupted them with their worship of money and machines, and with their foreign language, in which Thomas has written the poems we are reading. There are glimpses of a shadowy fighting past, of Glendower, and there are poems that might almost seem inclined to torch the carpetbagger's bungalow.

There are solitary lives in these poems, and solitary deaths. Darkness falls, and rain falls. In one of them a poet sends his work and is told to bury it 'as a cat its faeces'. To aspiring poets the muse shows a 'cold' face, just as a hill wife shows 'the cold seas of her eyes' to those sons and lovers who seek, and find, a safe island in her strength. Thomas's own poems are written in the 'cold' shadow of his strong and simple farmer, Iago Prytherch.

The beasts sold by his farmers for money suggest a 'shoddier altar' than the one that carries a crucified redeemer. Are we to think that the second of these altars is, or has become, shoddy? The poems reveal a piety which is troubled by doubts and difficulties, and which attends to a cold God. Christianity's ancient strain of rejection is much in evidence; hope, charity and redemption have to be searched for. The poems say that we won't become dust when we die; there is a something after, which incorporates correction. God's kiss consumes.

They also say, in memorable fashion, that

> He is such a fast
> God, always before us and
> leaving as we arrive.

This absconding god is also human – dark and inexplicable enough to seem part of the poet's nature. Late in his life, God is a Rapunzel who lets down no 'visible plait'; the movement of a curtain, however, may have been detected.

Good poems don't have to be kind (though they often are). The poetry of the Anglo-Welsh George Herbert is less consoling than we are apt to remember it: God's love is perceptible there, but so are the many from whom it is withheld. Herbert's spirit gasps: 'O show thyself to me . . .' And Thomas's poetry may be that bit sterner still. It is a measure of his sternness that you feel so relieved when he appears to let up – as at times in the honest poems about his marriage – and to speak of the love that human beings feel for each other.

That poem of his, 'On the Farm', presents three ominous, backward labourers. Two of them at least are 'no good'. But there is a girl on the farm whose pale face is the lantern

> By which they read in life's dark book
> The shrill sentence: God is love.

I'm not sure how much relenting has occurred. Perhaps this is a fast poem whose meaning slips from your grasp. But it is as interesting as it is beautiful, and it seems to bring a kind of comfort.

I have a bee in my bonnet about literary obscurity, but I don't think it drones from some shameful preference for a paraphrasable content or a meagre rationality. Starts have been made – by Allon White, for instance – on an understanding of the rise of obscurity in the modern period, but there is much here that remains unsounded. Stalwart reputations, André Malraux's for one, have taken in their stride the hurdle of a sham profundity, and the reviewing of verse has long since involved the heavy work of trying hard to find something to say about the hard-to-follow. This may seem plain enough. But it is also plain that many difficult poets are worth the trouble, those visits to the interpreter, and I have sometimes found it hard to follow poets of the present time who are among those I most admire. Anne Carson in America is one. Others are Tom Paulin and Craig Raine, mutual friends who now and then fall out on literary matters, but who are neither of them as fierce as controversy represents them. Tom can be as benign as an evening of Gaelic airs, or as those which seemed to fill his head, once, as he rowed his boat round his little holy island off the coast of Donegal, with Errigal rising to the east through opal mists, shining greens and the blue sky of an illuminated manuscript: journal argument, broadcast discussion, had been deserted for the very rich hours of the duke of Portnoo. A sharp polemicist nevertheless, who has written

well about the 'redemptive ethic' postulated for literature by some of those who still believe in the saving of
souls.

Hugo Williams is as far from a farm poet as it's
possible to get without tumbling off the cliff. Nor is he
at all combative, or redemptive. Paraphrasably and otherwise, his poetry is more lucid than most. My own attitude
towards intelligibility was affected by the Movement
indoctrinations of my youth, but was to grow more
pronounced in later years. When I found myself publishing Hugo in his comparative transparency, I was drawn
to reciting the following defensive mantra, which was
also an imprecation: 'Hugo Williams is a very good poet.
But we must not say so. Why not? Because he writes
about being a child, about being the son of a film star
(Hugh begat Hugo), and about having once (and always)
been to a prep school and public school. Because he isn't
difficult to understand, and is enjoyable to read. And
funny.'

I was overdoing it, of course; there was no need for
this mantra, with its reference to John Berryman's complaint about the boringness of human life ('must not say
so'). Hugo Williams's poems were never to excite the
indignation that savants would direct at the rude shocks,
humour and didacticism wrought by the popular Clive
James and the witch Fiona Pitt-Kethley: savants would
think of them in such terms, and insist that their
pentameters were defective and their jokes not funny.
About these poets too I would feel protective, and recite
my mantra. But Williams was spared the metrical objection, and the other one as well. And it may be that I was

imagining or exaggerating a right-thinking disapproval of what he was up to, that I was rescuing a Peter Pan who wasn't in fact being burned at the stake. In any case, his poetry isn't the easy ride the mantra might suggest. It is easier to celebrate, and to feel protective about, than to discuss.

It's entirely evident that much of it is preoccupied with what it is to have been the son of his gilded parents, to belong to a world of mirrors, good looks, gardenias, breakfasts in France, a nanny *and* a governess – which is like being both enjoyable and funny. After the war, according to the poems, came money troubles and relatively hard times for Hugh Williams, who, having been wounded in the fighting, would limp to the bus stop to attend auditions in London (as a Thirties star he'd been above them), and then miss the bus and be watched by a horrified Hugo from his bedroom window. Into all this he peers as into a window which reflects his features. He is a Narcissus whose face includes his family and their times together: 'The past stretches ahead, into which we stare.' There's a lot of staring in the poetry. He pores over his father's clothes, and gets going on his own. Soon we are in the Sixties:

> I carried on that way
> till my father died
> and allowed me to grow my hair.
> I didn't want to any more.

Some of his finest poems are more or less uncomplicated retrospects of this past – so far as such looks can ever be uncomplicated. Several of his poems are not. A doubling, or rather multiplying, of himself takes place. This is a conscious procedure on his part, and it's examined in a poem whose opening line is Racinian in its energy, plangency and concentration: 'God give me strength to lead a double life.' 'I have been smiling and looking innocent,' he wrote once in a journalistic piece, 'ever since I was seven.' The role here is that of the juvenile star with the little gold head who was six at one point, and to whom, as it happens, a double life has been attributed:

> Hush, hush, what could be worse,
> Christopher Robin is having his nurse.

Duality interests Hugo Williams, and his interest originates, as the phenomena of psychic division are often thought to do, in the pains and uncertainties of childhood, and the roles that childhood can seek to play – roles that seem to have been accentuated, for Hugo, by the presence on his stage of an actor father.

He writes as his older self, and at times as his father, and the day came when a mixed creature walked on in the shape of Sonny Jim, a catatonic, invalid, aerial, mismated clown alter and adult. Jim takes his cue from a cereal ad:

> High o'er the fence leaps Sunny Jim
> Force is the food that raises him.

Sonny Jim's leaps, as executed by Hugo Williams with a re-spelling of the name that filializes the creature, can bring to mind the surrealistic, unlike the recollections of Hugo's youth. The funny-fearful poem which anticipates growing up, growing not so much up as infirm, growing up to be like one of Larkin's 'old fools', leans towards Jim's antics but doesn't cross over into surrealism: 'When I grow up I want to have a bad leg . . .'

This emphasis on multiple personality has to be kept under control, though, if it isn't to tangle with what those who admire his work want to say on the subject. They want to say that it is not complicated, that it is bell-like, clear, clean and direct. It has 'attack'. Many of his poems might seem to be entailed by their opening lines, and almost always manage to live up to them. Many of his lines have the air of performative utterances, such as 'God give me strength', or:

> Now that I am cold
> Now that I look like him
> I put on this warm grey suit of wool
> In sympathy with my father.

His is a directness which can accommodate effects of laid-back casualness — such as the phrase 'for some reason', used more than once.

This directness, naturalness, unencumberedness, tends to be present, though not invariably or unrelievedly, in most of what he does. Such qualities might indicate that he lisped in numbers, that he started young, that he embarked at a young age on the eternal youth of his subject-matter, and so he did. On the subject of his early start there's a masterly maternal insight that was turned into a poem. His mother asked if he was making dams as he played in the mud by a stream, or was he making poems about making dams. He is sometimes to be found making a poem about making the poem we are reading.

'I have put on a grotesque mask' rings out neoclassically loud and clear in line one of such a poem. The poem explains that he has put on the mask in order 'to write these lines', and proceeds to show him staring at himself in a mirror, by the light of a candle. It is a poem which some might groan about for being one of his put-ons, for sticking out, as it eventually does, a tongue which declines to speak, for being an occasion for a poem, and the props for one, rather than a poem, for delivering the conjuror's cape and cane without the trick. That isn't how it looks to me. It brings you into the writer's head in the most dramatic way, and invites you to think about speech. This is not a Narcissus who has been struck dumb by self-love. Early in the poem Hugo writes:

> I hold up my head
> like one of those Chinese lanterns
> hollowed out of a pumpkin,
> swinging from a broom.

The poem is in his collection of 1994, *Dock Leaves*, and this passage returns us to an earlier poem where the boy bursts in on his sleeping father

> with a head hollowed out of a turnip
> swinging from a broom. There were cigarette burns
> like bullet-holes in his pyjamas.

I saw his bad foot
sticking out from under the bedclothes
because he was 'broke'
and I thought my father was dying.

The child's slide from injury to bankruptcy and death is a characteristic effect. Meanwhile his father's ghost walks, with the recurrence of that lantern head, and can be glimpsed again when Hugh's bad foot is found to walk in step with the bad leg that Hugo wants to have when he grows up.

Neil Rennie, poet, ukelele-player and South Sea scholar, is a friend of Hugo's, and is no less 1920s elegant. In Neil's Bloomsbury kitchen stands a Cargo Cult life-size head and bathing-trunked torso of his chum, moulded from the living man in some state-of-the-art dental plaster. Here stands Hugo's double, and a sight for the sore eyes of Narcissus – for others, a touchingly funny sight. R. S. Thomas would loathe it.

You may be wondering if I wrote a poem about my experiences, mentioned earlier, in front of the fire in Scotland. Reader, I did. It falls short of being a sonnet, and of being one of those poems which I have quite often wished I could write. It was based on a dream I had in which the poet Betjeman took part:

Poor fellow, caught beneath some bed at school,
Taken out and tasked and beaten for his pains,
A school that has lasted for a thousand years.
He's told to look into the hearth and write
The language of the fire. His poem reads:

'Terms from my grammar book begin to show
In the changing picture of the flames. A noun
Of coal is followed by the verb to burn.
Down comes a hanging participle of ash.
Wow! At a longer look the grammar melts
Into the churning and becoming of the fire.
"Parse me no more," the scarlet stuff exclaims.'

10. Teaching English

IN 1974, SHORTLY after leaving the *Listener*, I turned up at the end of a very long table in one of London University's high marble halls of conclave to be interviewed for the Lord Northcliffe Chair of Modern English Literature at University College, which has been thought big enough, and busy enough, to count as a university in its own right. This mooted return to academic life was not like Satan suing to Heaven for his job back: but a certain amount of gall was required for a submission to interview. Noel Annan, Provost of the College, had invited me to apply, and Frank Kermode, the departing Northcliffe Professor, had encouraged me to do so, while warning that there might be those in the English Department who would not want a journalist as the Northcliffe Professor of Modern English Literature. The chair had been endowed by a press lord, and its incumbent compared to the Mammon Professor of God, Mammon being another of the fallen angels: but that, so far from making it all right, may have helped to advertise the impropriety of appointing a journalist to an academic chair. The department had two established chairs. The other was held by the renowned linguist Randolph Quirk.

I had been an undergraduate at Cambridge, and then
a postgraduate, there and at Harvard: but I'd broken off
to go and work for a while at the Treasury. I was at this
very much later point finishing a book, *Cockburn's Millennium*, which dealt with the Scotland of the early nineteenth century, and revived certain of the preoccupations
of my postgraduate research. As this might indicate, I
was interested in the subject I was aspiring to teach. On
my arrival in the Department I found I liked the teachers
and felt welcomed by them. I remember a searching look
from Antonia Byatt, who was both a novelist and a
lecturer in the Department, and who asked me publicly,
on my arrival, why I wanted to come among them. I
think I said I was interested in the subject. She'd made
the same journey herself, I felt. But she was quite right
to ask her question, and this scarcely amounted to trouble.
Nor did I have any with the professors in the College at
large. Among the friendliest was a man who could be
trenchant in his distaste for intruders on the academic
scene.

Notes of disapproval were no doubt sounded outside
the College, but the only ones to reach my ears ('There's
always friends,' said Mary McCarthy once) came from my
old associates Philip Larkin, Donald Davie and George
Steiner, literary men who were also university men,
veterans of the promotion ladder I'd omitted to climb.
You were or were not 'one of us', teachers and scholars
would occasionally say. When, at University College,
Conor Cruise O'Brien, then the *Observer*'s editor-in-chief,
was due to give his Northcliffe Lectures on Edmund
Burke, whose life and works had cost him decades of

abstruse research, my friendliest of professors was heard to say that O'Brien was 'not one of us'. The expression is also said to have been used in Cambridge, by the outsider Leavis, of George Steiner, who was being considered at the time for some fellowship or lectureship, or for admission to some coffee-room. And now here was George using it of me, uttering the same cry of solidarity. I was another one who was not one of us.

Eligibility and exclusion had been a topic of conversation, between the two of us, in the past. During my time as editor of the *Listener*, I'd had lunch with him, and we had discussed what it took for the BBC to think someone suitable to deliver the Reith Lectures. Over the years I had published many reviews of his work, some of them hostile; and we were both aware that the Cambridge we both knew was a place where rhetorical brilliance and an engagement with ambitious themes could be judged shallow and journalistic. I listened with sympathy to accounts of the snubs he'd received there. But he may have reckoned that he'd seen through a mere show of interest on my part. As we sat face to face, like BBC Television's dialogic Smith and Jones, in our cramped restaurant booth, George's talking head said, in effect, that there should be no more about George – let's talk about you. He went on to ask: 'Why is it that for the past twenty years you have been systematically persecuting me?'

'Nor from the heaven of heavens,' says Satan of God, in *Paradise Regained*, 'hath he excluded my resort sometimes.' Over the previous fifteen years I'd had a lot to do with university men and women, some of whom had risen in their profession for reasons that included their contributions to the journals I'm describing, contributions for which some colleagues would initially have blamed them. 'Journalistic facility,' spat Leavis, himself a journalist. And Alan Taylor was a journalist, in high places and low, who was spat on by academics for selling out to Fleet Street. He said one or two strange things in his various places. But so in his comparatively heavenly place did Leavis.

The teaching of English literature strikes me as in many respects identical with writing it and with writing about it, and I felt at home in combining my work as a teacher with that of editing the *London Review of Books*, when that activity began in 1979 – with no objection on the part of the College, though I doubt if they ever got round to taking it in the Housman Room, where teachers drank their coffee. I knew, though, that the universities were something of a different world from journalism, that dons had their defects, that they could be narrow, jealous, hostile to outsiders and to one another, past masters of the art of *sauter pour mieux reculer*. I had witnessed, and indeed taken part in, the comedies and acerbities of academic life.

A friend of mine, then a member of the professoriate of another place, once wrote to rebuke me for publishing 'a transparently malevolent review' of one of his books. I looked up the review not long ago. It did seem spiteful. But it started off with praise, and by distinguishing between my friend's abilities as a scholar and his abilities as a journalist, infinitely preferring the former. The book with which the reviewer went on to find fault was an in-between based on a series of televised academic lectures. My friend always forgot but never forgave, never argued and never explained, or so he explained in the letter, which reported that 'a just judgment of God had fallen' on the reviewer. 'While there's death there's hope,' he wrote, 'but not in Michaelmas College: they will doubtless elect, in his stead, some harrowed toad, his unhappy pupil, or some clerical maggot who will creep up into the daylight now that that life-diminishing batrachian is no longer there.' The letter carried a marginalia, in the same hand, with sweet little drawings of a caterpillar and a toad. It was the hand of a man whose letters would quite often refer to 'the enemy'.

University College London stands opposite to the *Spectator*'s old Gower Street offices. Its portico'd Classical main building of 1828 resembles that of my school in Edinburgh, the Royal High School, which went up at the same progressive, public-minded time, and which was to be earmarked, by a later public mind, for the deliberations of the parliament of a devolved Scotland. Progress meant that there should be this godless Gower Street institution, this 'radical, infidel College', as a contemporary joker referred to it, which would give degrees to Free-Thinkers, Dissenters and Jews; and the reforming Whigs of Edinburgh and the *Edinburgh Review* were among its founders, in the persons of the politician Henry Brougham and the poet Thomas Campbell. I liked all that. And I liked it that the College was such a plain, worn and purposeful last-century environment, laid out for learning.

The environment of any more or less ancient university — each with its history of encounters between knowledge, love and friendship, between youth and age – was capable, I had found, of casting a spell: in part, a nostalgic spell, which could seem to re-immerse me in a childhood spent in the scholastic town of Edinburgh. Göttingen bowled me over when I got there, and I am moved by the depictions of three old men in three other old European universities – by the steep staircases and Gothic arches of the early German film *The Blue Angel*, with its infatuated professor, by the alma mater of Bergman's film *Wild Strawberries*, and by Chekhov's 'A Boring Story', among the most authentic of any of the scenes from academic life that are known to me, with its interesting pupil who fails his exam, its seeker after dissertation subjects, its colleagues and gloomy corridors, and the parting thoughts of the cross, famous medical scientist, an ancient person of my heart, who contemplates this scene and loves his adopted daughter.

Around and to the rear of the main building in Gower Street is a kasbah of converted houses and warehouses, dusty classrooms, initialled desks, equationed blackboards, pointers, slide-projectors, and of tall science blocks. 'Realism without the magic,' said the novelist Vikram Seth, relishingly, of the back half of the College. As we stood there in Foster Court, I shared his relish of the place, while thinking myself perhaps the more susceptible to its charm.

I was head of the English Department for seventeen years – jointly, at first, with Randolph Quirk, and then solo. I did not hope, and was not fit, to become a Faculty Dean, and I imagine I was thought to lack bottom so far as the higher counsels of the College were concerned, with their grant-computing algebraic formulae. I made up my mind to be a department man, to defend against deflection and dispersal what seemed to be working well: to do what I could, that is, to help us to deal with the mounting pressure of accountability and interference which the Thatcher Governments brought to bear on the universities during these years, and with the less acceptable of the innovations which the universities brought on themselves – in response, at times, to American precedents. We agreed that we should try to put off, for as long as possible, incorporation in faculty-wide modular arrangements which would have meant re-organizing our courses to make them generally available for selection by students outside the Department and to permit our own students to opt out reciprocally.

This was not an instance of the phobic recoil to which academics are felt to be prone. What lay behind this reluctance was a desire to stay with the integral and relatively self-determining approach to English embodied in the University College-based (rather than London University-based) syllabus which had been devised for the Department in 1970 by these Manxmen and former schoolfellows, Frank Kermode and Randolph Quirk, and it is gratifying, for those teachers like myself who have favoured this approach, to know that the English Department has yet to go modular. Frank's high standing in the profession, his role in reshaping the syllabus, and the very successful departmental graduate seminars on theoretical questions which were conducted in the high summer of his own engagement with the subject – these and more made him a hard act to follow. I hoped it might help me to keep my end up when I became involved in the attempt to develop a journal of international interest, knowing that it would take the best part of ten years to count for anything in academic eyes.

Modular arrangements were a threat to what we took to be the principal advantages of the Department's syllabus and teaching practice, which made each student known to the teachers and gave access to a rich but clearly delineated field of study. We were strong on history. The theory that was taught included Plato and Quintilian, and the anti-theoretical theories of Leavis, and was expressly deficient in any mandatory prescription of the various Post-Modernisms, though these were discussed too. The course ran chronologically from a little light Old English to the present day, with a movable stress on periods and topics of special interest. Our reluctance to adopt modular arrangements, to course-unitize in the sense proposed from time to time, did not entail any barring of the way to comparative studies or to the work of other departments. As time went on, we built into the foundational teaching lectures on foreign and ancient literatures and on other disciplines, and we did more than before with the social and commercial history of English literature and with Anglo-American literary relations. Best-sellers were taught, and films were taught.

At the heart of the whole thing was the one-to-one fortnightly tutorial. The desultoriness of the under-structured seminar was a fault of ours at this time, as of other English departments, I think, and the single-student fortnightly tutorial session made up for that. I never lost my pleasure in these sessions, I learnt a great deal from them, and I smile that they are still in place at University College. From other English departments, such sessions have largely disappeared. There was far less individual tuition in the Cambridge I knew as an undergraduate, though it may be true that the residential collegiate system has remained in some other respects friendlier to students than the urban universities have managed to be. The University College English Department has been protected from destructive change by performing satisfactorily in the eyes of the Government's inspectors-general, and its practice under the current head, John Sutherland, deserves and has received their continued forbearance.

Bitter experience of Oxford English persuaded Kingsley Amis that literature should not be taught in universities, and there's a modification of that doctrine which has it that Horace should be studied because he presents difficulties and has to be learned, but that George Herbert and Kingsley Amis should be left alone: both of the last two writers are studied at University College, and the difficulties they presented were in my time very rewarding. For all the nonsense it contains and encourages, literature is truthful and intelligible, and it can and should be intelligently studied as part of the university curriculum. A fully-functioning English department, moreover, programmed for a wide range of instruction, seems an indispensable element in higher education. Reading and writing skills are not usually impugned as pointless or deleterious, and it's often forgotten by controversialists that they are taught both in schools – by hard-working teachers incriminated by journalists and politicians – and in university departments of literature. This, too, is as it should be.

Our not being chauvinistically theoretical, our being supposed old-fashioned by chauvinists, did not, as I've already said, mean that we took no interest in past and present philosophical approaches to literature. The teaching effort was aimed at a comprehensive account of the subject, which was reflected in the wide range of books produced by members of staff. The Department had a well-known language-study element, in the care of the Quain Professor. This chair is not at present held by a linguist, but the study of grammar and usage is still pursued. On the staff, too, were imaginative writers – not 'in residence' merely, not just on call, but doing the work that everyone else did. Antonia Byatt had been there for a while when I arrived, and another novelist, Dan Jacobson, was appointed during my early years. No academic who was in a position to observe their work as university teachers would have been inclined to murmur that they were not 'one of us'.

The policy of admitting journalists and imaginative writers to the teaching staff has its nineteenth-century precedents at University College, and, in modern times, has been a feature of the English Department since the days of Frank Kermode. I am its beneficiary, but may perhaps be allowed to suggest that such arrangements are worth having. Such teachers should not be seen as specialists (in, for instance, 'creative writing', the creative writing of the student enrolment), or as the sort of specialist who is absolved from taking a full part in the teaching programme. And they could be seen as a form of mediation, as a way of responding to the division between the academic and the literary worlds, and to the failings to be found on both sides of that division. The humanities, and the universities at large, can exhibit an isolation from what goes on outside their walls, and a regard for techniques of exclusion, while literary journalism – so often undisciplined, opportunistic and cavalier – has exhibited a no less confining isolation of its own. Over the past fifty years, however, with the spread of tertiary education, literary journalism has sometimes appeared to have reached an accommodation with the universities, and to have been the better for it, while it may also be true that English departments have been none the worse for letting in qualified outsiders to help with the teaching.

These things may have happened. But it is doubtful whether they will go on happening. The cold wind of government cuts has been blowing in this direction; and the need to safeguard the position of young teachers is likely to curtail the 'mature' appointments – of those who have been out in the world practising some allied trade – which are required by arrangements of this kind. It may be that a tighter professionalism, on the part of the universities, a closing of the ranks, is in store. And it may also be that newspapers and certain journals have become less tolerant of academics than they were twenty years ago.

A veteran of the Department was Basil Greenslade, the student, and possessor, of a seventeenth-century eloquence, one of the Cromwellian people I have admired (without being all that keen on Cromwell). He wrote me, on my arrival, an invaluable memorandum on how to conduct myself as departmental head, and at the end of a subsequent academic year, and of a staff meeting, he handed me a bunch of flowers. I was startled — it lay before me like the Mace on that table in the House of Commons. And I was abashed. He should have offered the bouquet to himself. His fierce and equal commitment to his studies and to his pupils did much more for the Department than I was able to do.

The Quain Professor was in charge, not only of language studies, but of the work of the Department's Medievalists, some of whom were apt to be anxious about the survival of their mystery in a hostile climate (their mystery has survived, and their numbers are now greater than they were in my time). One of the few rows in which I took part at University College was jurisdictional in character, but involved no clash between the literature people of the Department, in their preponderance, and the language people, though some may have thought that it did, and clashes between language and literature people do sometimes happen. Randolph Quirk's successor in the chair, Sidney Greenbaum, who died not long ago on a lecture platform in Moscow, fell into a disagreement with a probationary lecturer on the language side, whose research had come to diverge into historical phonetics, an area more or less remote from the Department's teaching programme. Sidney and I had fallen into disagreements of our own before that, but, at a later stage in what became a multilateral battle of wills, I felt I had to support him on the issue of how closely the research interests of a teacher due for tenure should relate to what the Department taught. There were those in the College who held that we were bound by the doctrine that a lecturer, once appointed, should be allowed to research as he or she chose.

The lecturer in question eventually withdrew; she had had a hard time of it. And there were colleagues in the Department who would have spared no flowers for my share, as they saw it, in her hard time. Several of them were also to disagree with me over a proposal that a course in women's writing should be taught by teachers from outside the College who specialized in the subject. I thought that our syllabus, premised on inclusiveness and independence, made it desirable that we should as far as possible teach the course unaided, while making it difficult, at times, to do so. Half the staff were women, all of them interested in women's writing but not all of them convinced that it should be treated in this way. Feminism had by now asserted its rightful claims in the context of university life; but not all the cases that had arisen for debate were clear-cut. I was never myself in favour of 'positive discrimination' – another demanding new issue of the time – either in the field of appointments or in that of admissions. The problems it seeks to address – at some risk to the integrity of university education – need to be dealt with by securing the improvement and proper upkeep of state schools.

I was surprised to discover, in the later Seventies, that Leavis's ideas were as important as they were to the teachers of the Department. By that time, for some readers, they had dated, and they had come under the curse of literary theorists. 'Theory' – an ideological composite derived from French and American initiatives and perceptible to some of its adherents as a form both of science and of socialism – had entered the academic culture, and the intellectual development and promotion prospects of research students and young teachers had come to depend, in a number of universities, on an ability to wield the new terms. Appointment committees, whose members could sometimes appear more sensitive to reputation than to literature and scholarship, grew kind to the reputation-generating appetite for theory. An engrossing book could be written about the operations of the will to power which emerged, legitimately enough, in this quarter – about the appointments, curricula and teaching practice which resulted from this re-invention of what a teacher should know.

I was keen on the arguments expressed in Christopher Ricks's article of 1981 in the *London Review*, entitled 'In Theory', where he wrote, as he has continued to do, in terms of a commitment to principle and example, as against theoretical elaboration – a commitment to be seen as authorized by the 'practical criticism' of Samuel Johnson and of Empson and Leavis. But I have trouble, in this context, with any sharp separation of principle from theory, and I had long had trouble with Leavis's postulates, in more than one of their applications, and with the dogmatism that constrains his inquiring or exemplary approach, his intended dialogue with the reader. I had learnt to dislike his insistence on the single author and the major work, and on the distinguished interpreter of that work, and I had never liked his proscription of popular culture, his refusal to be anything other than hostile about it. I think I understood, therefore, when the time

came, what it might be to seek relief in this new collecti-
vism, and in this new stress on the self-contradiction to
be detected in books and in the truths they affirm.
Nevertheless, I went on feeling, as did others in the
Department, that Leavis was a writer of consequence
whose best work was able to show why books matter.

His writings were of a kind to give structure, at one
time, to the hope that reading books may contribute to a
perfection of the soul. Few of his pupils, however, in their
mid-century corner, can have expected miracles in this
respect, and his behaviour as a controversialist can't always
have encouraged them to do so. His pupils were in a
position to know that it is hard to read your way out of
certain forms of distress or disturbance, out of the
mistakes, many of them by no means peculiar, many of
them very familiar, which these sufferers are apt to make,
and the hostility they are apt to feel.

Before I began at the College, a student of the
Department – a good one, according to some of its
teachers – had withdrawn from his exams and failed to
obtain a degree. As I remember it, my only part in his
troubles was to notify him of their outcome. Undergraduate writings of his had spoken cleverly of blood and of
sadism, of applications of meaning to the world and of
their validity. He now started stalking me, in Gothic
style and with lots of literary references, for my part in
his troubles. There were messages – notes, phone calls,
chalkings – which would evoke a Germany of the mind,
the Allemagne of Anglo-American Romanticism. A Mr
Wolf phoned to say that 'the road to Berlin is almost
open again and the ruling class will become Edgar Allan

Poe's Mr Valdemar. All systems go.' Postcards were signed 'Von Braun'; one of them showed a cathedral, with the words 'Here's a picture of Votre Doom.' Mr Wolf had ancestors at Koenigsburg University 'at a time when bakers were simply mud'. Bakers and millers are not far apart. Mr Wolf took to calling himself by my name, and to calling me at midnight from a point of surveillance purporting to be near my house, and on one occasion he visited the College and was directed to my side by a colleague: 'You've come to see Karl.'

In a deserted students' common room, Karl saw Karl, who asked why he was persecuting him. A stern silence. A burly young man with receding fair hair and the darkly displeased face of a literary critic denied his messages. Here was a reader of books who would not have been out of place in a book by Dostoevsky, and who at one point had been charged with assaulting a policeman. After a while I changed my phone number and the messages ceased. Had he not withdrawn from his exams, it's possible that he might have passed them. I felt for him – for his struggle to make sense, and to look for it in books, while also finding in them material for his hostility and turning that material into a poem of a kind.

Literature is itself subject to the delusions it is unlikely to cure, and delusion has been known to obtain, and to deserve, an honours degree for excellence in the study and appreciation of literature. These considerations are related to difficulties that can arise both for teachers of the subject and for its students. But they can't be thought to settle the question of the redemptive reading of books, and they provide no grounds for leaving literature off the curriculum. Delusion has also been known to do well at mathematics.

One or two of the Department's students came across as period figures – claimants of their rights and inhabitants of the post-war culture of complaint – and I wouldn't have thought they had all that much to complain about, so far as relations with their teachers were concerned. My colleagues were scrupulous people, interested in their pupils. I didn't especially endear myself to the student body, but those of them I had most to do with endeared themselves to me. One student – whom I first met when he submitted himself for a scholarship interview with the air of a man about to make a citizen's arrest – was to melt sufficiently, after I'd left, to invite me to edit with him an issue of his magazine, the *London Quarterly*: more will be heard, I think, of the arresting John Bradley from Samuel Johnson's Lichfield, a natural born editor.

11. The Making of a Magazine

CULTURE AND ANARCHY are no longer what they were when Matthew Arnold wrote about them, and the word 'culture' can now give a sense of instability which registers this change. We don't always know what is meant when we hear it, and we aren't always sure that we want to hear it. A twentieth-century division has occurred. Does it mean, we may have to ask, something large, compendious, nationwide? Or something small and special? There are times when it means an excellent something which is felt to be under threat, or hard to reach. Those who wrote for the papers I worked for were conscious of a national culture composed of a diversity of mutually responsive elements: but we were also prepared to try to contribute to the intellectual life of the country, and prepared, in so doing, to publish material that many might find opaque. A journal whose writers think of it as national or compendious doesn't have to have a large number of readers. Many would have found the *London Review of Books* difficult to read, had they picked it up: but it was more of a problem that we found some aspects of the national culture difficult to read. We did not wish to seem narrow. Nor did we wish to seem gruesomely highbrow in comparison with the *Listener*.

There are those who have taken to asking if a literary culture or an avant-garde survives in Britain. This is to ask two different questions which can both be answered with a yes. Television has not destroyed these bits of Britain, though it is sometimes rumoured to have done this. As an element in the larger entity of the national culture – that compendium of books, films, football, the natural sciences, the National Curriculum, the National Lottery, and lots of other sublime and ridiculous things – its importance is very great, and is unlikely to diminish. But it has yet to destroy either the literary culture or the avant-garde.

It's worth going back, when thinking about these questions, to the decade that preceded the Second World War, and to the way things were then – so far as cultural entities were concerned – in America. In a memoir of 1993, Diana Trilling mourned the loss of the intellectual world she'd known there during the middle years of the century. 'No weight is now being put against the popular culture,' she regrets to say. Many of the inhabitants of her brave old world were grouped, as writers and readers, round *Partisan Review*, a journal which was successively Communist and anti-Stalinist, and which was for much of its earlier career self-consciously revolutionary in its prescriptions for both politics and literature. She cherishes these intellectuals, and she also castigates them. They were persuaded that 'they were of an essentially different order of being from the rest of mankind'. They were 'advanced'. So advanced were they that 'the war was not

Partisan Review's war until America was well into it'. The only good war was a class war, the editors believed, and this one did not count as such during the run-up to America's involvement. The editors also felt that America would become fascist if it fought fascism. After Pearl Harbor, however, they changed their minds and joined in the struggle against Hitler. They had come to see what a fair number of Americans had already seen – that they had better fight. An advanced journal had caught up.

The term 'advanced' confers an air of superiority, consigns you to some forward march, or to your dug-out on some battleground, and has been used to make light of the presence, within a given national culture, of an irreducible diversity and promiscuity, as opposed to an apartheid of high and low brows – and of middlebrows, those in-betweens denounced by Partisan Reviewer Dwight Macdonald. About what it is to be advanced, as I've suggested, Diana Trilling was in more than one mind. She was a woman who wanted to push against the popular culture, treating it as of an essentially different order of being from the literary culture with which she felt at home, but who was also to make a point of opposing alienation and romantic individualism and of befriending ordinary life, including married life and nine-to-five wage-earning – what Cyril Connolly and the British Fifties used to refer to as 'the pram in the hall'. Not that the two points can't both be made. Not that the two positions can't decently coexist. The complication for the British was that it had become hard to tell by the Fifties which of the two positions was the more advanced, the further forward.

Post-war British culture was to incorporate a push towards popular taste on the part of quite a few of those who would once, as in Diana Trilling's bygone Manhattan, have pushed against it, doing so on behalf of an idealized working man, who had to be shielded from the seductions of the mass entertainment business. Pop went the weasel. And the weasel also turned against the modern and against the pretensions of avant-gardes. For a number of the new writers, newness was finished. Revolution, in art as in politics, was finished. Forward was backward. The role of the path-breaker, of the Bolshevik of artistic experiment and exploration, was a joke, and barricade Bolsheviks were a joke too.

The reference here, of course, is to the lead given, the path broken, by the Movement school of poets and novelists, consisting of Kingsley Amis, Philip Larkin and a few other choice spirits; an influential minority poured scorn, for a while, on influential minorities. But the same pressure could be noticed elsewhere in the literary culture at large. Leavis's stance was equivocal. He can be seen as an avant-gardist, positing a deep division between minority culture and mass civilization. But he could equally well be seen as someone who, in squaring up to the handful of conspirators who managed the London literary world, had taken the side of the common reader and of a provincial wholesomeness. On the left, including the erstwhile revolutionary left, a similar contradiction was detectable. The New Left, with its review, could sometimes appear to share the outlook of the Partisan Reviewers of the American Thirties – to be keen on behaving as a vanguard for progress both in politics and in the arts. But New Leftist Raymond Williams stood for the Jerusalem of a culture grounded in community, a culture in which you wouldn't be hearing all the time about what it is to be ahead of, or better than, other people.

Since then, the élite forces of the avant-garde have taken to the popular as never before. The avant-garde that survives here consists, as its predecessors did, of a set of avant-gardes, some of which, as in the past, constitute, or are linked with, pace-setting, fashion-forming agencies and enclaves, and are now setting paces in the field of mass entertainment. 'Low Culture for High Brows' has been the motto of the *Modern Review*, a review of films, football and rock stars as well as of books. Applicants for the job of literary editor on a national newspaper were expected, not long ago, to have read the *Modern Review*. The magazine could be seen as a piece of your authentic influential avant-garde, and as proof that the avant-garde now has to know about, and to be advanced about, mass culture. It has, however, been argued that the magazine has been at fault in perpetuating the distinction between high and low culture, while at times appearing to be seeking to abolish the distinction. I'd say that it might be a good idea to abolish it, and to stop taking for granted the need for an avant-garde, very much including the kind that specializes in low culture.

The espousal of popularity which has taken place is discussed in a recent book by Eric Hobsbawm, a book which says that this has been 'the century of the common people', and that it has been 'dominated by the arts produced by and for' the common people, a book which indicates how far we have come since the days when it was natural for clever people to speak of battling the popular, and which indicates that an American popularity rules. Diana Trilling's book describes an American élite which imitated Europe; Eric Hobsbawm's book describes a Europe which imitates America. According to *Age of Extremes* (1994), the final volume in his serial history of the modern world, a common culture very different from the one spoken of by Williams and a revolution very different from Lenin's have come about. 'The common culture of any late twentieth-century urbanized country was based on the mass entertainment industry – cinema, radio, television, pop music – in which the élite shared, certainly from the triumph of rock music onwards, and to which intellectuals no doubt gave a highbrow twist to make it suitable for élite taste,' writes Hobsbawm.

But despite this highbrow twist, he believes that the old Western avant-garde has died. And he also believes that art itself, 'in the nineteenth-century sense of the word', is ceasing to be valued. He describes a life after 1960 in which not even 'the children of the educated classes in the rich Western world' were as interested in reading as their parents had been, in which, except for educational purposes, few people have 'read books seriously', or paid attention to Shakespeare. Can quality survive, he wonders, in competition with sales figures and hype? How with this rage, as Shakespeare wondered, shall beauty hold a plea?

Considering the empty and ostentatious behaviour of more than one vanguard of the past, it is possible to imagine a generally stoical response to the death of the avant-garde. But it is surely still alive, at the abstruse end of the general culture of this country, and given over, as ever, to the mentioning of foreign models. There it still is, containing, as it has always done, a loose collection of cells and circles, and of lone rangers, and of emotive self-descriptions. There at the abstruse end, with some at least of the attributes of an avant-garde, are Post-Modernists and literary theorists. 'The public' has not tried to understand what theory says, and very few published authors have tried to do so either. It is a form of dialectical scepticism which sets out to expose the self-contradictory nature of literary utterance. Left-seeming or subversive-seeming as it has sometimes been, it has also looked like an alternative to politics which began to beguile at a time when a defeated left-wing politics had come to seem futile. You will rarely encounter, in such writings of this kind as may lie ahead, any reference to Tony Blair, for whom, in turn, as he goes on succeeding at what he does, there might never have been such a development as literary theory.

I've been supposing, then, that there's an actually existing common culture in this country to which an actually surviving avant-garde belongs, and that television, which is thought by some to have captured this wider entity, has yet to quench its literary constituent. A more or less jubilant Marshall McLuhan, that renegade literary man, used to predict that the printed word was about to go down to television. Thirty years later, such a defeat remains to be seen. Nevertheless, such jubilation can still be heard, usually in literary circles. Irvine Welsh has been saying that 'it is ironic that I'm a writer, because I've always felt that the book is both technologically and spiritually obsolete ... I hope the author will soon be dead.' But he won't be if Welsh goes on causing stirs with his comic scenes and his scenes of horror, with his delirium of addiction and the Giro young, and with a spin-off of books into plays and films which goes to show that literary initiatives can still be a motor for the other arts. The punishing severity of his remarks on this occasion is itself, moreover, noticeably authorial. You'd think it would take a very real severity to construe as terminal the information that, in 1995, his novel *Trainspotting* sold 135,000 copies in paperback.

A dislike of the avant-garde is not the same as being against difficulty, enterprise and innovation, or against small specialist groups. It seems clear that we need a two-way traffic between the special and the popular, that the pushing spoken of by Diana Trilling is and should be reciprocal, and that in any complex cultural environment there will be pushes all round, an incessant copying and rejection. And it seems equally clear that the art of the past has yet to lose its push. An interest in art in the nineteenth-century sense, and in the arts of the nineteenth century, remains a feature of the wider culture of the present time. A large number of common readers – once more, over 100,000 of them – took to reading George Eliot's novel *Middlemarch* after its recent appearance on television. And some of us have been reading Tolstoy's novel *Hadji Murat*. It's about the nineteenth-century frontier war between the Chechens and the Russians which might seem to have returned with the recent slaughters in the Caucasus. Hadji Murat is a tribal chief who goes over to imperial Moscow and ends up as a severed head. 'Keep rigidly to my system of razing dwellings, destroying supplies in Chechnya and harrying them with raids,' commands Czar Nicholas. Russian soldiers have been doing again what they did then. Eric Hobsbawm says that an interest in art in the old sense is an interest in quality. And it is also an interest in history. Here are two good reasons for going on reading *Hadji Murat* in the days of Czar Yeltsin, and we'd have to be a worse country than we appear to have become to have lost the sense of what these reasons might amount to.

So people still read the fiction of Tolstoy, together with the fiction of George Eliot, which was at one point decried by an avant-garde. Few of the writers I published were drawn to the decrying and exclusiveness that protects cultural élites, and many possessed a breadth of taste which matched the aspirations of the journals they wrote for.

One of them, Ian Hamilton, has said, of the upbringing of the novelist Salman Rushdie, that 'low culture was not perceived to be a threat', and Hamilton himself does not perceive it to be a threat. He is a poet who is also a critic, a man of letters who is also interested in football, and persuaded that football is cultural, an art. He is neither at the front nor at the back of the culture he inhabits. He is neither high nor low. He wouldn't present himself as a path-breaker – and yet a path was broken by the magazine he edited, the *Review* (eventually the *New Review*), a magazine written by a small group of culturally-motivated people.

Salman Rushdie grew up to like low culture, to write books, and to figure in the stories which have been circulating about the flight from books we are meant to be witnessing. One or two of these stories depict aspirant literary editors assuring their appointments committees that they don't read books. Another has a quality newspaper ringing the sequestered Rushdie at his safe house to inquire if he'd be their literary editor. What about the difficulty posed by the sentence of death passed on him by Moslem holy men? Rushdie spoke of the snags that lay in the way of his showing up at the office to look at the review copies and make all the little arrangements. 'Don't worry,' replied the quality newspaper. 'We can get somebody else to do that.' Who is to say that it might not have worked?

There have always been such stories, and the literary culture is still around to be scared and diverted by them. The flight from books is not beyond dispute, and has yet to reveal itself, to any demoralizing extent, in the sales figures of publishers. At the same time, there's no point in attempting to deny that the print culture is under pressure from the new media, and it's not surprising that the avant-garde should sometimes appear to have given up on it, and to be directing its energies elsewhere — which is part of what it would mean to say that its historical 'moment' may perhaps be over, but that the thing itself is still alive, in this country as in others. Still alive, though changed, no doubt, from what it once was, in Thirties Manhattan, or in Old Vienna.

The changes are not such as to impede recognition of the Frenchman Jean Baudrillard as the avant-garde incarnate. He is reliably reported by a critic of his writings, Robert Hughes, to have been suggesting that 'anything or its opposite can be true', and he has found in America a triumph of sign over significance. He is fascinated by a country which has become its television programmes: the medium is its message. Such have been his vertiginous interpretations, as he deconstructively refers to what he writes. In this voiding of America can be caught a more thoroughgoing television capture than any so far adumbrated for Britain. But it is a capture in which it is impossible to believe, and which he has chosen to describe in print. Advanced Americans are said to have opened his books and been excited by this phantasm of the glamorous worthlessness of their country and by 'the death of reality' which it represents or portends. Baudrillard and Welsh have enlarged that sizeable body of evidence which suggests that the books which are still being written, by the avant-garde, by bibliophobes, and by others, are still being read.

The idea of a highbrow magazine which concerns itself with popular culture would have been thought as outlandish as the desire of the star for the moth by the high-culture loyalists who edited the politically revolutionary journals of the Thirties. By the autumn of 1979, when the *London Review of Books* was launched, it was an idea whose hour had come. But the journal was no embodiment of it. The *London Review* was not intended to be a highbrow magazine, in any very strict sense of that term, though we realized that it would sometimes behave like and would often be taken for one. You could say that we were too broad to be truly highbrow. Our compendiousness was among the features which failed to suit the classification which the early circulation figures might have appeared to earn. The magazine took in, but did not prefer or exalt, the popular arts, and it took in a wide range of concerns. Some of these were the concerns of small minorities. Others were not.

In the year in question, there was an eleven-month lock-out at Times Newspapers which silenced the *Times Literary Supplement*. It was felt that a journal might be started to fill a gap which the common reader may not have spotted. The *New York Review of Books* financed the launch and kept the paper afloat for six months. I was asked to edit it, and did so with two former colleagues from the *Listener*: Mary-Kay Wilmers, who became its deputy editor, and Susannah Clapp. At very short notice, a matter of two or three weeks, we began to appear – folded, initially, inside the *New York Review*. When the Americans pulled out, or pulled us out, the paper was acquired by the deputy editor, who became the editor thirteen years later. We were also, from that early point onwards, in receipt of supplementary financial support from the Arts Council, which drew complaints. There were journalists who called it disgraceful that such a journal, a journal of opinion, should be given money by the state. After two issues, the Mistress of Girton – the college, not the man – declared in Cambridge that we were not as good as the *New York Review*.

At one bound we were free, however, with the start of this paper – to the extent, at least, that constraints due to other people's precedents and to institutional preconception and necessity were gone. Once we'd conveyed to publishers, and to those of their advertising managers who were paying attention, that we were able to muster a full coverage of new publications and were not dilettantes, we felt we could put in what we wanted to put in and leave out what we wanted to leave out. We felt entitled to be as funny and as demanding as we were capable of being, to write short or at solemn length, and to be strange and daft when the spirit moved. At most times it was very like hard work for a microscopic staff, each issue being the length of a 50,000-word book. Each issue was bookish, too, in affording themes and variations and contradictions; a particular piece might be seen to qualify and interpret another one placed in its vicinity; we must sometimes have looked like the living opposite of the doctrinaire journal of ideas, like a fully deserving recipient of public funds.

In offering at one stage to describe what it meant to make a book of ourselves with each issue, building up, pointing up and co-ordinating themes while also trying for contrast, variety, vagary and surprise, I referred to the issue of 20 September 1984, assembled and laid out by my two editorial colleagues when I was off on holiday, looking out for fireflies in the Tuscan night. It still seems a good example of what we thought we were up to in the matter of co-ordination. They had gone for a harmony which embraced, among other elements, Ian Hamilton's praise of Martin Amis's riotous novel *Money*, Frank Kermode's inspection of some 'Old Testament capers' on the part of Muriel Spark, Craig Raine's birth poem 'The Prophetic Book', Michael Screech's homage to Rabelais, Denton Fox's mocking account of Rabelais's prodigious seventeenth-century translator Urquhart, Fiona Pitt-Kethley's Rabelaisian poems, and Denis Donoghue's examination of a new edition of *Ulysses*: a harmony that trembled to the themes of language, invention, divinity and misrule. Such a system of correspondences and contradictions requires a surplus of material to choose from for each issue, and it requires a willingness to be late (or early) in responding to the publication dates of the books under review. We wanted to be prompt, but we wanted even more to try for the qualities I am describing.

The paper was laid out according to a simple and serviceable formula. There was no front and back: we ran on from first to last like the *Edinburgh Review* – in no set thematic order and with very little in the way of segregation. Long broadsheet pages tended to make those issues which were light on advertising look too thin. We used to fill the cover with a single illustration, frequently taken, like most of the visuals inside, from one of the books under review: an apt and thrifty solution. Letters were placed early, as a sign of respect and as a temptation to the reader, and they were allowed to be stormy and to make a case.

In my time, the paper did not do enough, because it did not know enough, to deal as they deserved with the popular arts. Unlike Coriolanus, we 'loved the common people', who did not love the paper, God damn their sweaty night-caps: but, as I've said before, it would be wrong to think that the failure to make what we hoped to make of rock music came about because we were not, in the colloquial sense, a popular paper. We did not know much about science either, or about Classical music. I am a listener to Handel and Rossini, but am deaf to a lot of later music; and I've yet to be a reader of Stephen Hawking's history of the world. Where we felt we did not know anything at all, and lacked guidance, we'd refrain from publishing. *De omne scibile* did not apply, editorially, on any of the papers I've worked for: but I was never shy about publishing the thoughts of the geneticist Peter Medawar, or the music criticism of David Drew and Hans Keller. I was happy to let Hans trail his coat of many colours.

We knew enough about the logistics of literary journalism to accept that the road to profit was never going to be easy, and that we might never get there. Unless we'd felt that we were making progress towards a circulation figure of 20,000 we would probably have stopped publishing. But we were aware that an intellectually demanding paper is hard put to it to get to that figure, and to be seen by the trade and by advertisers as having a market value. Hard put to it, therefore, to make a profit. Failure to reach that figure has to be compensated for by the florid advertising support which an occupational or vocational connection might attract, but which a lower circulation figure would otherwise be almost certain to preclude. This means that demanding papers are likely to be privately or institutionally subsidized. As the Eighties wore on, publishers' advertising budgets were tightened, and the practice gained ground of turning to mass-circulation papers, in order to place expensive advertising displays designed to protect an investment in those few books on which large advances had been laid out. Many, many books are now neither advertised nor reviewed. From the standpoint of the more exacting, the less bankable author, the word 'publisher' has begun to take on a note of irony.

The *London Review* was no different from the other journals I've worked for in functioning as a specialist paper of general interest which exhibited a blend of minority and majority concerns, many of them no different from the concerns which exercised most people up and down the country. The nation cared about spies, and so did we; Neal Ascherson wrote a piece on what it felt like to be wooed, in a more or less literal sense, by MI6. The paper came into existence when Margaret Thatcher came to power, and when the Social Democratic Party – formed by Roy Jenkins and other veterans of the *Spectator* and the back half of the *New Statesman* – embarked on its chequered career, its changes of name and of fortune, and its eventual escape from the deadly shade of Jenkins's Upas tree, David Owen. The paper shared with the SDP the objections to Old Labour which were later to be enshrined – to the point of Thatcherite exaggeration – in Labour Party policy. It also undertook a criticism of Thatcherism, which had burst on the scene in government form, with very little in the way of warning. Ian Gilmour, W. G. Runciman, Edward Thompson, Ross McKibbin, Peter Clarke, Tam Dalyell and R. W. Johnson were chiefly responsible for lodging objections to the Thatcher triumph.

Throughout the world could be heard the withdrawing sigh of the socialist ebb-tide. The despotic variety of socialism moved towards a collapse into misery and disorder. Meanwhile, in Britain, the democratic variety dropped its head. In relation to democratic socialism, the paper did what it could to help to initiate a work of renewal and reappraisal. Writing in the paper as early as 1981, Garry Runciman foresaw the emergence, 'for the first time in British political history', of 'a New Left which is to the right of the Old'.

In the autumn of 1984, a dispute arose when Michael Stewart wrote a review of Arthur Scargill's miners' strike. The strike was a challenge to the Government's intention to effect a drastic reduction in the number of pits, and in calling the strike, Scargill refused to ballot his members. Stewart claimed that this was a violation of democratic principle. I agreed with the claim, agreeing, furthermore, with the customary view that the country should be governed by the government it elects. But then Stewart was to point out in his piece that the elected Margaret Thatcher had also been a flouter of democracy: braced by a huge Parliamentary majority on a vote of only 31 per cent of the electorate, the Prime Minister had behaved in an arbitrary fashion, forcing through contentious and unpopular legislation, as in the case of the abolition of London's presiding local authority, the GLC. 'Mr Scargill must be defeated,' wrote Stewart, 'but so, in a sense, must Mrs Thatcher.'

The allusions to Mrs Thatcher's highhandedness did little to qualify the exposure, which struck me as un-answerable, of Arthur Scargill's. But the case against Scargill was to split not only the troika that ran the paper, but the readership as well. Having won their battle, Conservative ministers proceeded to shut down and sell off the country's pits and to thrust the mining communi-ties onto the dole. So that's what came of speaking up for elected government, while also publishing, as so often, its critics: Stewart's was not the only view of the strike to be printed in the paper. Subsequent pieces included one by my son Sam which reported on a visit to the village of Grimethorpe and on the efforts made, mainly by the women there, to deal with the hardships brought about by the strike. There were those in the area who hoped that there would be no return to a patriarchal reality. Twelve years later, the reports are that Grimethorpe, badly hit by unemployment and by crime, is on the way to becoming a ghost town.

This was not the only war in which we took part. We fought two others in the shape of the Falklands War and the Gulf War, arguing an unpopular case which stressed constraints on military engagement, at the start and finish, respectively, of these wars: but I don't think anyone on the paper believed that Saddam's aggression could have been handled purely diplomatically, which was what we'd hoped for in the case of the Falklands conflict.

Late in 1987, a Diary in the paper by Tony Blair said that Thatcherism, rumoured to be invincible, could be beaten. A certain impatience with the Labour Party was perceptible in the Diary. 'People only listen to those they trust,' he wrote. But there was 'nothing more ridiculous than the notion that socialism is inexorably dying'. The 'trick', as he put it, was to 'refashion' old approaches, to be 'modern'. And modern meant, among other things, that a party which 'restricts its appeal to the traditional working class will not win an election': this was a time, the day before yesterday, as it were, when the traditional working class had come to be thought – by influential commentators such as Peter Jenkins – to have turned into a wasting electoral asset, and when Thatcher had moved to force it into an under-class. So Blairism had set out its stall some ten years before seizing the Party and contending for government. Shortly afterwards, a Diary by R. W. Johnson argued, with all of Paul Johnson's power of disparagement, that the Labour leader Neil Kinnock had to go. Confrontational cradle-Catholics, these Johnsons – a red-haired duo, with a Scottish Border, a Border-fighter name. In the Sixties, with apologies to Conan Doyle, Maurice Richardson liked to talk darkly of the League of Red-Headed Men – meaning John Freeman and Paul Johnson – who edited the *New Statesman*.

Contributors to the Letters columns were quick to join in on one side or the other of the disputes that arose on a paper prepared to disagree with itself and to entertain more than one view of most matters. Though not of all matters. Like Hugh Greene on the subject of journalistic impartiality, we believed there were limits to the dialectical approach. Especially productive of disagreement, both in public and in private, was a miscellany of issues to do with truth, reason, literary theory and authorial identity. When a professional writer, Al Alvarez, published a book on divorce which criticized his first wife in a chapter of autobiography, we gave it to the first wife, an amateur, for review. This offended editorial advisers, one of whom said that the personal lives of authors should not be discussed in the paper. Then came an article by Norman Stone, containing strictures on a former colleague, the historian E. H. Carr. There were lots of strictures on this obituary onslaught, parts of which were to appear to some of us, in retrospect, as malicious, and, perhaps, as a breach of privacy. This was to concede that there are limits which should be placed on discussion of the personal lives of authors.

Other controversies had to do with the disgracing of the Deconstructionist Paul de Man as a consequence of the discovery of his pro-Nazi writings in wartime Belgium; with the reputation of Raymond Williams; and with that of Shakespeare. They were controversies which raised once more the question of the presence of authors in their works, while also raising the question of the admiration of authors which fastens on that presence and thereby contributes to a mythology or mystique. In our intentness on their achievements, we may well have struck literary theorists as being pre-theoretical, archaic. But it must have been obvious enough to others that we were in a broader sense markedly theoretical: hospitable to writers who were both for and against theory, to philosophical inquiry in general, and to the theorized investigation of literature's social provenance.

Individual authors whom we took up, as favourite subjects, too often consisted of authors whom we'd taken up in the past, and there were authors whom we should have taken up and didn't. I don't remember publishing anything more than a few first-rate paragraphs by Robert Taubman about Joseph Roth, whose masterpiece of 1932, *The Radetsky March*, evokes the last days of the Austro-Hungarian Empire, with its Moslem peoples and its province of Bosnia. So it's as up-to-date as *Hadji Murat* and another reason for there to be journals which attend to literature and politics, quality and history.

There were articles which spoke of the making, as opposed to the discovery, of truth, which spoke of reality and of rationality, and of meaning as a union of opposites and a locus of contradiction. The American academic E. D. Hirsch identified Derrida's axioms for the journal: among them, that 'everything can be given at least two equally cogent explanations', and that 'in the temporal process of thinking about anything, one explanation collapses into its contrary'. As a student of traditional duality, I was intrigued by these axioms, but also deterred by their 'anything' and 'everything', which might remind one of the maxim assigned to Jean Baudrillard by one of his critics: 'anything or its opposite can be true.' Hirsch dwelt on the traditional nature of this part of Derrida's procedure, before declaring against the procedure. Hume and Blake said such things too, wrote Hirsch, concluding that Derrida doesn't do enough with them. What Baudrillard does with them, in his sloganized version of Deconstruction and of Marshall McLuhan, would no doubt be too much for Hirsch to bear.

The issue of 17 April 1986, whose cover depicted two Wyoming miners made by Richard Avedon to look like two looming black-and-white minstrels, led off with the first of the American philosopher Richard Rorty's Northcliffe Lectures of that year, in which he gave an account of what it means to take truth as made rather than found. Here was a respect for contingency and invention, a refusal of the belief that truth is 'out there' and other than language-dependent, other than metaphorical. Here was a refusal to worship the corpses of ancestral metaphors which was also the acceptance of a dialectic of alternative explanations and vocabularies. Rorty's article deserves to be seen as a brilliantly suggestive exposition of his views even by those who think of his views as Hirsch thought of Derrida's axioms, or as the man did who told Rorty after one of his Northcliffe Lectures: 'What you have said is wicked.' The Welsh are alleged by their detractors to have no word in their language for truth: Rorty's progress as a philosopher had taken him close to suggesting that the English language could afford to drop the word. It is certainly true that it is often abused.

In the issue of 23 November 1989, Bernard Williams reviewed the book of Rorty's Northcliffe Lectures, saying that, having once cared in his own way about getting things right, Rorty had now lost the sense 'of anything that needs to be got right'. Williams's 'anything' may be set for contemplation beside Derrida's, and beside the one assigned to Baudrillard. He conveyed that the kind of accuracy that matters to the structural engineer matters to other people too, and declared that 'Rorty cannot get rid of the truth as lightly as he pretends.' Williams and Rorty – fellow Nietzscheans of a sort, of different sorts – had fallen out.

The difference between them involved competing assessments of ideas that were important to the conduct of all four of the journals I'd been working for. These journals showed, I believe, something of a special attachment to the idea that truth was in some measure dialectical, and that doctrine should have in it the tolerance and forbearance that are likely to accompany an acknowledgement of diversity and of difficulty. But we had no inhibitions about using the word 'truth' in the sense that associates it with the word 'accuracy'. We made use of the contested terms 'objectivity' and 'impartiality'. And we believed in the need for policy and purpose, and for the decisions that pertain to them. We were in no doubt that the journal which fails to decide fails to survive. We made up our minds, and we made attacks. The *London Review* did not lack decision, any more than it lacked idiosyncrasy. It was different from other papers. It was itself. And in the message imparted by this idosyncrasy, as by the decisions, derisions and aggressions that went every fortnight into the paper, the limits of any dialectical approach – whose journalistic possibilities include featurelessness and tedium – are inscribed. It is in the nature of magazines to attack, to suspend whatever stress they may choose to place on the uncertain and the undecidable, on the virtues of a dialogue between forbearance and aggression, and to reveal themselves in so doing. The paper was never as alarming as I am making it appear, but it was at least as decisive as it was dualistic. My concern here is to say that it was both, and that in being so it revealed itself as at once socialist and liberal.

Richard Rorty's position, with its bid to unsettle widely accepted conceptions of truth, has been construed here with reference to the dualistic or dialectical tradition in literature and philosophy, and my own view of the dispute was affected by my interest in the tradition. But this did little to impede my appreciation of what Bernard Williams had to say in his review, which was capable of persuading many of those in two minds about the two-minded dualistic calculus to make them up, on this occasion, by moving towards a distrust of Rorty's version of it. Williams could be thought to have his own version of it, one should add. He, too, is interested in this tradition.

Rorty's position belongs to a disposition of mind which has echoed about us, both for better and for worse and in a variety of registers, for a long time now. There are American professors who have been saying that it's all right for them to advocate their political opinions in class, and – or but – that there's no truth in what they advocate, and a British psychoanalyst is saying that the job of the analyst is to allow the 'compelling' story told by psycho-analysis to lie on top of the no less compelling story told by the patient. This is Adam Phillips, a writer for the *London Review*, who has found a really interesting way of letting it be known that the truth is a copulation of stories and an accumulation of stories, and that there's a sense in which authority needs to be deposed in favour of the ignorance professed by a new kind of expert. The psychoanalyst must 'contain within herself' an Enlightenment Freud and a post-Freudian Freud, and become 'an expert on the truths of uncertainty'. At one point he remarks in effect that you can't trust the statement that truth is based on trust. Phillips's paradoxes can be vexing, and might even seem wicked to some people: but they can also argue very well on behalf of this disposition of mind, to which – at the risk of blaspheming against the reckless voice of the unconscious – I've been responding here with grudging talk of limits and of rational intent, of decisions and purposes, in the knowledge that by most experts on uncertainty these often fallible and inconclusive decisions and purposes would be consigned to Rorty's accumulations, to his layer-upon-layer of guesses and stories, improvisations and figures of speech, to the monumental human heap imagined in his writings. In the knowledge, too, that if there are experts on uncertainty by whom the lies that take part in literature are redescribed as strong inventions, there are other experts on uncertainty who behave as if they need to be told that there are inventions which are best described as lies.

The dialectical, and the limits of the dialectical, could be glimpsed in the *London Review*'s tendency to be neither highbrow nor lowbrow, to provide a subject-matter that was both popular and abstruse. They were apparent in the attempt that was made, on all of my four papers, to go for a common knowledge fed by different disciplines and to bring together journalists and artists and academics. And they were often apparent in the discussion of political questions that was conducted and reported there. In 1965, a White Paper reduced entry vouchers for Commonwealth immigrants from over 200,000 to under 10,000. The Labour Cabinet felt badly about cutting the intake, but worse about risking unrest, and the Labour vote, by letting in too many people. It seemed to some, to many, that both aspects of the question had to be taken into account. Nevertheless, there were lots of people on the left who were ready to cut this knot – who held that to entertain the prudential argument was a 'betrayal': that was their word for it, as for much else, and I knew hardly anyone who doubted that the two main parties were wrong to employ a criterion of race in enforcing their Commonwealth exclusions. Richard Crossman, Minister of Housing at the time, a time of financial crisis, was to encounter the bitterness, on the subject of immigration, of a former journalistic associate and former immigrant, the cartoonist Vicky: the encounter might well have reminded them of the conflicts that had sometimes characterized their revolutionary and conservative journal. Immigration, Ireland, Europe – the major British problems of modern times resemble one another structurally; each has its note of the intractable or insoluble or impossible; and they express, I think, a fundamental British uncertainty. They are the problems of a nation that lives with the idea of invasion and with the enigma of a diminished international role.

Disputes can poison magazines and destroy them, but they are none the less – to persist in the dualistic vein – an aspect of their vitality. Rorty and Bernard Williams were one of a series of quarrelling pairs of *London Review* contributors, and we would have been nowhere without these clashes. On one occasion Christopher Ricks wrote of a volume of essays by Clive James: 'these reviews, some of which appeared in this journal, don't amount to much.' Worse was to come on this occasion. 'Even good reviews,' he went on, 'are ephemeral, honourably so.' The editors felt that a good reviewer, in mediating and interpreting what someone has written, may add to it. Not only is this honourable. Such a review is a literary work more valuable than many books manage to be.

In 1986, I wrote that it was a blessing to belong to a small staff where one might hope that there would be less bother with 'conflicting aims and "halves", and the formation of coteries and conspiracies'. The intervening years have caused me to feel that this was to worry too much about conflict, and that there's little to choose, in this respect, between small magazines and big ones. In respect of the related subject of editorial freedom, the editoriality which is among the pieties of the modern world, there can often be little to choose between individual and institutional ownership. The majesty and authority of editors, invested with the power of their circulation figures, is a romantic notion which is evident in the writings of Thomas Carlyle, and which has been flaunted ever since. Carlyle asked: 'Is not every able Editor a Ruler of the World, being a persuader of it; being self-elected, yet sanctioned, by the sale of his Numbers?' But Carlyle, whose words and capital letters are not without irony, knows that this rule will end if the numbers stop selling; and it will also end if the self-elected proprietor cancels the editorial prerogative.

There are sound reasons for preferring editors to proprietors, as many people, and most editors, would appear to do. I'm not sure myself how you'd set about demonstrating in principle that an editor should always be, and that the owner who appointed him should never be, free to publish what he wants to publish. But this is not to deny that proprietors should, as far as possible, be subject to safeguards and to the oversight of independent boards of trustees, or to deny that a paper will struggle when editorial control is disputed – when owners interfere, or when institutions do, or when decisions are allowed, for internal reasons, to degenerate into contests and compromise. There can be the finest of lines, or none at all, between torment and the accommodation of a productive dissent, between rancour and the orchestration of opposing viewpoints, between confusion and the complexity of duality. The response to duality is an exercise of the mind that can be overdone. We may need to see double, but we also need to set limits to the discovery of contradiction. This being the case, it would seem that a good editor is likely to be one who is able to rule over a divided paper, and that a paper should have just the one editor. These are my two more or less congruent golden rules for periodical journalism.

Despite the delegation which occurred at intervals on the *New Statesman* of the past – a delegation suggestive both of dualistic interpretation and of dual control – there was, in the last resort, just the one editor, who knew how to put together a good paper. The journal has in recent times been struggling – as opposed to staggering, in the manner of the past – and has now been relaunched. I'd say that it has long been much the worse for shedding most of its literary part, its rearward challenge and garden of delights. Less contentiously, this loss of ground could also be attributed to boardroom inertias of the late Sixties and to the journal's later submission to the purported democracy of committees, interested parties and in-house tactical manoeuvre. Not that the opposite pole of outright owner-authorized editorial despotism would necessarily have been an improvement, or that the staff should have endeavoured to prolong or restore the romantic notion of the editor as hero.

Such arrangements and relationships can make or break a magazine or an editorial programme. And they used to communicate a paradisal air to *I. F. Stone's Weekly*, the American journal owned and well-written by Stone, dispatched by mail from their home by Stone and his wife, and profitable with it. Not many could do what these two did, but the new technology makes life easier than it used to be for those on small papers who have something to say and are willing to suffer the experience of trying to do their best with the early issues, while all too aware that very few eyes may fall on them. This is what we went through on the *London Review*, wondering whether there were any readers out there who were attending to the best we could do. Eventually our creatures from outer space made contact.

I left my university in the autumn of 1992, and at that time too I left the paper, having ceased to get on with the colleague who owned it. The relationship reached a crisis which can be precisely tracked by inspecting the unsightliness and tormented typography of a succession of compromise covers. I was lucky to have had, for well over thirty years, so free a hand to do what I so much liked to do in journalism, and as far as this last period of thirteen years goes, I owe a debt of gratitude to the colleague with whom, in the best traditions of our paper, I had failed to agree, and to those who worked with us so zealously.

The journals I have been discussing embodied a collective attempt to see the sense that literature makes, to insist on that, at a time when contradiction had been discovered, when ambiguity and irony had been discovered, and the truth to be found in books had been thrown into uncertainty, an uncertainty which was not without its appeal for the journalists who made the attempt. There was a place for literature in the blood-stained environment which has become known to some as the people's century, and it was sometimes felt that there was a place in the literary culture for anyone who wanted to join it. In recent times it has been felt that the literature which is more widely accessible has come to need defending. But there are no grounds at present for claiming that market forces, or any others, are bound to put a stop to it. Ten years ago Richard Rorty's arguments about contingency used to produce reminders of Stevie Smith's sly translation of the sonorous Latin tag: *Magna est veritas et praevalebit*. Truth is great, said Stevie Smith, and it will prevail for a bit. Literature, too, is great, and is likely to prevail for a bit longer than the end of the millennium.

12. Infamy

I LOVE THE GAME of football, and I do so in ways that can remind me of the satisfactions I have gained from reading books and of my procedures as a reader. With regard to football, for one thing, I commit the biographical fallacy identified by literary experts: I believe that the personality of a given player helps to decide games and to account for their appeal. In both fields, personality can flourish as the stardom that compels the imagination and may hold the interest even of the austere. Stardom can be impugned. It is impugned in this book. But it can never be left out of account, and it has its own very great intrinsic interest.

Such a player is Peter Beardsley, the least meretricious of stars. He is still playing at thirty-eight, and has turned out in recent years for Newcastle once more, where he began, all dressed up in its vertical black-and-white stripes – the quintessential soccer strip, I reckon, perhaps because it was that of my village team, the first I ever watched, whose pitch was the first on which I ever played. He looks like a little boy on the field, but there's an old head on these hunched shoulders. 'I often get called

Quasimodo.' Quasimodo got called Goldenfeet by his
father when he was even smaller than he is now, and told
not to worry: 'You'll make it.' Peter Beardsley of the firm
jaw, open mouth, Newcastle-coloured white face and
black hair, oozy fronds standing out over his collar at the
back of his head in the heat of a game, has many qualities.
He is reserved, contained, but a straight talker. He is a
play-maker, both a maker and a scorer of goals, a man
who can never have directed an act of vengeance or undue
violence at an opponent, by foul means or fair.

The manager who took him to Newcastle, Kevin
Keegan – an emotional man, an 'Islamist', a great talker
about resignation ('I'm off!') who resigned during the
blizzards of January '97 – built, for a financially profligate
club, an exhilarating but precarious side, with Beardsley
tucking in for a time behind the sound and productive
Shearer, the striding, heading Ferdinand, the squirming,
spaghetti-like Asprilla, with his Colombian voodoo, and
the suffering god Ginola. Keegan had the sense to sign
Beardsley at a point in the player's career when other
bosses had taken to dropping and selling him for being
too old. There is something that can touch the heart
about the people of the North-East of England – very
much apparent in the television serial *When the Boat Comes
In* of several years back – and its name is Peter Beardsley,
who would have played to perfection in the serial. The
fans and the players wanted him to succeed Keegan.
Instead, the directors chose another 'Islamist', a spectacu-
lar one, Kenny Dalglish of the repressive-depressive
mumbling managerial style. Ginola's French flamboyance
was soon to be gone from St James's Park, and so was

Beardsley's reserve. He had been dropped by Dalglish in the past, and in his prime – at Liverpool.

I am not threatening to spread out my favourite football players in a fan of cigarette-card likenesses. What I'd like to write about here is an aspect of the game which has always been hard to miss and harder than ever during the Nineties: this is the fascination with the exceptional or untoward player, who can sometimes be seen as alien or exotic and is now quite likely to be foreign, a fascination which can turn to loathing, a loathing which journalists help to incite. It can all seem at times to amount to a desire for the destruction of talent. This destructive work was familiar enough when the foreign player was still a rare bird in Britain. But then team sheets suddenly began to read like mellifluous menus. Ravanelli, Juninho, Vialli, Zola – there were sides half-staffed with foreigners, and a real Quasimodo seemed about to arrive at any moment, on the wings of a transfer fee of millions of pounds. Malice might have been defeated by this embarrassment of imported talent. But it has gone on raising its sneer – foreign players are mercenary, said the *Independent* in 1996, but 'not all' are lazy – without so far removing from the general mind the impression that the English game is that much more beautiful, by and large, as a result of the imports. No doubt there will be tears before bedtime. Some of these players are over the hill. There were some who were immediately reported homesick. Some have gone home. And as the Frenchman Eric Cantona has pointed out, foreigners are the first to be dropped when a team runs into trouble.

This Foreign Legion is a recent development which was preceded by a certain awe of the nevertheless decried foreign game, and it would already seem to have done a little to diminish the jingo racism which has been found at football grounds. Black players and white get on fine, in the main, whether as partners or as opponents; they seem to like each other, and can even seem exemplary. But colour remains a theme in the name-calling din from the terraces, and it creeps into television commentaries in the form of insinuations about unreliability, inconsistency and lack of bottle. 'You never know what Asprilla is going to do,' commentators tell you, the ones who also make it clear that alien goalkeepers of all complexions are liable to be effeminate – 'suspect on crosses', like Kingsley Amis. On the tabloid and broadsheet back-pages, prejudice seems mainly to fly in the direction of Caucasians from abroad.

On 25 January 1995, Manchester United were playing away, in London, against Crystal Palace. Their French star Cantona, who'd been on the end of the hassling managers call for in order to stop stars from playing, kicked out a little at his marker as he went forward. It was more of a flick than a kick. It was like the fly-catching flicker of a Midi lizard's tongue. In another game that day, another foreign star, English-looking, English-speaking, English-playing Jürgen Klinsmann, then of Spurs and a favourite of the fans at White Hart Lane, was clattered by a far from effeminate foreign goalkeeper, an Australian Croat, in one of the most violent interventions I've seen on a football field, and was carried off unconscious on a stretcher. The referee allowed the goalkeeper to remain on the field; neither a red card nor a less grave yellow card was awarded. Cantona had no such luck. He was sent off.

Eric Cantona: My Story, translated and adapted by George Scanlan, pre-dates this disproportionate sending-off, and its momentous sequel, but might be thought to predict them. The book details earlier scrapes and scuffles and shows Cantona to be a resenter of unfair treatment. There can't be any doubt that he was in a state when he left the field on this occasion, at which point a youth descended the terraces to scream xenophobic scurrilities at this 'French git'. The French git then entered the crowd, or the margins of it, and took a flying kick at the youth – a karate leap, allegedly. And that's when the really bad violence began.

The incident was discussed by the Saturday-night soccer experts on BBC Television. It was not yet known whether Cantona's assailant had come to any harm; none was later reported. Nor was it yet known that the assailant had been in the hands of the police as the result of an attack on an Asian garage-man, and had been linked to far-right racist groups. The *Match of the Day* presenter, Desmond Lynam, for many, as for me, a sympathetic figure, called Cantona's action 'infamous' – an adjective which he was afterwards to re-apply to the action, and which has gone on being applied to it by journalists ever since. 'Infamous' contains a response to Cantona's being famous, and perhaps also to his being foreign; if you and I had done what he did, some other word might have been used. The former soccer star Gary Lineker said on the programme that Cantona's behaviour was inexcusable, or was it unforgivable, and he was solemnly uncertain whether this man would or should go on earning his living by playing football in this country.

Cantona was fined by his club and banned from playing for the rest of the season – a ban which was extended by the Football Association until the end of the summer. And he was sentenced by a magistrates' court to two weeks in jail. He had no previous convictions, and the charge of common assault which was obtained by the defence rarely receives a custodial sentence. This remarkable penalty award was influenced, according to the chairwoman of the bench, by the prominence of the defendant ('You are a high-profile figure with undoubted gifts, and as such you are looked up to by many young people'), and was described by the *Guardian*'s legal correspondent Marcel Berlins as 'one of the most outrageous magisterial decisions I have ever come across. Quite apart from their apparent disregard for the obscene, hate-filled provocations which the so-called victim heaped on Cantona, I have no doubt that, had it been an unfamous person in the dock, with – like Cantona – a pregnant wife and small son and no previous convictions, and pleading guilty, custody would hardly have entered the justices' minds.' The sentence went to appeal, and on 31 March it was replaced by a spell of 120 hours' community service, accompanied by some welcome observations from the appeal judge. This was a relief. But the custodial sentence was to remain in the mind, as was the journalism which preceded the custodial sentence, and followed it too. The *Guardian*'s headline on the reprieve from prison was rather more typical of its coverage of the affair than the article by Berlins. Cantona, it sneered, 'ducks the cells'.

Meanwhile, at the beginning of February, when their team went a goal down during a friendly match between England and the Irish Republic, a number of Englishmen, some of whom were reported to be members of the neo-Nazi group Combat 18, smashed stadium seats and threw them at the crowd. None of these thugs was sentenced to anything at all, as far as I could learn. So it seemed that there was racist aggression on the terraces, and that the authorities' way of dealing with it had included an attempt to send one of its victims to prison.

Famous Eric Cantona's action was infamous, said the papers, and they also said that what happened in Dublin was infamous. But very few papers that I saw made any attempt to connect the behaviour of Cantona's assailant with the affray, or provocation, in Dublin. That would have been to make Cantona's behaviour less inexcusable, and to call attention to the routinely hateful treatment, in many football grounds, of enemy players, rather than to an act of retaliation in the face of such treatment. Newspapers continued to run with the story of 'shit hits fan' and with the cry of inexcusable, in one of their biggest displays of canting obloquy.

When Cantona started his English career, journalists gave out that this moody man was temperamentally unsuited to the wholesome national game, in which he then went on to extraordinary success. Now they were saying that 'the Frenchman' had to go. Some of them alleged that his retaliation under attack showed that standards, those ever-falling things, had lurched on down, that it showed a rampant commercialism, a collapse into bungs, bent managers and overpaid stars. Amongst the pack was David Lacey of the *Guardian*, who likes to be sour about star footballers' failings. It is natural to wonder if he read the words of Marcel Berlins in his own newspaper, and if so, what he made of them.

On 27 January David Lacey wrote: 'If professional football is to retain any lingering pretensions to be a part of sport, as opposed to a product guided by market forces, then Eric Cantona has surely played his last game for Manchester United.' Lacey is more of a stylist than a prophet. Some might feel, he said, that on that previous Wednesday 'a *poulet* came home to roost'. A year later, almost to the day, he was writing about 'the kung-fu kick which earned Eric Cantona an infamous place in football history'. Three months later still, two things happened. Lacey referred to the occasion when the Frenchman 'kung-fu-kicked his way to infamy', and the *Independent* reported that 'the football fan who provoked Manchester United's Eric Cantona to launch his infamous kung-fu kick was jailed for several days for contempt of court yesterday after attacking a lawyer' – in the court where he was being sentenced for the original assault. It was sometimes to seem that journalists write the words that other journalists write and that they don't know what this word means.

One of them said in the *Observer* at the time that Cantona had 'always seemed consumed by a dangerous self-belief masquerading as hatred of injustice'. The autobiography I mentioned suggests that he has sometimes been unjustly treated, while also suggesting that he regrets nothing, in relation to earlier brushes with authority. He fell out with the megalomaniac financier Bernard

Tapie, who was later jailed for attempted bribery on behalf of the club he'd presided over, Marseille Olympique; he spoke ill of a manager of the French team; scrapped with a team-mate; threw down his shirt when ordered off the field. Nothing greatly untoward here. His disciplinary record isn't an object of horror, though it's true that he has sometimes retaliated and has made some violent tackles.

The book presents him as a romantic individualist, proud to be 'different', intolerant of stupid bosses. A key episode has him, as a boy, dribbling halfway across a field in order to score an important goal – only to be pulled up at the last minute by 'the official' for having a bootlace undone. He is interested in betrayal, and worried about being betrayed. He speaks of his 'dream'. He is like the Italian-Australian wing three-quarter David Campese, whose 'free-spirit drivel' was said by a captain of the Australian team to have got on his nerves, and who must count as one of the best of all rugby players. The book doesn't have many insights into what one can concede to be Cantona's inflammatory temperament and thin skin, or into the mysteries of his superlative play. What does emerge, however, is a contrast between his self-willed and self-endangering side and a strong sense of dependency. He likes reading and painting – tastes sneered at and smiled at by journalists unable to abide pretentiousness; and he has taken to appearing in films and in calamitous free-spirit advertisements.

Of Italian and Spanish stock, Cantona grew up outside Marseille in an amenable, aromatic South of France. His grandfather took part in the struggle against Franco. He is Mediterranean man, and in bad moods can look like the sort of Southern peasant who might be feared to be up to something in a wood. But at other times the body language is very different. In this book there's a snap of him with the rebellious actor Mickey Rourke in which he is the soul of deference; Rourke appears to be telling him that he did it *his* way. Keen as he was on his family, and on his native Caillols, he soon felt he had to leave them in order to get to the top in football. His family can be seen as both a presence and an absence in the book, which has him down as a self-elected orphan who has tender feelings about his kin, as someone at once dependent and independent, a stayer and a mover-on; about his wife and son he is wholehearted and more expressive.

Not everyone in this country yielded to the media disposition to behave towards him, when he kicked his fan, like some scandalized judiciary. There was next to none of that from professional players, whose Association had previously voted him their player of the year, as the guild of soccer writers had not. The very 'different' Rodney Marsh, formerly of Queen's Park Rangers, said straight away that if anyone should be banned for life it was the fan who got hit, and current British players were heard to speak generously of Cantona and of his game. The injustice that was done to him would have been as serious, though less intelligible, if it had happened to a less distinguished player, but the 'undoubted gifts' mentioned by the magistrate are a vital part of the picture, if only because it is that much more satisfying to hound the gifted. He has never been at his best on a losing side or when playing for Manchester United on a foreign field

(England has suited him, as Italy he thinks would not have done, and, like Ginola, he hasn't suited the present manager of the French team). But he is an unusually imaginative athlete who has performed in strange ways that the other players in the side have had no difficulty in understanding and exploiting.

The treatment he received in 1995 is unlikely to have been extended to someone who was not, or who could not be represented as, a foreigner, and it rates as a significant episode in the eventful history of post-imperial British xenophobia. But it also mattered that he was a star, and in some sense an artist. He was at one point called 'mon genius' by his manager at Manchester, which was a bit unsettling given that British football is a place where geniuses often fail to fit in. But it seems all right to think of him as an artist. He has the artistic temperament that not all artists have, or would want. There are moments in his book when he assumes the anachronistic air of some bohemian solo turn from the nineteenth-century provinces. Romantic individualists are, as a rule, less forthcoming now than they used to be, and than he is willing to be, and there have been seasons of dislike for the modern equivalent of the grieving and scowling masks which furnished the nineteenth-century pantheon of art. But no retreat from the idea of artists as different, and of art as having a great deal to do with suffering and separation, is to be expected soon. The idea is still around, and so is the behaviour to which it can be attached. Art continues to be obliged to the romantic exception who is sometimes in danger of being sent to jail. Suffering and separation are going to go on being widely ignored. In the arts and in sport, however, they will still be in there with a chance of attracting money and the services of a good agent.

This was one of the interesting aspects of the Cantona crisis. It shed light on the peculiarity of artists, or of some artists, in the contemporary world, on the paranoia that gets into art and its reception, on the wish to have artists blamed as well as praised, rejected as well as enjoyed, to disapprove of them in the press and to drive them to live up to your disapproval. George Best, another artist, became for a while the George Best of the diatribes and hype, and the same can be said of artistic Paul Gascoigne, who is still on the field and is still entangled in a brutal and relentless publicity premised on notions of talent, delinquency and disaster; to be a football writer has been to specialize in saying that he has brought the game into disrepute. It may be that, in England, Cantona's dream, with its threat of betrayal, came true. Unable to speak the language without difficulty, while wanting to know what was being said in his vicinity, bombarded with praise and blame – what a treat, and what an ordeal, for the naturally suspicious, for the 'errant Eric' of the headlines, famous and infamous.

There are players, according to the individualistic, socialistic Pat Nevin, late of Tranmere Rovers, whose 'extreme personalities' are 'inextricably linked to their brilliance and almost always eventually contribute to their downfall'. True. But Nevin would be likely to agree that further contributions are made by those in and around the game and into it on the terraces. This is one of the ways in which someone's troubles can be inextricably linked to the troubles of others – many others or just the one. It can't have been difficult for those who knew him to predict that there would be trouble when Cantona's ambivalence came into collision with a communal ambivalence about foreigners and stars – stars being, from one point of view, foreigners anyway.

The Cantona crisis said more about injustice than it did about football's collapse or decadence. The game is not in the desperate state that journalists have occasionally alleged. It has not been ruined by rising rewards, by the fact that sought-after players are paid as much as high flyers in the arts are paid, or by the knowledge that huge bribes have been offered and accepted. It is still a sport, and an art, and a pleasure. All the same, it has been damaged, and continues to be threatened, by the buying, as opposed to the rearing, of talent, and by recurrent failure on the part of those in authority. It took Arsenal months to decide that there was some sort of decisive objection to their manager's willingness to accept hundreds of thousands of pounds of 'unsolicited gift' in connection with the purchase of two undistinguished players: the manager in question, by whom Cantona was, at one stage, thought to be a cissy, was then speedily re-employed at another top club, which had once employed Cantona and had told him that he was still learning and would have to work harder. There was no talk here of a custodial sentence, and the manager has remained publicly unrepentant and chat-show popular. Such developments have been sickeners which could well have put some people off watching football. Its spell, though, for those who feel it, is very strong.

I went on watching, and sat down before the box for the Euro 96 tournament, held this time in England and attended by English journalists not noticeably less brutal and sanctimonious than the ones who had tried to exclude their Frenchman from the national game. The prime focus, as on so many occasions in the past, was on Paul Gascoigne and his misdemeanours. He has always been at fault in the eyes of reporters and, in his early days, of coaches. A few years back I'd written about him defensively, in a piece that would be referred to later, sometimes with an air of surprise. Here was a piece about a man reckoned stupid by the press, though not by his peers, a piece by a literary journalist who taught at a university, one of those foreigners' pieces about football which are apt to irritate sports journalists, among others.

On the eve of the Euro 96 tournament the England team flew off on a Chinese tour. Just before the game in Hong Kong the television camera panned across a patch of crowd and zoomed in on a face whose owner stuck out a tongue which gyrated like a shirt in a spin-dryer, between two ear-to-ear rows of neat predatory teeth. Oh God, moaned the viewer, here's some thug who thinks he's Gascoigne. It then dawned on us that he *was* Gascoigne.

It was his birthday, and in the evening he went drinking with his mates. On the Cathay Pacific flight home a bit of horseplay broke out during which a TV set and a foldaway table were damaged and in which Gascoigne was accused for a while of playing a key role. There is no reason to believe the rumour that at one point he attempted to fly the plane. At some earlier point in the drama of their departure from the East a cocktail with the fiendish name of a Flaming Lamborghini had passed between these rows of teeth. All hell broke out in the press. A Tory MP popped up like a toaster to call for his dismissal from the team. Martin Kettle thundered in the *Guardian* that 'if human societies were organized on the consistent moral and civic principles which politicians and pundits seek to proclaim, then there is no doubt whatever that Paul Gascoigne should have been sent packing from the England football squad in disgrace and that he would probably still be helping the police with their inquiries into his alleged behaviour' on the aeroplane, part of which, he alleged, was 'wrecked'. Kettle was incensed because he feared that the alleged behaviour would be glossed over by officials. In thereby anticipating the findings of the Football Association inquiry which had been put in hand, he was no different from the chairman of the FA, who rapidly announced that he was especially interested in investigating the role of Gascoigne.

The Cathay Pacific infamy produced less of a commotion than the Cantona kick. But it risked reviving the tension which has endangered Gascoigne's game, and disturbing an England team that had yet to settle. This clearly mattered less, to the more patriotic papers, than did the prospect of a vampable horror story, with plenty of blame attached – to offset the poor showing expected of England in the tournament. I thought on the eve that England might possibly find itself in the course of it, as happened in the 1990 World Cup – but failed to allow for the return to form on Alan Shearer's part which was to help them to do so. And I thought they would need Gascoigne: for his constructive eye, for his tight-situation contrivances, and for his fighting spirit, which had taken him over the top, but which could still be a force for order and purpose. Newspapers didn't see it that way. In the course of the run-up to the tournament and of the opening games they went after him as never before. Fans have always liked him, and were quicker than managers and scribes to see the point of him. Scribes – a name for them from the days when they used to call goalkeepers custodians – like him too, in a closet sort of way, but have tended to behave as if they owed it to themselves to destroy him. He is never as fit as he should be, they write. And he is not as fast as he used to be. The truth is that he has never been as fast as he used to be. That is not his game.

Against Scotland, pacing himself, he did all right in the first half, while playing too deep and too defensively (that is not his game either), in a team which was at that stage struggling. In the second half he lit up. With his new frowning face and marigold hairstyle, he made a very well-timed long forward run to gather the ball and score a goal that only a very smart and fit player could have pulled off. At half-time BBC Television's Jimmy Hill had suggested that he should be replaced.

On the Sunday after, the papers praised the goal, but there were sneers too, which gained in volume as the week began and the game against Holland loomed. 'Say what you like about Gazza, but the boy can certainly play,' said one man, who'd been saying what he liked a few paragraphs before: that Gazza was 'below his best'.

Ever since he entered the game there's never been a time when he hasn't been below his best. But members of the Scottish team reckoned that he was the outstanding English player on the park in England's opening game, against Switzerland, and the German Franz Beckenbauer, a great player and a great authority on the game, named him at one point as 'my player of the tournament so far – the intelligence of his playing has been simply fantastic'. There is more than a touch of the tightrope about Gascoigne's game. It trembles on a brink, and can make anxious watching. Off the field, he has appeared laughing and restless and Tourettic, but with a glower of depression settling on him in recent times. On the field, he can seem tense – as if laced into the corset of the pressures he lives with. Nevertheless, he played shrewdly and courageously throughout the tournament.

England saw off fancied Holland, scoring four goals, and went on to hold Germany in the semi-final, going out in the penalty shoot-out by one missed kick. More 'culpable' than the man who missed the kick, wrote David Lacey, was Gascoigne, who had missed by an inch in extra-time with a sliding strike on goal. England had not played as well as this for years, and the press seemed, for the most part, quite unable to appreciate what the team had achieved.

Euro 96 was poorly refereed. Amidst a cascade of red and yellow cards penalties were wrongly and inconsistently awarded. Intrusive refereeing has become the chief curse of the modern game, together with the diving and faking which has developed in response to it. A good deal hangs on the concept of intention, which keeps coming up in discussions of foul play, and indeed of dives and feigned injury. Except to prevent an otherwise certain goal, few players *intend* to commit a flagrant foul in their own penalty area; the foul play which is, and may often have to be, penalized as such is mostly accidental; and intention is on many occasions an undecidable factor, if not a chimera. Referees and commentators would seem to be much more confident of players' intentions than the players themselves are. When the ex-Tottenham mid-fielder Nayim scored recently for a Spanish club against Arsenal with a shot of the century from halfway and over by the right-hand touchline, a shot as remarkable for its power as for its placing, English journalists in their jingo meanness shouted that he hadn't meant it — it was a freak shot: but it later turned out that he'd practised it for years. When, during Euro 96, Tony Adams played the ball and a Scottish player fell over his leg, he was deemed to have meant this, and a penalty was given which, had it been converted, would have made nonsense of the England-Scotland game. Justice, however, was done, and a second later Gascoigne was doing some more of it with his goal, in that below-his-best way that he has.

Why is it that so many patriotic soccer writers have failed or refused to acknowledge the qualities of intelligence that Beckenbauer sees in him? Why has the press worked so hard to victimize him? Why has he been systematically persecuted? He could well be too clever for some of these writers. That may come into it. And jealousy must come into it — the jealousy expected of the readers for whom they have made him a celebrity, and their own jealousy as well. The frustrations experienced in a struggling country once aggressively pre-eminent in a number of spheres may come into it too – with Gascoigne to blame for England's failure to win soccer tournaments.

The pursuit of Gascoigne has targeted a human being more complex than he seems to the majority of scribes. Without having met him, and quite without wanting to sleep with him, as one show-business personality has proposed, I like him. There's a stiff North-Easterly attraction to him, apparent in his wit and in his play. The North-East is a football stronghold which dates back to the fighting Border tribes of the later Middle Ages, with their Charltons and Robsons on the south side of the divide: there's a place called Charlton in the Debatable Land, within hailing distance of which I went to live for holiday seasons in the Seventies, and Charltons and Robsons have a place in the history of football. Footballers are fighters – restless, bold, playful, physical people, many of them; their behaviour has to be understood in the light of what they are in that respect, and what they have to be; and before they were footballers they were moss-troopers. Gascoigne's behaviour certainly needs to be understood with reference to the nature of footballers, and to the history of a region, perhaps as much as it may also need to be understood with reference to the nervous tic or peculiarity which has been surmised. His Northerliness takes effect at several levels. There are those in the South for whom he is the spirit of old England, but there are others there for whom his version of Geordie speech is a species of Norwegian, for whom he is as much of a foreign-language player as Cantona. This foreigner's decision to move from Rome back, like the salmon, to the ultimate North of Glasgow Rangers was, on that view, only fitting.

To say these things about him is to attempt to contribute to the case in his favour. But there's also a case against him, which can scarcely be disregarded simply because it's all over the newspapers, or because it must be a strain to be rich and famous and to lead an outrageously demanding life. He hasn't always been at his cleverest. He has often been out of his depth in the world outside football. And, like other victims, he is capable of acting in ways that are impossible to defend. Spying on him in their investigative fashion, journalists have been able to come up with a picture of his wife's face, bruised by him in drink. There was a tingle in the air when that happened – as of the sense that this time he'd done something really bad. And so he had.

Maybe they'll kill him. But if he lives long enough he may turn into a national monument, a heritage feature. Just before Euro 96, BBC2 gave over an evening to honouring the talent of George Best, whose shots and shimmies were run and re-run as twilight deepened into midnight. Best, too, was disgraced and vilified in the course of his playing career, for getting drunk, sleeping with girls and missing appointments. Now, though, as unveiled in an eventide interview – which nevertheless managed to convey that he'd once been 'infamous' – he was as lovable as he was good and great. Meanwhile, in an interview with Desmond Lynam on BBC1 shortly after Manchester United's achievement of the Double, Eric Cantona was shown to have taken rather less time to become, for the media, lovable and respectable. He's a very interesting man who has weathered his troubles tremendously well, said Desmond Lynam in the gravest possible tones. The year before, he'd been infamous.

The year after, though, Desmond Lynam was still applying the word to what Cantona did as he left the field in January 1995. This happened on a page of the *Observer* (2 March) where it also happened that the word was used correctly – with reference to the detective who beat up a suspect in the Carl Bridgewater murder inquiry and saw to it, by faking evidence, that four innocent men went to jail for many years.

In the spring of 1997, when a painting was unveiled which alluded to Piero della Francesca's risen Christ and portrayed the player in Imperial Roman armour at the heart of the Manchester United team, Cantona bought it. He is his own triumphal arch. Then, in May, came the news that his game might be up. At the end of a season during which he had done very well, which had brought another League Championship, but which had also brought missed chances, missed kicks, previously unheard-of on his part, and other signs of fatigue, he announced his fairly early retirement, at the age of thirty-one, the age at which Yeats lost his virginity. He wanted to leave while he was at the top. But then he'd wanted in the past to call it a day. The odds are that he still has a few more leaps left in him for the football field. I hope so.

13. My Books

I AM ATTACHED – well beyond the call of theory, of the adhesive theory of authorship to which I am also attached, whereby books are the people who write them – to the books I have written. When reviewers condemned them, I suspected that the reviewers, even those who were known enemies, might be right, but remained on the book's side – rather as a parent feels when confronted with a teacher's letter telling of some enormity at school. I don't mean to review these books all over again now – only to peruse them a little, to look at material relevant to their concerns which has subsequently come to light, and to wonder why they are so Scottish. Most of my writings in book form are about Scotland and its writers, and one of the first books in which I appeared was a collection of essays, *Memoirs of a Modern Scotland*, edited by me and published in 1970, which evoked the literature of the place in which I grew up and of the country at large. This may seem mildly odd in an anti-patriotic semi-Scot, not sold on the ethnic boasting and hallucinating that gets into literary history.

The first book which was all mine came out in 1975. *Cockburn's Millennium* is the portrait of a pugnacious, militant, mercurially wise Edinburgh Whig – a historian, advocate, judge and politician, a drafter of the Scottish Reform Bill, consequential on the English one of 1832. On the eve of these twin triumphs he exclaimed: 'The Scotch Millennium seems to me to have arrived.' To put the matter another way, one that Cockburn himself would not have favoured, the journey towards a democratic franchise had begun. The book was priced out of the market by its London publisher; it was barely reviewed in my native North. By a miracle of unsolicited curiosity, however, some younger Scottish readers did become aware of it. This was the first full-length book to call attention to the merits of Henry Cockburn, the Tacitus of Scotland, as he appears to me. It is not the study of an inordinately-studied, securely canonical author; for every syllable ever written about Cockburn there are pages on Walter Scott. And yet he writes better than Scott does, in those of Scott's several spheres which approximate generically to the writings of his friend and political enemy, whose copious letters – the majority of them still unpublished – strongly assist this claim.

I was set going on the project when a friend, John Clive of Harvard University, invited me to do an edition of Cockburn's *Memorials of his Time*, and I became eager for all traces of my man, the invasion of his manuscripts a joy of undiminishing returns. The effort to trace him was daunting, initially, for a fearer of libraries, but I made it and learnt to like it. I soon had to correct the mistake I'd made of supposing him to be more left-wing than he was. He was fired up by Enlightenment ideas, and by the French Revolution, when he was young, but was never a radical; he went on to fly 'the Whig flag of sense and justice' for the rest of his life. He wanted change, demolition: but he also wanted anything that was old, old buildings not least, to be let alone. This liberal took to worrying about what would happen to the politics of reason when the force of numbers made itself felt in the course of the new century – as it would first, he thought, in Russia. The difference in outlook between Cockburn and Burke – Cockburn's 'great and accomplished, noble and lovable' Burke – was to diminish with the years. Though never keen on the umbrella'd saints and roaracious sermonizers of the Kirk, he remained, as I was to find out, a believer, and a connoisseur of old-style Presbyterian piety: another upset for the researcher's preconceptions.

I used to puzzle over a passage in his annals – made up of the *Memorials* and of his *Journal* and his *Circuit Journeys* – which describes a fire of 1824 in Edinburgh's Medieval High Street. Old buildings came tumbling down, and a wall had to be blown up. A fog of white lime dust arose. 'It was sublime,' he puns, maybe inadvertently. Through it could be heard the cry of 'the people', who were watching the explosion and were being watched from above by Cockburn. What did he mean by these words? I decided that for Cockburn the expression could contain 'the mob', and could also contain 'the public' – a category which included, as he saw it, the 'general reader', and was due to be strengthened and enlarged with the advent of a wider franchise. It was with the second of these senses in mind that he was to rejoice that the people had 'arisen'. Meanwhile, as he grew older, the word 'democracy' started to sound like a doom. The passage in my book about the passage in Cockburn about the High Street fire never did come out quite as it should have done. Its imagination of the writer's aloofness slips into the fanciful.

The book explores the romantic culture which began in Cockburn's Edinburgh to cultivate the notion of duality, following a transmigration from the German of doubles and second selves. In the year of the High Street fire there appeared duality's masterpiece, the *Confessions of a Justified Sinner*, which he nowhere mentions, though he speaks respectfully of James Hogg and of the Scots language produced by him, and for him by ghosts, in *Blackwood's Magazine*. 'Romantic' was, for Cockburn, a word to be flirted with rather than embraced, and he was indulgent neither to Germanism nor to Hogg's Toryism. But he made use of the language of duality, and his poems responded to those of Wordsworth. He was prepared both to contribute to his friend Jeffrey's *Edinburgh Review*, where Wordsworth came under attack, and to praise its romantic Tory rival, *Blackwood's*.

His life was seen in the book as a system of opposites. He was an Anglophile Scottish patriot, a classical romantic, torn between town and country, between his pugnacious efforts as a public man, pledged to 'wealth and sense', and the pursuit of 'nature and romance' at his tower of Bonaly in the Pentland Hills, a man for whom kinship was a complex matter, a double business, and for whom political reform and Presbyterian piety were each of them a double business too. His early life, that of a father-resisting upper-class son, preceded and resembled the early life of Robert Louis Stevenson, another dualistic master, a wearer of Hogg's plaid in that respect; but he would not have believed, as Stevenson did two generations later, that a fellow could be two fellows. To most intents and purposes, and on the streets of Edinburgh, he was exceptionally sure of himself, a monolith, one of the pillars of the place. He was not like Dr Jekyll and Mr Hyde. The aim here was, as an examiner might phrase it, to compare and contrast him with Stevenson, in the context provided by the developing literature of the double. But too much space was spent on the attempt.

Over the years that followed the appearance of my Cockburn book, manuscripts by him, or about him, turned up. One of them was a letter of 1808 by his friend Elizabeth Hill from her house, Woodhall, out by the Pentlands, where his circle of friends used to foregather, where they tramped the hills, wrote poems, singly and in unison, and compiled a commonplace book composed of unattributed favourite pieces of verse, with the high points of Wordsworth's 'Tintern Abbey' transcribed there. 'Nature never did betray,' copied Cockburn, 'the heart that loved her.' The letter helped me with a problem I'd agonized over: the authorship of the poem 'Geraldine', attributed by me, in the book, to Cockburn, but thereafter to his friend the solicitor and flautist John Richardson. It now seemed likely that the poem was two poems, but for the most part Cockburn's. There were poems in the commonplace book which were like that – round robins, communal in the sense of exposed to the criticisms and rewritings of the house, anonymous in somewhat the way that the *Edinburgh Review* was anonymous. The *Edinburgh*

Review was the local rag of the Whig romantics evoked in this letter – among them the poet James Grahame, who had moved to England and to whom the letter was addressed.

Another manuscript letter – which I carried in the *London Review* 170 years after it was written – counts for me as a cardinal text for the history of literary journalism and of literary coteries. It was written from Woodhall by Cockburn on a sunny Sunday in March 1810. 'It wants but seven days of the vacance, and the weather is getting good-natured at the very thought of it. From where I sit just now in a nook of the window the universal operation of the Secret Spirit of Spring is visible and pleasing. The stream and the sky are trying which can be bluest; the trees are putting out their hands, with nerves at the ends of their fingers, to feel the mild breeze; the blackbirds trill so shortly that it is obvious they do not believe it has returned again . . . All within doors is as well as all without them.'

This letter also was addressed to the exiled Grahame, and it gives news of Edinburgh and of its chattering class: 'except that we have got a new new town to the West, one to the North, one to the East and one to the South, there is no change in Edinburgh, morally or materially, since you left it. Its pleasures, too, of nocturnal parties and a sort of half-fashionable, half-literary slang about Science and reviews, are still the same.' Walter Scott 'still keeps the printer's devil chasing him for sheets, like a fool. I know no poet who has committed such suicide as Watty.' Mutual friends are thriving; one of them is perhaps no better than so-so – but then 'a man is not to be like a column that stands in the desert and desolation of all things, and at the end of 1,000 years still says, This is me.' Which is what his own writings, those of an Edinburgh pillar, still say, at the end of their second century. A friend, James Pillans, had been delated for Jacobinism, but, 'to the great delight of the worthy', had nevertheless been awarded the rectorship of the High School, my High School, and Cockburn's, which had yet to quit the Old Town and ascend the Calton Hill. Someone else's 'whole house is creeping with weans; there was one of them caught and enclosed all night in the rat trap lately. It had gone in after the cheese, and the lid closed.'

The poet James Grahame, an Anglican curate, was stationed for his health near Bath, where his 'worthy lungs' were exposed to a damp church. 'And godly Grahame chant a stupid stave,' wrote Byron at this time, squeezing himself into the narrow interval that separates the two letters with an outpouring of slurs on the Edinburgh that dispatched the letters. The Scottish poet is also known as 'sepulchral Grahame' in the poem in question – Byron's satire 'English Bards and Scotch Reviewers', where the incipient Rector of the High School is known as 'paltry Pillans', and where, in a prose postscript to the second edition, Jeffrey is known as 'the great literary anthropophagus' of the North. Sepulchral Grahame was soon to be in his grave. Here was a Scotch bard who styled himself the 'poor man's bard' and who wanted to be a Scotch reviewer, and who wanted to receive a worthy notice in the *Edinburgh Review*, now almost ten years old. He was a humanitarian Whig, against field sports and subject to fits of depression ('indolence') and drink; Cockburn's letters to him talk of the consolations of religion and preferment. And he was the author of a long poem in Thomsonian vein, *The Sabbath*, and of the *British Georgics*, which was now up for review and in which 'beauties' alternate with bucolic lectures.

Cockburn's letter advises as to the role of the reviewer and the role of the reviewed. It portrays his editor friend Jeffrey as 'a Dictator', and describes a code of practice in the matter of reviewing which has yet to disappear, and which literary anonymity – 'concealed authorship', in Cockburn's expression – did much, originally, to promote. Jeffrey managed his two brisk horses of politics and letters under cover of darkness and with the firmest of hands. He freely rewrote the material sent him for publication, and reviewers were expected to shut up about it. During the Seventies of the present century, what remained of anonymity, so far as journals of opinion were concerned, was badly hit when John Gross brought signatures to the *TLS*. In journals of this kind, however, as on the books and arts pages of newspapers, the practice of rewriting has gone merrily on, with many of the practitioners, both here and in America, very bad at it. Why did you hire me, Edmund Wilson asked the *New Yorker*, if you don't want to print what I wrote?

The relevant portions of Cockburn's letter open with a response to Grahame's eagerness for a favourable review of his poem:

That, says Jeffrey, depends on what you call favourable. It must be reviewed fairly; and that fairness, according to my views and feelings, is a great and sincere love of the general tone of the whole poem, and of a great number of pleasing passages, with an unqualified condemnation of the whole agriculture as not sound – and as totally unfit for poetry even although it were sound. This was Jeffrey's general opinion. He objected a little, but not much, to some want of spirit and nerve in the language, and praised the uniform Scotticism of the scenery, sentiment and manners. These are minor considerations; the above is the general scope of his general opinion. Whether this will be favourable or not, it is your business to judge. It seemed, and seems, to me who heard what he said and saw how he said it, that either according to my opinion of the merits of your poem, or as conjecturing yours, the review will be favourable. If the other passages be well praised, you may afford to have the Agriculture respectfully abused, for I don't suppose you ever thought it the crop of your poem yourself – and you know that so far as my judgment goes, it has been abused disrespectfully already. Moreover Jeffrey's approbation is always powerfully and feelingly conveyed when it is sincere, and even his disapprobation can make its object amiable where he chooses. Now his love of the excellencies of the *Georgics* has been uniformly true, and I know, and he said, that his perfect esteem for you would make his censures, however decided, completely respectful. In these circumstances, I am satisfied that unless your poetical pulse be peculiarly feverish, this review will be thought by you favourable. It should have been in this number if Jeffrey had not been obliged unexpectedly to do something else; but he intends, though of course can by no means positively engage, to put it into the next.

This – and in particular the last two sentences – is the kind of thing that literary editors and their friends continue to say to hopefuls and innocents: it's as if the last two centuries had forgotten to happen. Jeffrey's eventual review was measured and not dishearteningly unfavourable. 'The poem before us, we fear,' states the notice magisterially, will not remove the objections that apply to the Didactic Muse. It may be 'divided, more certainly and commodiously than most of its family, into the two great compartments of the legible and the illegible' (on a previous occasion, Jeffrey had consigned Wordsworth's 'Immortality' ode to the compartment of the illegible). But the descriptions were all right, and for the sake of these, 'we must pardon Mr Grahame' for his bucolic lectures and for 'all his dullness about drains, fences and manures', items as low and vulgar as anything found by Jeffrey in Wordsworth. But think what Seamus Heaney would one day do with such items.

The letter then turns to poor Grahame's hankering to become a reviewer himself. To do so would be to submit to the dictator who drove the dark horses of the *Edinburgh Review*, and whose rules, thought Cockburn, were candid and judicious.

Jeffrey says that he takes the unquestioned and unlimited power of alteration and rejection of all reviews into his own hands; that he never once came, and never will come, under any obligation, even to the mightiest literary giant in the island, to insert whatever they send; that they are always told not to be surprised if their best efforts be sent back unopened, or published so changed that they cannot recognise their own offspring, or only recognise them so much as to be horrified by the change of their dress, manners and opinions; in short, that he takes and pays every contribution according to his own opinion of its merits solely; that under this unyielding, and necessary, and only respectable condition he will be delighted to receive any contribution as you may honour them with; and that if you be disposed to write you must give him some notion of your general subjects, as well as of each book you wish to review, else half a dozen will to a certainty be engaged at the same work.

Cockburn's revealingly sympathetic, not to say complicit, account of the Jeffrey despotism, of these early Scottish practices in the field of editorial control, exaggerates, no doubt; it is tuned to the note of humour, for the comic effects which came naturally and blissfully to Cockburn. But it can't be claimed that any of these practices and prevarications has become archaic. The processing of copy under cover of anonymity, and as an exercise of individual editorial autonomy, enabled the journalism of the time to function as a political instrument. But there would seem to be more than that to Cockburn's emphasis here on subjection: it is an emphasis which might remind one of his pugnacity, and of the taste for mastery which can sometimes seem to underlie the libertarian Whig politics of his earlier life, with its promulgated 'death to dictators'. It was also the case that the anonymity of this journal was by no means spotless. Authorship could be revealed when articles caused a stir. It appears probable that such articles were not among those which had been heavily rewritten.

The sore thumb of duality which obtrudes in *Cockburn's Millennium* signalled an expanding interest in the subject, on my part, which led ten years later, in 1985, to the publication of a history of dualistic literature in English, from what could be termed its revival in the eighteenth century to the present day and the contributions of Martin Amis. This book, *Doubles*, has barely more than a chapter on clinical duality, and has some scepticism to express about the autobiographical divided self; it mostly pre-dated, and might otherwise have been inclined to suspect, the testimony of those in contemporary America who see themselves as multiples and have formed themselves into clubs. But it speaks up, as does the present editorial autobiography, for certain varieties of dualistic interpretation.

A collection of essays entitled *Authors* (1989) makes the anti-theoretical plea that the individuality of authors be respected, while seeking to stay clear of the idolatry of the great writer which has seldom been out of fashion with teachers and students. If Hogg is the central figure in *Doubles*, the central figure on this occasion is Louisa

Stuart, a Scotswoman of royal blood, the long-lived and 'far-descended' daughter – the enthusiastic adjective is hers – of the eighteenth-century Prime Minister Lord Bute, and a gifted writer who hoped never to see her name in print. Her memoirs and letters are discussed in relation to Richardson's *Clarissa*. Clarissa was an author too – a posthumously-published author, you might say, like Lady Louisa. Stuart judged herself precluded from the literary life by her sex and patrician status. Her writings – Austenian in manner and outlook, and reminiscent of some of Cockburn's too, for all the party differences that divided these compatriots – are as shrewd and as funny as they are little-known. Had she been the Englishwoman she took herself to be, she might have come before the Southern public more often than she has. But then her short-lived contemporary Robert Burns, who had no trouble in thinking himself Scottish and whose lexicon gave trouble to English readers, was nevertheless very soon well-known to readers in the deep South, such as Jane Austen. I had earlier paid homage to Burns's Scots and to the epistolary element in his verse, in the form of an essay and a selection of poems.

James Boswell's blood was as blue as Louisa Stuart's, and his far descent transmitted a disturbed mind, shared with a brother and a son and daughter. His ambitions, elations and despair ran in the family. His talents – much maligned, much condescended to, and at times belied by an entanglement in the contradictions of a tormented life – were extraordinary, and so was his at times virtually invisible capacity for hard work. I wrote about him in a recent pocket book, *Boswell and Hyde*, which had him down as a precursor of the Stevensonian divided man, an unstable mixture, or, in the lastingly influential language of alchemy, a 'strange compound'.

In 1996 I did an edition of Stevenson's unfinished novel *Weir of Hermiston*. The introduction dealt with his place in the dualistic tradition, with his debt to Cockburn, whose Lord Braxfield is a precursor of the novel's hanging judge Lord Hermiston, and with the decisive presence in his fiction of the Scots speech which enabled him to re-imagine his youth. A few months before that, there had been a salute of mine to yet another of these Scots people, in an edition of John Buchan's *Three Hostages*, a romance which exhibits both the power of the preposterous and a remarkable play of mind and display of learning. My youthful distaste for Buchan had been largely overcome, though it was somewhat re-inflamed by the discovery of a likeness between certain of his activities and those of another Scots lord, John Reith, each of them a son of the manse, the aspiring worldly son of a pious Free Kirk Glasgow minister. Buchan, however, less liberal than Cockburn politically, was a lot more liberal than the dictatorial founder of the BBC.

The memoir of my early life and adolescent self-pity, *Rebecca's Vest*, which appeared in 1993, was sited for the most part in Scotland and is full of it. There's a tender chapter on the seventeenth-century Scottish sonneteer William Drummond, who cried his shy heart out and attained his orphan's public eminence in the library of his dizzy little castle of Hawthornden, looking down from the skies at its glen and its river Esk, a bus ride from my bungalow near Gilmerton.

The ethnic tendency in what I've written makes me wonder if I am, despite myself, a Scots patriot. I suppose that in a certain sense I must be. But I am not the sort of Scots patriot who wanted to have it conveyed, as it was on television by the leader of the Scottish Nationalists, that the massacre of children at Dunblane, which had become a source of distress for practically everyone on the island, was a grief for the Scots alone. And I'm not the sort who is altogether sure of being Scottish.

Those who are Scottish can be thought by the natives of the South to be more Scottish than they are. National stereotypes are rarely more coercive than they are for expatriates. This particular stereotype is apt to contradict itself, even in respect of its supposed contradictions. Are Scotsmen split (Scotswomen have been spared most of this), or are they the monoliths they would sometimes like to be? They have been seen as split by those who are aware of Scotland's pioneering part in the literature of duality, and who used to mention, while trying to avoid having to spell, the 'Caledonian antisyzygy' – an old highbrow tag for the divided Scottish self. Are Scotsmen rugged, outspoken, self-righteously puritanical? They are sentimentalists and rash romantics as well. They are both drunk and sober. In the South, I've been seen as a John Knox whose black clothes were the badge of an unrelenting nature. But no one has called me Jock.

Once upon a time there was said to be a *perfervidum ingenium Scotorum*: do Scots people still have passionate minds? Many don't. Alec Douglas-Home's *ingenium* was not like that. He had the manners of a Sassenach landed gentleman quite as much as a Scots one, and it would not have been staggering if his real name had turned out to be Peregrine Worsthorne. Did his ancestral connection, the Border philosopher David Hume, have a passionate mind? He had a Scots one, but it wouldn't be worth going on about it for very long. I detect in him a touch both of the *seigneur* and of the sardonic Berwickshire provost or shepherd – but am probably dreaming.

Let me dream on. Temperamentally, I am more Irish than Scots. I see myself in the exasperating Irish, with their wrongs. In particular, I see snatches of myself in the behaviour of the Scots Irish – abrasive, dreamy folk, some of them, abolishers of the difference between irony and sarcasm, the absolute opposite of Yorkshire man – and I feel that I know where the scornful Glasgow-Irish novelist James Kelman is coming from. They're the absolute opposite, too, of a large number of Scotsmen, of various conditions and genders, though I imagine I'm one of *them* as well. My Scots-Irish friend Andrew O'Hagan was entering, the other day, a Glasgow hall seething with fans who had come to hear the drug-culture novelist Irvine Welsh, the enemy of the book, and who were far from in tune with the kind of fan who normally attends book readings. One of them threw back an enraged head and yelled at Andy: 'You Irish Catholic writer from London, you!' It would be a delicate task to identify the most venomous term in that description. Andy is, in fact, as Ayrshire as Robert Burns, though he's a convivial Londoner as well, like the expatriate James Boswell and the expatriate Henry James.

My maternal grandfather crossed the Irish Sea to work in Ayrshire and in the mines of Midlothian, where disaster-loving William Drummond well-nigh foundered in a coal pit near his poet's castle. This grandfather was by all accounts fairly full of himself, and a tease. I am not empty of myself, as Frances Partridge had occasion to point out. But I am not sure what nation I am. Uncertainty, rather than its self-proclaiming opposite, is the true note of nationality; it can be as hard to know your own nationality as it is to know your own nature, or to listen to your ancestral voices. National is multiple, and so are you.

A devotion to Scotland went into these writings, and into the several summers I spent with my family in the Seventies at Polwarth, near Greenlaw, in the Borders, down the road from Ninewells, where David Hume grew up. We lived for these seasons in a rufous nineteenth-century Gothic farmhouse, let me for a song by the local laird, Robin McEwen, which looked out to the south at the Cheviot Hills. Not far off lay the River Tweed, and the moors through which the roads north ran up to Edinburgh, where my mother, aunts and uncle lived. There's an eighteenth-century song by Allan Ramsay which has lads and lasses dancing round the ancient and supernaturally important thorn-tree 'at Polwarth on the green'. Polwarth is one of my good places. My children danced away their seasons there. We played football on a dwarf pitch, steering through the thistles beneath the socket and surviving stones of Redbraes Castle.

I can't say I have avoided the tortuous and precarious guesswork so often entailed by literary criticism's re-imagining of the imagined, and sometimes feel that I'd have done better to have been a lot less literary critical, and to have told more stories. In the Cockburn book, what I like best, in such moods, is the plain-dealing law chapter, and in the book about doubles, the relatively clinical and least literary chapter on Sybil, the celebrated American multiple who was presented to the world, as if by Svengali, in the Seventies. Oh well. One thing I am happy about is that I have written from time to time about people who were little-known, and that I have contributed comparatively little to the cult of the great writer. The procedures of this cult are not in every respect preferable to the self-delighting exercise of adverse critical judgment.

Judgment has endeavoured to choose its small number of writers and to make light of the rest, while literary theory has endeavoured to make light of judgment. This ground has been fought over for many years now. The canon has been under attack, but in none of the arts has it been abandoned: an art critic I know was recently told that he should have been a disc jockey, with his Top Twenty. 'Woe to the country,' Fredric Jameson has said, 'that needs geniuses, prophets, Great Writers or demi-urges.' Jameson is against 'the bourgeois ego' which needs and is these things. He is in favour of a collectivization of literature. In an article in the American magazine *Raritan* (Summer 1996) Richard Rorty responded to Jamesonism by writing in praise of imagination, inspiration, nonsense, hero-worship, 'the idea of greatness', romance and hope, including 'the hope for a religion of literature'. He explains that Jameson eschews judgment – 'the indignant moral denunciation of the other', in Jameson's words – while nevertheless helping to produce in academic common rooms a knowingness and dryness comparable to what prevailed in English-speaking philosophy departments under logical positivism. Knowingness and dryness hold out no hope, Rorty thinks, and it is easy to grasp what he is talking about. But then it's possible to want to see accommodations here, dualities here, to want to avoid a sterile polarity. It's possible to feel that without knowledge there may be no hope worth having, to be keen on literature without making a religion of its great books, and to be fed up with great books without enlisting as a Jamesonist.

'A book is a book,' said Louisa Stuart: 'fair criticism' pays no attention to the sins or virtues of its author. The need to separate a book from its author has accompanied the approach to authorship which devotes itself to great books and to saints' lives. Separation can look like a way of worshipping both the author and the dissociated work, and for much of the present century – though not without evidence, in recent times especially, of doubt and abstention – Yeats, Lawrence and Eliot have lent themselves to a worshipful approach whose adherents have sometimes been persuaded that the writings of these three men are an escape from personality. For Eliot, separation and salvation, the impersonal and the eternal, can appear to be related. I would have thought that a fair criticism would do well to decide that the worship of authors, and the elimination of the author which takes the form of a proscription of biography, are both of them likely to lead to misrepresentation. A book is its author – however obscure, oblique or athwart its relationship may be with the human being known to biography.

All three of these men pursued the hope for a literature of religion, and possessed a strong aesthetic interest in religious exaltation. They believed, religiously, in the few; most people were spiritually dead. They took part in the rise to credit, and to power, of European Fascism. Two of them, Eliot and Lawrence, threw stones at the Jews, with Eliot advising exclusion for the free-thinkers among them. They are all three among the sources and principal exhibits of a rhetoric which treats great books as sacred, and as alien to democratic state systems. Meanwhile, they have been industriously but selectively explained, with blind eyes turned to their human deficiencies – none of these, in my view, dissociable from their work. For the justified artist, grace abounding and the benefit of the doubt ... I had better explain that I am not arguing for retribution here, or for exclusion. There would be no justice in a 'demolition' of the sort that Leavis supposed he had accomplished for Milton.

The previously unpublished poems by Eliot which appeared in an edition of 1996 were received with the deference, and suspension of doubt, which have long been customary in this quarter. The first reviews praised, with reason, Christopher Ricks's edition, and said that the poems were welcome, as indeed they mostly were. Among them were 'sister' poems to the published ones, and it seemed that there were very few weak sisters. Here, said the reviews, was a command of language which could speak of a black man's 'knotty' penis – and, one might add, of a housemaid's 'crimson hands'. Letters to the press then said that one of the items, in which a woman is heartily disembowelled, contains snatches of old rugby songs; it reads like the most bespectacled rugby song ever to regale a dressing-room. Of the scabrous poems in the collection, you might say that they give pain and that they show pain. They are far from being impersonal. But it is doubtful whether they have much to communicate, at the level of personality, or of the all-too-human, which was not already known.

There was a man at the court of Charles II who liked, said the King, to 'tell us our faults', and Eliot took to doing this too. In recent times, as never before, even in the days when his early poems could be found strange and offensive, his own faults have been at issue. During the successive debates about his anti-semitism which have occurred in this country over the last few years, it was conceded, by some of those who objected to it, that good art can be inimical, in this way among others, while defenders felt that it was 'politically correct' – malevolent and stupid, therefore – to imagine that we should think less of his writings because of their anti-semitism. The debates took a Prufrockian turn recently, when a leading writer on this subject was barred from membership of a literary dining-club in London for his attention to Eliot's injurious preoccupation with race. The poet's defenders have been inclined to ask how preoccupied with it he really was, noting that he doesn't write all that often against Jews. Even in the years before the Holocaust, it would have seemed at least indecorous – decorum being a concern of Eliot's – for a poet to have gone on about them a lot, in this vein. What matters in literature is what, not how much, is said. A little can go a long way; a word can do it, or a phrase, such a phrase as one which appears in the previously unpublished poetry, where there's a to-all-intents authorial reference to 'a bastard jew named Benny'.

In 1936, the same author published a review pooh-poohing the persecution of Germany's Jews, a review which, without surprise though sometimes with regret, was at one time attributed by Eliot scholars to Eliot. The discovery that he had not written but had only published the review was thought by certain of his recent defenders to absolve him from responsibility and to make all the difference. Tom Paulin has argued that the quarrel about Eliot and his work should be seen in relation to 'the redemptive ethic which informs a great deal of literary criticism'. So it should. And I agree with Paulin that it ought not to be a matter of indifference when the work of good artists can be shown to be unfeeling and unjust. A fair criticism should care about it.

The kindness of writers is an expression that might be greeted with a wintry smile. There are writers who are kind. But it is also clear that there are good writers whose personal lives are objectionable, good writers who are cruel, whose very gift is for cruelty. I had a friend at Cambridge, Geoffrey Strickland, who died recently. He was high-minded and generous-minded – the two quali-ties don't always go together, but they did with him. And he wrote good poems when he was young. He was to notice that Stendhal had once reviewed himself, favour-ably, and he called this 'an unaccountable breach of integrity'. The poet Thom Gunn reviewed his own poems at Cambridge, but his review was regarded by those who were in on it as a piece of high spirits and a real attempt to state his faults. Stendhal's review may have been more of a scam, but Geoffrey's response seemed overdone. We can live with Stendhal's reviewing himself, as with much else. Nevertheless, Geoffrey had a point. We have to live with the place there is in art, and in the artist, for worse than that, and with the place there is for the inhumanities in any university curriculum. But there's also a place for knowing what we are doing when we do this.

Bizarre as it may appear to be saying so, art is, in general, kind. Its transactions rest on a shared humanity and on a sympathetic interest in the way people are. Writing about his experience of an American delirium of pain and anger, Ralph Ellison's black 'Invisible Man' arrestingly says: 'In order to get some of it down I *have* to love.' And you might imagine that a rancorous art, dependent on a shared hostility, is likely to defeat itself, though such an art, in its various new forms, has had its successes in the course of the present century. These are among the reasons for objecting to the unpleasantness, and for insisting on the errors, of important writers, and for refusing to turn these writers into pantheon material for a religion of art, with each of them treated as some sort of god, the sort of Border God said by a farmer in one of James Hogg's novels to be entitled to 'his ain way o' things. He's no likely to gang far wrang.'

Leavis had his own way of things, which embodied the intensification of a familiar approach. Literature was religious and a small number of authors were saints, none of them likely to go far wrong, even when, as in the case of Jane Austen and Lawrence, their outlooks were utterly opposed. Leavis's 'Lorrence' – the name was spoken by him, with such warmth, as if it were that of an august friend who was still alive and with whom no quarrel could ever have taken place – was subjected, in print, to an exercise in querulous, adjectival praise and extenuation. The murderous, suffering Lawrence, who hated England, hated India, hated the human race, who would profess to despise Tolstoy and Dostoevsky, to believe that Turgenev wasn't a patch on Fenimore Cooper, that Chekhov, as a pet of Middleton Murry and Katherine Mansfield, was so much potted shrimp, is let off lightly in Leavis's study of 1955, while Lawrence's enemies and false friends are chased into footnotes and asides and stabbed to death. This is an exercise in which Lawrence and Leavis can sometimes appear to coalesce.

Lawrence's rise to eminence, and its sequel, are, for readers of my generation, one of the dramas of modern literature. When I was a pupil of Leavis's I saw nothing strange about his enthusiasm for Lawrence. I shared it. I drove up into the 'big, unbroken spaces' of Lawrence's New Mexico, up through the sage brush towards the relics of the sage beneath the Rocky Mountains, to stare at his grave, with its phoenix carving, as I'd once stared at Robert Burns's Ayrshire farms, and to sit in the open-plan creosoted shack where I was told that he'd stayed. At Cambridge, a rakish undergraduate friend would ask visiting writers, in tones of Leavisian reproof, if they'd 'read any Lorrence'; one of these writers was the taciturn gin-drinking patrician, Henry Green, whose novels were unknown to me then and are admired by me now, and whose response to the question, now forgotten, can't have been effusive. I tried then to make sense of Lawrence's philosophy of the senses. Was the blood wiser than the intellect? Didn't we need both, and how could we tell them apart? What was it for lovers to be 'apart but in constellation'? To a young man at the age of twenty-three and on the verge of the Sixties, that sounded like an auspicious arrangement, and I wrote about it like mad in my Tripos exams.

I feel differently about him now, and it would appear that the recognition of Lawrence's importance which Leavis's book was intended to promote, but which had already happened, has declined. I feel that his descriptions of landscape, and of birds and animals, and of an animal humanity, are a work of genius, that the English literature of the present century can barely be understood without reference to his imagination of the unconsciously-determined life, and that there's a rhetoric of genius in his saying, for instance, in one of his letters, that the truth is hard work, and that 'the problem of truth is: How can we most deeply *live?*' But then there's the nonsense — partly explicable with reference to the fact that he was ill, and grew steadily worse. Talk of 'the live, really lovely phallic self' grew desperate and formulaic as 'the hurts and the bitternesses sank in', as they began, together with his illness and as an aspect of that illness, to 'waste' him. These are his own words. Their implications were to be obscured by the modalities of recognition and reputation, and have yet to make themselves known for what they are to some of his more devout interpreters in the universities. 'He said I was dead,' said E. M. Forster once, as we walked through the fault-finding precincts of Downing. Death was a fault that Lawrence was given to finding. He went about saying that people, quite often friends, were dead, and in a sense – Lawrence's sense, one might think – he died of it.

The sweetness and courtesy of his Nottingham friend- ships were recalled in a *Listener* interview of 1967 with one of these early friends, Helen Corke, then in her eighties, who spoke with great strength of mind about what deserves to be called the enlightened sexuality which she had discovered for herself at that time. She and Lawrence had occupied a middle ground, she said, between male and female, and it was Jessie Chambers whom she had loved sexually. The interview was testi- mony to what Lawrence forfeited when he left the scenes of his youth. His early friendships were replaced by relations of tutelage and convenience with privileged people – not all of them unimpressive, admittedly, not all of them, one might say, with Ottoline Morrell in mind, eclipsed by Helen Corke. He became an expert on human nature who thought that Forster should 'take a woman' and advised him not to go to India, and who sneered at Katherine Mansfield, who was to die before long of his own illness, for malingering, for 'doing the last-gasp touch'. His letters keep insisting that he doesn't give a damn, while damning everyone in sight. He was a hater who denounced and enjoined hatred. He was a true- blue English grizzler, who had a particular dislike of moaning minnies, and was to endure his illness, the long distress of his 'bronchials', patiently and wittily. The humour that went with the appreciative energy of his young days was never to wear out, and was to place its brake on many a sermon: 'So long as there's a bit of a laugh going, things are all right.' But it had to be an *honest* laugh.

Then came the last laugh, the last gasp. He had travelled the world and had thought to rule it, an enemy of the will eaten by a will to power. A posthumous fame, inseparable from the sufferings of his lifetime, and from that will to power, was soon to be consolidated, and is more than likely to rise again after its current decline, if that is what we are witnessing.

Leavis's performance as a controversialist leaves no more doubt than Lawrence's does that there is a bitterness which can participate in a commitment to literature and which can enlist a following of disciples. A friend of Geoffrey Strickland's, and of mine, at Downing was Morris Shapira, who became, for a time, Leavis's right-hand man and heir-apparent. No cross words were to pass between us, though he wouldn't have approved of my immersion in Leavis's denounced 'London literary world', and cross words flew freely then, and not only then, in Cambridge.

During our time as students I stood with Morris on a verge outside Cambridge in an attempt to hitchhike to London. The two priggish scholarship waifs exchanged glances. I looked at myself and back again at Morris – at the bald brow and watchful oval face, at his shorts, his college blazer, college scarf, orange briefcase and rolled umbrella – and reckoned that between the two of us we'd be lucky to get a lift. But we made it to the big city, where, in North London, I met his likeable elderly-seeming Jewish parents. His father worked in the garment trade; his mother chose his neat wardrobe for him till well beyond graduation day; eventually, he went into motorcycle leather. He loved music, loved his records, and was poorly read when he came up to Downing. Thereafter he moved rapidly into possession of what Leavis had to teach, and learnt to expound it in what was on occasion to prove a challenging fashion. Leavis's dauphin leant towards the lawyer-like, and would have made a frightening inspector-general. I remember one unpromising inspection, proposed by Morris. Asked by him to apply with him to the BBC for the same holiday job, in order to find out whether the Corporation was anti-semitic, Thom Gunn firmly declined.

Morris's judgments were both Leavis's and his own. Like those of other disciples of Leavis then, in their schools and universities, they were neither tolerant nor relenting. He published next to nothing, but there was a sentence somewhere to the effect that Frank Kermode was a poisonous nuisance. The language of Lawrence's more hostile letters, and of the ethnic cleanser. In part, at least, because of his lack of publications, the Downing Governors denied him the succession to Leavis's College post. Leavis had wanted Morris to succeed him. But after this came rows with the Leavises, and more especially with Leavis's wife Queenie, in which Morris was to the fore. The Leavises were called liars. The *Scrutiny* jihad on behalf of literature and standards had gained, in its time, the allegiance of able and honourable people. It had had to survive the touchiness of the Leavises, rather as Lawrence's touchiness had constrained and postponed his Rananim, the small company of like minds that might one day rule the world. Now it had dwindled to a quarrelling parish. A fight broke out over who should be the first Leavis Lecturer at Downing. Leavis didn't want his former associate H. A. Mason to be appointed but was circumvented by his current associates. A friend of Morris's in their undergraduate days, Patrick Harrison, commented not long ago, from the standpoint of a veteran civil servant who knows about appointments boards, on the lectureship affair, and on Leavis's run-ins with the Governing Body of the College. Harrison wouldn't be surprised if Leavis had been 'a bit of a blister' in committee. But on the matter of what happened to him over the lectureship he writes: 'I suppose one has to charge up some of the disregard for ordinary civilized proprieties to ignorance and innocence, but Shapira's behaviour, and also that of Harold Mason, allegedly caught trembling like a guilty thing surprised on meeting Leavis unexpectedly in Sylvester Road after accepting the lectureship on a permanent basis without having told him, was shifty and inexcusable.'

Having moved off to teach at the new University of Kent, Morris became eccentric, went somewhat wild. He began to conduct Lawrentian nude supervisions, displeasing his students, who complained to the authorities, and he began driving his car to Canterbury Station and giving lifts to back-packers and hitchhikers from the Continent, one of whom, in 1981, killed him. Others have written about Morris – now me, and not for the first time. What I have wished to do here is to mourn him, and to reflect on the uses of literature. I think of him as he was at the start of his adult life, on the verge of that road to London, hoping for a lift, and for a future. And I think of the figure of speech prolepsis, a term applied in the schoolbooks of the past to certain forms of anticipation, and illustrated there by lines from Keats about a pair of intending assassins:

> So the two brothers and their murdered man
> Rode past fair Florence . . .

Here were two brothers, Morris and I, with one of us a murdered man. An early scene looks forward to a later one. One lift leads to another. This is among the symmetries or coincidences which can be felt to matter, in some occult way, by those who experience them.

In a curt allusion that appears in Ian MacKillop's life of Leavis, where Morris is awarded a considerable role, what transpired in 1981 is described as 'a random act of violence'. It wasn't really that. Among the strains that weighed on him may have been the conflict between Leavis's outlook – in which a hostility to homosexuals became apparent – and Morris's sexual nature. And there was a further conflict which can't have helped him and which could at times appear to have escaped him: the conflict between literature, which depends on sympathy, and the jealousy and enmity displayed in the Downing academy of letters. The Leavisism of the young which flourished in the Fifties was overtaken by the events, the student protest, of the Sixties. These events look self-indulgently parochial when compared with what happened in America over the Vietnam War, or with what happened some years later in Peking's Tiananmen Square, when students risked their lives for freedom of speech and association, having been preceded by a generation of protesters who had risked and ended the lives of others, charged with dissent. Some unrests are plainly better than others. As for the Leavisism of the Fifties and before, I'd say that its message deserved the attention it received.

There is a story which Leavis told of himself, in 1971. It has, but is unharmed by, the elaboration which gained on him with the years. During the Great War he served as a medical orderly. At a much later time he found himself discussing with an 'obviously nice' young American the deaths of the 'innumerable boy-subalterns' who had advanced from their trenches to be mown down by machine-gun fire. A remark of Leavis's had drawn a comment from the young man:

> The comment, quietly sure of its matter-of-fact felicity, was: 'The death-wish!' My point is that I didn't know what to say. What actually came out was, 'They didn't *want* to die.' I felt I couldn't stop there, but how to go on . . . 'They were brave' – that came to me as a faint prompting, but no, it didn't begin to express my positive intention; it didn't even lead towards it. I gave up; there was nothing else to do.

There is some self-consciousness here, and his whole point can't have been that he didn't know what to say, since what he managed to say is in its elemental way so good. One might also feel, and think it a pity, that, for Leavis's purposes, the naive young man had to be American, and the brave men all officers. The story may nevertheless be worth retelling. It has the element of debate which he thought that criticism should embody. And it has the decency which he never lost, which his struggles threatened to destroy, but which can somehow be surmised in the dementia reported of his last days.

In the course of this century, writers have suggested that most people are spiritually dead and that some people should be excluded or removed; and an effort has been made to put such sentiments into institutional effect. They have since been expounded for educational purposes, in the schools and universities of this country and of others, and they have not ceased to furnish an education. The works of the German philosopher Carl Schmitt, an enemy of liberals and Jews who believed that politics is enmity, and who was distrusted by the Nazis he served, for being a Catholic who'd had Jewish friends, have been revived, and are currently the admiration of the European Right and of sections of the European Left.

It is just as well that the majority of writers have not felt the need to use this language. In 1963, Eliot moved to distance himself from it, when he asked his lawyers to write to the *New Statesman* to say – in response to something said there by Christopher Ricks – that he'd never been 'in any way sympathetic' to fascism. Readers of the journal must have understood the urgency of the disclaimer, and yet been a little surprised by it: this was a time of unrest, of calls for socialism and democracy, which was nevertheless a time when the presence of fascist sympathies in literature and on the curriculum was widely overlooked.

In 1985, a story by Christopher Burns appeared in the *London Review*. A disaffected country priest, sequestered in the middle of Europe, tells of being summoned one winter's night to ride to a farm in order to be with a sick girl, who recovers from the fever which is threatening her. As he leaves the 'rich' farmer, this 'saviour' secures the present of a ham. Riding back, he sees a halted train, and a string of trucks crammed not with cattle but with people, whose hands stretch towards him through grilles. The train resumes its journey, passing him, the arms 'still stretched out with spread hands, like strange white growths opening into the night'. The story is about exclusion, and safety, and coincidence. It describes a chance encounter between salvation of a sort and its unequivocal opposite.

I have never forgotten the story. It is not a humanitarian transaction. It is art. It is subtle and austere. But I value it not least, though not only, because it shows pity for people whom writers with messages have thought it necessary to exclude. Writers who can teach should teach. But the teaching of gifted writers reveals a huge quantity of ugly error.

There are artists who must be accounted thinkers, even if they think that some people should be excluded or removed, even if they believe in enemy races and enemy classes, and there has long been an appetite for the production of doctrine by novelists and poets, a feeling that they should aspire to be philosophers or prophets. Artists' doctrines – which include and attract the doctrine of artistic impersonality – are rarely as hostile or untrue as the ones I've been complaining about, moreover, and it's difficult to suppose that literature could do without the desire to produce them. They are, of course, ancient. They reach back to the general knowledge formerly thought to be within the compass of the individual thinker, and, indeed, to the time of oracles. At the present time, however, the appetite in question would appear to be thinly served, and to have lost its edge. I doubt whether, among the imaginative writers of this country, there are at present many wise stars of the old sort, of the Carlylean sort, professors of anything and everything, minded to give advice on the punishing work that politics can do, or on the replacement of politics by leadership. The novelists I have lately been reading, Ian McEwan, Martin Amis, Penelope Fitzgerald, Beryl Bainbridge, Julian Barnes and Patrick McGrath, are gifted writers who may be interested in causes, such as salvation from nuclear war, but are none of them either didacts or seers. Nor do they appear to be – in the way that Beckett, for instance, sometimes does. They are artists, and they are artists who enable you to put up with the present shortage of sages, of writers prepared to tell people what it all means. What it has all too often meant in the past, as with Carlyle, is that some people should be kept out, or down.

Those who go on about exclusion, as I do, are likely to have felt it or feared it – once and for all, perhaps, in childhood. But there is a lot of it about. And many of those who are tough about it, and who say that there should be a lot more of it about, are likely to have felt it and feared it too. Such is my own share in the piety directed towards Eliot, and towards Lawrence and Yeats, that I have been shaken by my complaints on the subject. In making them, I have felt an anxiety that has very little to do with the breach of an academic accord. It has more to do with a sense of blasphemy, of a broken tabu – these being all that's left, for many people, of religion. An indignant response by William Empson, in the summer of 1965, to Conor Cruise O'Brien's account of the Blueshirt Yeats kept whispering in my ear. Was Yeats a fascist? 'The first point to get clear,' wrote Empson, with an air of dispatch, in the *New Statesman*, was this: 'So were all the great writers in English in the first half of this century, except Joyce.' It never did become clear in the course of his article how much, if anything, this contributed, if true, to the defence of Yeats – an uncertainty, however, which did not appear to reduce the chances of its being true. I had already supposed that it might be, adding it to my bag of contradictions, and I dealt with it then much as I continue to deal with it now. Absolute greatness, I told myself, is a religious category, a form of salvation, from which literary discussion should stay away. Great writers who are fascist are less great for being so.

14. Between the Stirrup and the Ground

A LESSER NOVELIST than Lawrence, Graham Greene
has at times received almost as much attention in this
country. Two titles of his sat, not long ago, beside three
of Lawrence's (and a Delia Smith cookery book) on a list
of the '100 greatest books of the twentieth century',
compiled by television producers from responses to a poll
– Channel Four's Top Twenty times Five. Most of the
choices were British and some modish. Half of them had
been A-Level set texts or had been for other reasons on
the school curriculum, and quite a few had been filmed
or televised. Such polls can be mortifying. Britain's
favourite poem, I learnt recently, was an excellent one
about growing old disgracefully which had appeared in
the *Listener* before I went there and which I hadn't
previously read. The poem is by Jenny Joseph, with
whom I'd been friendly during our time as students.

Graham Greene died in 1991. Three years later no
fewer than four biographies appeared together. I reviewed
them, and took occasion to give my sense of his fiction,
as I'm about to do again. Earlier, in 1972, I had reviewed
his autobiography, *A Sort of Life*, and in doing so had
irritated him. He wrote to the *New York Review* to say

that I'd overrated the 'Franglais' food at the Etoile in Charlotte Street: I'd unguardedly spoken in the piece of lunching with him there. I should declare this episode, perhaps. It may have warped my mind, conditioned though it had been to take to him because of his admired brother Hugh. But it didn't stop me from liking some of his later books, his comedies or entertainments. I like them better than some of his more list-compatible earlier ones.

He was not, I think, the most gifted of the British writers of his time, but he was among the most efficient and productive, and, with the exception of Evelyn Waugh, he was the most famous of the novelists among them. Some of these novelists are surely very good – Waugh, Compton-Burnett, Elizabeth Bowen, Henry Green, Anthony Powell. Some have assumed the air of a lost generation. But Greene has never been hard to find. In some of their work can be seen an upper class prone to look down on a seedy poor – which requires to be led, enlightened, insulted or seduced – and on filthy foreign parts, prone to buzzards and to human dereliction. Greene's way with foreigners and the poor was a way of his time, and of his own, which helped to make his name.

The Greene bay-tree flourished exceedingly. His fame rested on an ability to reach large numbers of people by being both religious and left-wing, at a time, a time of war, when both outlooks were more than usually appealing, and when the embattled sexuality in which specialized was found acutely interesting. He was both a Christian and a socialist – according to Orwell, perhaps 'our first Catholic fellow-traveller'. And not only that. He was both a Christian and an agnostic. And it was also popular of him to appear to be what could be called an antinomian Catholic. He was a man who broke the moral law associated with his Church while continuing to call himself a Catholic – a man who was to say, 'I broke the rules,' and who wrote all about it. He wrote about sinners who are seriously sympathetic and in some sense 'chosen' – saved or damned, his readers may have felt, these sinners are with the just – and he wrote in so doing about a conflict between religion and ethics, salvation and conduct, faith and works. The 'filthy works' traditionally decried by certain Protestants were decried, for Rome, by Graham Greene.

This Catholic convert and justified sinner spoke for a time when the Christian clergies and laities burst some of their bonds, and he can be awarded a precursor in another Catholic convert, the sculptor Eric Gill, of the sacerdotal-sexual lifestyle laid bare in Fiona MacCarthy's biography. Greene's whisky priest in *The Power and the Glory*, with his illegitimate child, has featured in a landscape where priests have come out of closets, made love, marched in protest, and supported the Sandinistas and the IRA. Greene suggested that human beings might be able to participate in the divine intent, might 'help' the deity to do away with evil: such a suggestion belonged to a time when priests could be heard to propose a dialogue with God, in the form of a more democratic prayer in which you talked with Him man to man. Those days are now gone, or going. But it can safely be said that Greene's writings contributed to a revolution, and he was to resent the counter-revolution delivered, during the years that preceded Greene's death at the age of eighty-six, by Pope John Paul II.

The antinomian claim that misconduct need not preclude salvation, that the bad man may be touched by God's grace and need not go to Hell, is historically linked to the Protestant attack on Rome: it was once among the strategies of that attack. The strategy could be thought to have undergone a reversal when conduct became a Protestant shibboleth. But it can also be thought that the primacy of faith over works has been of interest to Catholics and Protestants alike, just as the Catholic concern with repentance and reprieve was to survive among the Protestant religions. The antinomian claim enjoins this concern, and the imaginative literature of the subject has dwelt on the horror of the unshriven death, of 'dying sudden', as *Brighton Rock* puts it. Repentance is a crux both in this novel and in *The Power and the Glory* — two compelling fictions. Each, though, is tormented by theological profundities which must often be accounted specious.

In the first of these novels there's the Catholic boy Pinkie, who was for Greene what Colonel Noriega was to be for Greene's friend President Torrijos of Panama: 'my gangster'. Pinkie is a gangster who is destined, by his novelist, as his novelist subsequently explained, to go to Hell, and there are worries in the book about what it is to die sudden and unshriven. At one point, in conversation with the simple girl Rose, who loves him, this unlettered homicidal adolescent, sympathetically and tellingly perceived, as Rose is too, quotes from an epitaph recorded by the Elizabethan historian William Camden:

'You know what they say – "Between the stirrup and the ground, he something sought and something found."' Rose supplies this something: 'Mercy.' The epitaph, 'for a Man killed by falling from his horse', reads:

> Betwixt the stirrup and the ground
> Mercy I asked, mercy I found.

Camden's Augustinian epitaph – Augustine being its source, and one of the authors of the doctrine of redemptive grace, and of an unregenerate human wickedness, which is at issue here – took root as a figure for last-minute escapes from perdition. Samuel Johnson spoke the lines to Boswell, with every appearance of concern.

Running, razor in hand, from his Jewish enemies, who've been trying to 'nail' him with their boots, Pinkie says to himself: 'You could be saved between the stirrup and the ground, but you couldn't be saved if you didn't repent . . .' Greene writes in the novel of Pinkie's state of mind: 'Eternal pain had not meant much to him: now it meant the slash of razor blades infinitely prolonged.' This is 1938. Orwell was presently to envisage a secular future consisting of the perpetual descent of a boot on the human face.

Greene is the novelist from Hell who ceased to believe in it. He also lost his taste for the sexual disgust paraded in this early novel, where it operates as a clue to Pinkie's worth, with its implied 'better dead than bed'. Fat, carnal, liberal Ida, his chief pursuer, is blamed by the novelist for believing in right and wrong rather than good and bad, in ethics rather than religion, and is informed that priests teach that sexual transgression is like murder. Ida retorts: 'Why, even Romans don't believe in *that*.' Greene's italics – for the notion of sex as mortal sin. As for Greene's Romans, some of them believe in it and others don't, and Greene was to move in time to a more liberal view of the matter. He remarked in middle age that opium was an improvement on the unimportant sexual act. In the old days the act had been damnably important, and he could be very good at expressing this. In *Brighton Rock*, a sleazy couple are glimpsed in an embrace: 'They might have been inflicting on each other the greatest injury of which they were either capable.'

Greene was also good at the depiction of pursuit, and had kind feelings about those who are pursued. Among Pinkie's pursuers is the ghetto of Jewish criminals which is imagined for the Brighton of the Thirties. Greene's dislike of Jews, when he was young, is more obtrusive than that of the early Eliot, but has gone until recently, as Eliot's has not, unnoticed. Pinkie visits a grand hotel in order to visit Colleoni, godfather of the Jewish gang, and is assailed by midgets: 'A little Jewess sniffed at him bitchily and then talked him over with another little Jewess on a settee.' In trips 'a small Jew', Mr Colleoni, 'with a neat round belly'. The small Jew's eyes gleamed like raisins . . . The little bitches on the settee stopped talking as he passed.' So grand is the hotel that it is Pinkie, not Colleoni, who 'looks like an alien'. But the real alien, we are to understand, is Colleoni.

A critic has argued that the distaste expressed in this passage – most of whose racial slurs were retracted in post-war editions – is meant to be thought of as Pinkie's rather than the author's, as an aspect of Pinkie's perception of what is going on at the hotel. I feel sure myself that the distaste was very much the author's too. And there can't in any case be much doubt that Greene has a taste for Pinkie, for his gangster, who is pitted against a Semitic criminality. Greene had a thing about 'foreign blood' when he was young, and as a film critic used to rail against the 'dark alien executives' of Wardour Street.

This antinomian life of Greene's is one that many might want to write but that few would find it easy to write. Of the four biographical treatments published in 1994, two are comprehensive explorations: but they leave parts of his life as dark as they are likely to remain. Some of it was designedly secret, and he seems to have relished the thought that his biographers would be baffled and 'misled'. He was a novelist who was also an adventurer and, like more than one of his relatives, a spy. During the Second World War, he worked, as officer 59200, for the British Secret Intelligence Service, and went on assisting it, on his travels, into the early Eighties. He was also susceptible to the glamour of disloyalty and of the double agent, and was to speak favourably, after Kim Philby's detection and defection, of his friend's covert activities on behalf of the Soviet Union.

During the Cold War, as one of the heads of British Intelligence, Philby 'sent his *own* agents into Albania and then betrayed them to the Russians', writes Norman Sherry in one of these biographies – Volume Two (1939–1955) of his long life of Greene. Asked to comment on this, Greene told Sherry, loyally enough: 'They were going into their own country armed to do damage to that country. They were killed instead of killing.' The loyalty in question complies with the Bloomsbury code of preferring friendship to country, and entailed a disloyalty to the service for which Greene had worked. Conversely, if you like, his abrupt departure from his SIS desk in London, towards the end of the Second World War, may have been influenced by an awareness of Philby's machinations on behalf of Russia, which may have had the effect of prolonging the war. This could well be among the 'complications' of his life which he claimed to relish.

In three of these biographies – the ones by Sherry, Michael Shelden and Anthony Mockler – there can appear to be more about the dark and dirty business of spying and sex, and about Greene's travels, than there is about his fiction. Does it resemble, and does it rank with, that of John Buchan? Buchan too has his spies and hot pursuits, his talk of evil and the equivocal, and of foreign blood, of friends and country. Such questions do not arise in these three biographies. The valuable criticism which has been devoted to Greene's art is virtually ignored. This is not an approach of which Greene approved: he took the familiar view – which accords as much with a regard for privacy as with a regard for theory – that we should be told about an author's works and not about his life. It would take a very zealous theorist, however, to deny that it can be nice to be told about both, in a fashion that assists an understanding of the author's works.

Greene's marriage had not lasted very long before he began to live apart from his wife – he had joined the Church, her Church, in the course of marrying her. Vivien

Greene would speak sweetly about furry animals and other such comforts, and she was to become an expert on Victorian dolls and furnishings. Slow to accept Greene, she was then to be, well into his desertion of her, fond and loyal, a Twenties Mariana at the Grange, who informed him in one of her letters: 'Bizet wrote Carmen, Wagner wrote Lohengrin. Nobody writes me: Gee, I'm lonesome.' In *Graham Greene: Three Lives*, a comparatively slight study, Mockler reports her as speaking generously of Greene after his death; it seems that she also said that he hadn't really been a Catholic, and that for most of their married life he had been a 'cold, unhappy man'. He blossomed into a handsome one, tall, and of beguiling appearance, with the unsettling stare of a pair of spymaster's blue-grey eyes that fixed me in the Etoile.

He was himself lonesome and unsettled. His principal mistresses – the word seems as obtrusive in discussions of Greene as 'infamous' does in discussions of Cantona – were a woman who was a warden with him in Gower Mews, Bloomsbury, during the Blitz, Catherine, Lady Walston, and a Frenchwoman, Yvonne Cloetta, who kept him company in Antibes during the last thirty years of his life. The three books allude to lots of other affairs, and to prostitutes and brothels. Shelden's book alludes, in addition, never very convincingly, to homosexual leanings experienced and denied when Greene was a young man: he has to work hard here at the evidence supplied by male bondings noticed in some of the early fictions. His book stresses the importance, from this point of view among others, of a traumatic episode of bullying and betrayal at school, where there were double-agent difficulties to do with having a father who was headmaster of the school. Greene's suicidal dicings with death have long been a topos for his commentators. Shelden writes of a blank cartridge 'safely loaded in the chamber' of the revolver. All three books pay attention to a depressive tendency, and there is a descent from depressives to be reckoned with, as I've tried to do elsewhere, in the context of my small Boswell book.

Greene's publishing partner at one point in his life, Douglas Jerrold, observed that 'in all this chatter about Graham Greene as a religious novelist, there is a confusion between being intensely interested in religion and being religious'. Jerrold declared that one of Greene's great themes was hatred, and is thought by Shelden to have understood 'the hostile nature of the big child' in the next office; his colleague's adult life was described by Jerrold as his 'later childhood'. Shelden agrees – that Greene never really grew up. The big child hated, held himself aloof, went off on lawless roads, journeys without maps.

Shelden does not trust Greene, and is zestful in trying to follow his trail. 'He was the Harry Lime of the literary racket.' Harry Lime is more than just elusive in *The Third Man*, and Shelden's anomic Greene, a version of the writer who thought Harry up, is said here to possess a 'tarnished talent' and a 'tainted imagination'. One of the images evoked by this adversarial account is that of a kind of duplicity – of the victim's friend who went in search of massacres and would thrill himself by diving about in the air with pilots whose job it was to blast the sampans of Vietnamese peasants.

Shelden thrills himself when it comes to addressing the subject of Catherine Walston's 'sexual odyssey'. She was an American woman drawn to celebrity and married to a Labour-supporting Jewish magnate. On her conversion to Catholicism she became Greene's godchild. According to one of those 'friends' who pipe up in biography, they set themselves to commit adultery 'behind every high altar in Italy'. She had 'a thing for priests', said one of her priests. Another was Father Thomas Gilby, 'a Dominican theologian and a professor of something called "Speculative Morals",' writes Shelden. 'He was a hearty fellow who wore tweeds, smoked a pipe, and spent a good part of his life drinking in pubs.' A sister of hers took note at the time of a less Chestertonian Gilby: 'He behaves *sexually* in the most possessive manner.' She felt that 'his behaviour shows a lack of dignity, coupled with a masked brutality'.

When Catherine's interest in Greene faded, he too became possessive. 'You are the only wife I've ever really had,' he told her, and he told himself that she didn't consider her marriage valid 'because it was not a Catholic marriage'. Shelden says that Gilby – 'a close friend of both Walstons' and the author of *Morals and Marriage: The Catholic Background to Sex* – may have advised that she and Greene might go on seeing one another, but without sex.

A further connection emphasized by Shelden is Greene's friendship with the Panamanian strong man Torrijos, who was anxious to obtain, and did obtain, his country's sovereignty over the Panama Canal. Greene responded to that endeavour, and treated with Fidel Castro on Panama's behalf. He didn't seem to mind that the regime was a despotism, and that it practised such suppressions of dissent as throwing a priest from an airborne helicopter, but he did subsequently admit that there was something about Torrijos's gangster, Noriega, that he didn't like.

A further friend of Greene was the novelist and elderly satyr Norman Douglas, whom he used to see during his stays on the island of Capri. Douglas is rated by Shelden as someone not altogether unlike a child-molester. By Sherry he is described as a 'close friend of Joseph Conrad (whom Greene admired)', and as a hedonist and sybarite, 'pagan in outlook'. Without having said in so many words that Douglas was homosexual, he proceeds: 'Greene's other friend Sir Harold Acton (himself a homosexual) was a little jealous of his friendship with Douglas.' And the passage ends with the switchback sentence: 'There must have been something special about Douglas, for he was a strange man for Greene to like, because he was a homosexual.' As opposed to a South American strong man.

Of rather more moment is a Sherry story about 'a large fat foreigner' who was injured in the Blitz and who showed the white feather. Despite his cries, the wardens had to lay him down because he was so heavy, and so on. The same story is discussed by Shelden, who points out that this coward is referred to, in Greene's published 'Notes from a Journal of the Blitz', as 'a large fat foreign Jew'. In order to bowdlerize, Norman Sherry has had to misquote.

Greene was a good writer who can sometimes seem to be writing to a deadline; even that striking sentence in

Brighton Rock about a lovers' embrace is a little badly written. And he was a good writer who is portrayed in these three biographies as a man who if he was a Christian at all, as distinct from the creature of the Jerrold hypothesis, certainly stood in need of some Augustinian escape clause. He is portrayed there as someone whose politics were as heartless as they could at times seem shrewd and prescient. The fourth of the biographical treatments of 1994 presents, however, a different man from the one who appears in the others. Leopoldo Duran's portrait could be said to correct them, while failing to dispel the impression they leave.

Father Duran is a Spanish priest who gave Greene absolution at the last, and went on to write this book about his friendship with him over the previous three decades. His innocence, his simplicity, his blessedness and holy foolishness are celebrated in Greene's engaging clerical comedy *Monsignor Quixote* – where they are seen as inherited from the tilter at windmills – and they are celebrated afresh in Duran's *Graham Greene: Friend and Brother*. The two of them used to gallivant round Spain on picnics and excursions. Father Duran kept taking snaps of his chum, the rogue Catholic, alias Sancho the Communist mayor in *Monsignor Quixote*, knowing that he hated being photographed. What in other men might have looked like holidays is made over into a work that can look like an accession to the lives of the saints. And there's more than one saint, more than one *sancta simplicitas*, on view, with Leopoldo's 'folly' a match for Graham's intermittent wise 'childishness'. 'What a great man, but what a child this famous friend of mine can be!' The exclamation is Duran's nearest approach to Shelden's arrested-development verdict on Greene.

He is not the modern sort of priest who longs for democracy. Duran is a fan of Franco and of Lourdes, and was resigned to the secret activities of Opus Dei; he prefers virginity to marriage. So his opinions were frequently at odds with those of his friend. But he is able to report that, for Greene, the absence of a navel from the Turin shroud 'provided proof of the virgin birth' – the sort of opinion, as espoused by Greene, that Norman Douglas used to laugh at on Capri. He is benign about Greene's dealings with Torrijos, and he praises what he regards as his victorious battle with the Côte d'Azur Mafia – which Shelden regards as an ineffectual attempt to turn into a *cause célèbre* the circumstances of a divorce obtained by the daughter of his 'good friend' Yvonne Cloetta, as Duran calls her.

Duran's simplicity can on occasion appear to recruit and to simplify his friend. The people of Antibes seemed to Duran to be 'polite and sensitive'; and then, when the two of them go off to buy for the priest a medal from Lourdes, they find that insensitive thieves have set fire to the shop. But they also find that the fire has spared the medals. Duran refers to the shopkeeper as 'the holy woman of the medals', and Greene is said to have seen in her something supernatural. Elsewhere, Orwell's expression 'our first Catholic fellow-traveller' is deemed a tribute to Greene's journeys in the company of kindred spirits. The Communist sympathizer in Greene, here suppressed, was one of the few aspects of his life which were not to his friend's liking.

Father Duran's memoir springs a late surprise. It becomes a better book when he writes about Greene's temperament and marriage, together with his love for the Trappist monastery at Osera. To his restlessness and self-contradiction – to those constant travels of his, among much else – Duran persuasively applies the ancient notion of balance, the old alchemical notion of a right arrangement of the human elements: 'Graham Greene recognized that his temperament was not stable; it was not perfectly balanced. Thus his moments of peace were often fragile.' And he adds: 'He would never be cured; some things never are. Some people may choose to call this sort of psychological imbalance an illness, but such conditions are ways of being.'

For his part, Greene recognized in his friend a certain old-fashioned sweetness of nature, and his depressions would seem to have been relieved by the presence of his foolish friend, known to him, in jest, as 'my whisky priest'. The comic flirtatiousness of their exchanges conveys a dependence on him which the closing stages of the book enable one to understand. Duran writes there with a disciplined compassion about the failure of Greene's marriage and about the human elements of Vivien Greene.

It is pleasant to come across these qualities in a man of God. Father Duran, author of *La Crisis del Sacerdote en Graham Greene*, is an old-fashioned priest who has remained unreconstructed, antediluvian, politically. Gallivanting, however, with his antinomian Catholic socialist famous friend – an old Catholicism hand in hand with a new, which had begun to suffer the enmity of Pope John Paul II – would seem to have gone along with God's grace in softening his more inhuman opinions, while hardly exempting him from some suspicion of hypocrisy. There have always been old-fashioned priests who have displayed – and failed to display – the qualities to be sensed at the end of his book; but Duran's display has the interest of causing the reader to think about the Catholic religion of the past fifty years. The changes which have overtaken the Church in the course of his lifetime are changes which its counter-revolutionaries, bringing to bear what Greene saw as their Counter-Reformation piety, may find it difficult to eradicate.

The novels produced by Graham Greene in the Thirties were not such as to remind people that there is such a thing as philosemitism. But there has been, and there is, and it can no doubt be detected in the present book. Writing in 1997 about a new novel by Saul Bellow, I found myself remembering the warmth which I and others felt in the Fifties for the American Jewish writers who were then emerging, for Bellow, Malamud, Mailer, Philip Roth, for older and earlier Jewish writers too – such as Isaac Babel and Isaac Singer – and for the work of Dan Jacobson, a Jewish South African come to London. It was now possible for those who may somehow have managed to miss it in the Thirties to discover that Greene's Jewish midgets could write books. There was at this point a real feeling in Britain for Jewish efforts in the arts, a feeling perceptible to me domestically, as furnishing a climate for Jonathan Miller's stage and television debut. It was, and was declared, ethnic of him to start off as he did, to be both bookish and funny, in the way that Woody Allen had started to be in America. Saul Bellow, likewise, has been Jewish and bookish and funny. His recent novel, *The Actual*, brought back to me this post-war philosemitic heyday (mention of which in print caused one Jewish reader to suspect with due ethnicity, as anti-semites might have felt, that the *New Statesman* had gone anti-semitic), together with the thought that a novel can be like a poem, and be a place where writers show their faces, their often complicated faces, much as they do in certain sorts of verse. Prose fiction has never been unable to behave in one or other of the many ways in which poetry behaves.

In *The Actual*, a very astute, very old Jewish trillion-aire is counselled by an astute Jew, no longer young, no longer poor, who has resumed relations with a first love, never forgotten. For Harry Trellman, a businessman, an importer, Amy Wustrin is 'the actual'. 'Other women were apparitions' for this narrator. 'She, and only she, was no apparition.' This is the centre of things in Saul Bellow's latest work of fiction. Not that there are all that many things for it to be the centre of. It is a short book – no different in kind from one of his long stories – and an oblique one. Are we to suppose, romantically, that only the first love matters?

Amy and Harry dated at high school, then drifted apart. She married Harry's friend Jay, a lawyer and pretender, one of those hustlers, gangsters and confidence men who stand close to the narrator or hero of Bellow's tales of mystery and imagination. He is a seducer of women, the sad emblem of an age of emancipation, according to the narrator, whose views on the subject are in line with those of Mr Sammler in the Bellow book of thirty years ago, a verdict on the space-travelling carnival Sixties: courteous, old-world Mr Sammler is given to reflections on the rise of the individual in the modern world, and on 'the peculiar aim of sexual niggerhood for everyone' which has come about in his own time. Jay, who had chosen to be buried next to his hostile mother-in-law, is now to be re-interred, in order to make room for his senile father-in-law. The story moves towards the transfer of the corpse, which is witnessed by Harry and his date from within the cocoon of the trillionaire Adletsky's limo. The scene suggests that Amy will live up to her promising first name.

Burials and re-interments are a thing of Saul Bellow's. In one of his stories a woman wants to dig her husband up for a last look. 'She said she just had to see him again.' Humboldt, in *Humboldt's Gift*, is climactically re-interred, together with his mother, in a cemetery scene which alludes to the necrophile raptures of the mother's-boy escapologist Houdini. Saul Bellow is an Illinois Old Mortality whose taste for graves can seem to incorporate a taste for escaping from them, and for the boundless beyond. In *Mr Sammler's Planet*, a novel much possessed by the idea of 'earth-departure', the 'actual' is at one point equated with the eternal. This new re-interment bestows, however, no such thoughts on the remains of Jay Wustrin, who can sometimes look, from the dualistic point of view established in Bellow's earlier fictions, like Harry's lower self. Harry may be fit to rise, but no one would want to see Jay again.

'It is of course impossible to guess what people know about one another,' claims Trellman. It may not be possible to know what people know about one another, but it is surely possible to guess, as Trellman's opening sentences have already admitted, in conveying that it's easy to see what people think they're doing and not hard to make out what 'they really are up to'. In the course of a *Listener* interview which appeared in 1969, Saul Bellow, in person, went so far as to remark that the individual 'understands what is in his own heart, and in the hearts of others, somehow'. So what does Harry know, and what do we know about Harry? Is the importer an impostor? He says that he has been a dissembler, that he is secretive. Amy says that he lets on to no more than a tenth of what he 'really thinks or knows'. And he hasn't always been in a position to observe what he reports.

A key scene in the retailing of which Harry's powers as an observer are apparent, but from which he was absent in the flesh, ensues when wildfire Madge – who once took out a contract, no marriage contract either, on a husband who later remarried her – tips a cup of tea into Amy's thickly-tweeded lap. The tea is spoken of as lukewarm and as scalding. The plant aloe vera is applied to the hurt. But Harry has to check with Amy later in the book: 'Did Madge Heisinger really pour tea in your lap? Were you scalded?'

Old Adletsky, who maintains a think tank or intelligence service, has hired him for the high quality of his gossip – for the higher gossip of which the novel itself appealingly consists. But we may sometimes wonder how much of this unreliable narrator to believe, and wonder, too, about the paradox of the Cretan liar, who told people not to believe him. It doesn't seem right to believe that Harry Trellman is Saul Bellow. But nor can it be right to see them as standing at a distance from one another; the physical descriptions can now and then be found to match, and we may be meant to notice this. Harry sees the often merely sour Adletsky as astute: does he think, as novelists are apt to do, that the rich are interesting? The book contains many references to their brand-named luxury goods and gains: one Chicagoan owns 'several Goya portraits, as well as some Picassos of my favourite kind', which is pitching it high, and may or may not be meant to seem like part of Harry's pitch. Do we take his word for it when he calls 'commonplace' most of the people he is gossiping about – among them, his elsewhere prodigious Adletsky – or Amy's word for it when she tells her resumptive boyfriend, in a language we associate with more than one of the heroes and narrators of Bellow's previous books, that he has led a 'high-level mental life'? These puzzles are intriguing. To make what we can of them it is worth turning to those of his previous novels where similar questions could be asked.

At the centre of many of them shines a solar ego. They transmit a strong personality, a strong will. In a discussion of Bellow's typical characters, Nicholas Spice has referred to them as 'variant hypostases of a central Bellowian godhead'. Out of this godhead there can issue a confessional comedy of the paranoid response, in which a narcissistic hero, or consciousness, is affirmed and ironized – as here: Trellman is aware in hindsight that for most of his species he 'generally had a knife within reach'.

Not all of Bellow's fictions answer to this account, but some do. It rests on the notion of an authorial presence which invests his narrators and heroes, together with their symbiotes and dualistic opposites: on the bi-part notion, in other words, of a strong self and of a mutability of the self. The novels and stories in question are dominated by the author and his avatars.

In order to speak generically of these arrangements, it might be appropriate to resort to the ancient categories and call him a lyrical writer, and a romantic one. The formal properties of the novels and stories in question, their dramatic structure, their endings and non-endings, are accommodated to the fact that their author has yet to end; it's as if each of them can only stop when the writer does. Somewhere in these intimations of deferment, and of immortality, may lie a reason for the 'looseness' benignly identified by Spice, and perhaps, too, for the writer's interest in the closures effected by funerals.

Those of Bellow's characters who aren't avatars, who are comparatively remote from the rays of this perpetual sun, are brilliantly evoked, and are the subjects of a proliferation of first-rate sub-stories or sub-plots: but it may be equally true to say that it is sometimes possible to mix them up and to forget — as can happen with characters in Dickens — which book they belong to. The books they belong to are works in which the writer may seem, for the most part, to be talking about himself and his enemies, and about first and further loves, in which he can from time to time be experienced as a divided consciousness, as a diversity to which enemies have access. This is not true, as I say, of all of his fictions; nor are they always as soulful, as ethereal and eternal, as they are at times. And it is not true of the one which is the most expressly dualistic, and which could well be reckoned one of his best. *The Victim* unequivocally ends, is quite tightly plotted, and would encourage no one to find in the mutuality and division of the pair of characters at its centre any unmistakable lyric cry.

These arrangements add up, in other hands, to a way of writing poetry. But they are also, and have long been, a way of writing novels, one which Bellow's way with words and outstanding literary achievement have served to perpetuate, as the axis created in Anglo-American fiction by Martin Amis's admiration for his work would seem to show. No more Bellowian book, in the generic sense, than *Money*. Over here in England too, the godhead.

In Edmund Wilson's diaries of the Twenties can be found a statement of the aesthetic I have been describing. Here are the rudiments of a dualistic art. He writes of what it is for a novelist to choose characters 'too remote from himself', and remarks that 'there is, of course, no such thing as real detachment'. Attachment can give life, and 'the more kinds of character a man has, the more kinds of characters he can create'.

15. Lads

OLD AGE IS a slow surprise, writes Patrick Chamoiseau in his fine folkloric Martinican novel *Texaco*, and this surprise may include the discovery that the pictures on which much memory depends are so few, and that the middle years of a life, in default of diaries and other documentary prompting, are a darkness. But even here, for most people, there will be points of light, a little gallery of pictures. One of mine shows me the moment when, on the *London Review* in October 1992, in the handsome Lutyens hallway by the lift, almost the only privacy achievable in a small office, I told my co-editor Mary-Kay Wilmers, the owner of the paper and an old friend, that I wished to leave.

Another picture, from two years before, shows me a scene in which a proprietorial right was asserted in respect of the material we published. Mary-Kay and I then carried on editing the paper, while debating what this development was to mean for its future. Ian Hamilton and Frank Kermode, members of the advisory board, tried to reconcile us, but the working partnership of many years proved impossible to restore. I was aware that my position could not be defended in law should another crisis blow up, and that I would have no desire to make the attempt. When I told her of my wish to go, I noticed in her vigilant eye what looked like a gleam of hostility, which made it seem like a good time to do so, and it came to me that this was odd. She should, on balance, have been pleased by my news. I had understood for some years that she would one day want to edit the paper on her own; the co-editorial arrangement that had eventually transpired – suggested by me, I think – was a step in that direction. It seemed unlikely that she'd disliked me for the thirty years we'd known each other. Once the break had occurred, however, a resentment is bound to have set in, or been exacerbated. When someone wondered whether I might thereafter be sent a copy of the paper every fortnight, she thought not. She knew me well enough to know that I wouldn't read it, that I'd been loth to read the other papers I'd left. Thirty years of friendship went into that refusal.

The episode has long since begun to partake of the darkness of the past, and I may at the time have missed part of its point. It was put about, in the usual way on such occasions, that I'd been difficult to work with. I can remember few departures, apart from my own, from the papers, or parts of papers, where I was in charge. But there is likely to be some truth in the complaint; I must certainly have given more trouble than I should have done, or than I wanted to do, during the overworked years that went into the *London Review*. Less plausibly, it was put about that I'd desired to keep Gore Vidal out of a paper he'd probably have been too grand to enter. The co-editorial eye-contact I am remembering, which was also a talk with my employer, was followed by a re-acquaintance with the hiring fair frequented by the freelance journalist, which occurred at a time when the old are less beguiling than they were when I was young, and old heads are seldom hunted for editorial posts. The conversation by the lift was both commonplace and bizarre. It was bizarre because of the depth and long history of the association in question. Equally, it's the kind of thing that is apt to happen in journalism. It leads me to ask whether the kinds of thing that happen in the journalism of politics and letters have changed with the years.

Two other darknesses have figured in this book. I have spoken of the darkness of nineteenth-century journalistic anonymity in the periodical field, a condition which could yield at the time to the glamour of the identified reviewer, and which in the fullness of time was to be drastically curtailed, but which, in one form or other, has yet to disappear, if it ever will, from the world of the reviewer. Then there's the dark horse of the unconsidered writer – newcomer or veteran; here, too, there can be a gallop into the light. These are darknesses which intersect, and which can at times be found to illuminate one another.

Two separate functions can be attributed to the reviewing of the present century. It has provided infor-mation and opinion about a plethora of new books, a service of vital importance to whoever needs to know what the books are about. It has also been a forum where articles appear which are meant to be interesting in their own right, and in their own write: good, bad or indiffer-ent, they are performances, utterances, the work of authors. These are functions which support each another, but can sometimes be seen to get in each other's way. The difference between them is, in part, a difference between criticism and an extensive something else which includes journalism and literature. Theorists of recent years have insisted that criticism is writing, is literature, in the course of insisting that everything is a text. Such thoughts have been considered disturbing. But they have their merits, and there must surely be ways of thinking them which permit a distinction between the informative and the expressive, and which don't force you to unthink the function of criticism at the present time.

'Criticism' is a word that can sound weary with hostility and personality, with the 'personalities' which it theoretically abjures. It was the great word of the literary undergraduate in the Cambridge of the Fifties. During my time there as a student, my immediate predecessor as literary editor of the *New Statesman*, the novelist Walter Allen, came, with lingering steps and slow, I have no doubt, to address the prigs of the English Club on the subject of reviewing. Here is another of the pictures that remain with me. The prigs were, or affected to be, shocked to learn that a journal's book pages were like a train due to leave every seven days, whose passenger seats had at all costs to be filled. This, at any rate, is what we thought we were hearing – that there might have to be one or two dummies propped in the seats. Brian Inglis used to say a similar thing on the *Spectator* – that there were 'cod leaders' which had to be written.

After that English Club meeting, or another of the time, I drank coffee with friends – among them, Joan

Bakewell, from Manchester, very rosy in her gown. She and I were Northerners, she felt, which was what Wordsworth felt when he arrived in Cambridge – 'a Northern villager'; and she was soon to become a very accomplished broadcaster. My friends and I talked about authors, and someone said, not me, my lord, that T. S. Eliot was 'a lovely man'. This is what young people felt then, those who were keen on authors. We were in a world where T. S. Eliot was a lovely man, and the departure on time, every seven days, with all seats taken, of journals of politics and letters was an event. Before very long I was to find out for myself that there were seats which had to be filled, and that there were pieces which were late and which due consideration would have spiked, but which had to go in. And I was also to find out that there was more to literary journalism than criticism.

Looked at in a certain light, London's literary pages were a space where the unconsidered author and the unconsidered reviewer had to struggle for access, and a night darker than that of nineteenth-century anonymity might descend on them both. One means of escape for such reviewers was to pass over the unconsidered author and to rail against the overrated, the past-their-best, the displeasingly famous. None of this has changed very much, as far as I can make out. But there are changes that I do seem to see.

The impact of radio and television, and of the expansion and diversification of newspapers, dating from the Sixties, has led to a featurizing of journal coverage. It has meant interviews, and fame, even more of that than before. But it has meant less of it too. Now more than ever dark horses may become also-rans or midnight black. Journalistic pages can resemble a visually-impaired attempt to resemble television programmes. And the academic input of the Fifties and Sixties has in most places receded. The scholar journalist, salaried or free-lance, has become a rare beast. None of this means that there are no good literary journalists under the age of fifty. But it seems clear that of the two functions I have ascribed to periodical reviewing, the second – the expressive – has gained ground at the expense of the first. This is not to speak evil of self-expression; a satisfactory discussion of literature tends to require it – while also requiring a suspicion of the journalistic self.

Reviewing is the business of a small professional group which has suffered its sheddings and curtailments in particular areas but which appears to have grown larger with the advent of exultation about the death of the author and of the book. Reviewers look younger to me now, as the policemen they sometimes impersonate are said to look to the old, but it seems probable that they really are younger. They could scarcely be more adversarial than reviewers were in my own early days. But they try. And adversarial reviewing is now accompanied by adversarial interviewing, thanks to the pioneering work of Lynn Barber. Neither interviews nor attacking reviews preclude criticism, but they don't encourage it either. Of all these developments, however, the most striking is not so much the threat to criticism as the editorial under-standing that criticism needs to be less literary than it has been in the past. This is not the death of the book. But it is something.

It is something which came to mind when I read an issue of the *New Statesman* (7 March 1997) and compared it with one of the last issues there in which I had a hand — that of 30 December 1966. Not an especially good choice, since, after the Christmas Books expanded issue earlier in the month, advertising was *Listener*-low in the water, and the number of pages was down. All this means for the present purpose, however, is that the difference I am about to detect would be even more marked if almost any other issue of the mid-Sixties were to be substituted for the one I've chosen.

In the old issue there were two poems, by John Fuller. The lead, by George Lichtheim, was on 'European civilization', in the light of a book by the Austrian scholar Friedrich Heer ('a learned controversialist writing about history, rather than a historian . . . It is no use going to him for information about anything that actually happened'). Then came V. S. Pritchett on Mrs Gaskell, E. S. Turner on Darwin as traveller, Peter Gillman on climbing mountains, the novelist Colin MacInnes on snaps, the novelist Frederic Raphael on the paranoid world of bridge-playing, the poet Norman MacCaig on a bare-knuckle bygone Edinburgh Police Chief, and a piece by Julian Symons on whimsical literary essays. Eight reviews, followed by a think-piece by Hans Keller which told the difference between art and entertainment (and kicked off with one of his provocations: 'The fact that the cultural history of this country started a new chapter when, at the age of nineteen, I descended upon it is too well-known by now to be in need of detailed discussion'). Then came a four-page arts section.

In the 1997 issue none of the contributors sported initials and there were no poems, and no novelist or poet reviewers. There was a strong arts section of six pages. There were six reviews, plus a piece on the publication of screenplays by the deputy literary editor of a Sunday paper. A review by Joan Bakewell discussed 'women, science and God' and remarked that scientists are keen to be thought on God's side. The agony aunt Claire Rayner gave hell to a film star who had written an autobiography and been insufficiently vetted as a candidate foster-parent: 'her fame was all that Mia Farrow needed to pack her life with small damaged children for use as plasters for her own problems.' There was an ecological piece by a special adviser to the Secretary of State for the Environment and a clever piece on the Internet by the *Guardian* journalist Charles Nevin, which opened with a tease: 'You will be familiar with the technique where a literary editor, intent upon enlivening his pages, commissions a review from a writer with a particular animus against a book's subject, or even better, against its author.' This book section was enlivened by a lead piece which exhibited the writer Bruce Chatwin as a monstrously camp and precious aesthete.

To compare the two issues is to witness a move from literature to current affairs. Both book sections contained current affairs: the decisive difference was that in the recent one very little sympathetic attention was given to works of the imagination or to the humanities. The front half of the paper – energetic and eventful, rife with interviews, with scoops and semi-scoops – has annexed the back. The pantomime horse has gone dark. I don't wish to suggest that all other book sections give the same impression, or that this one is uninteresting; and I realize that if the writers of the past sometimes get forgotten, they have had lots of time in which to become well-known and to take on a nostalgic interest which might affect comparisons of this kind, causing an unfairness to present incumbents. Nevertheless, in this quarter as in others, a change has occurred. There are more editors around now for whom literature doesn't matter.

Reviewers and journal editors have yet to become like ostlers and lamplighters, the dear old souls of a lost world; their skills are still of use. Of these skills, there were one or two which I was unable to deploy. Standoffishness and showoffishness can go together perfectly well, but they didn't do so in my case, which could sometimes seem to involve a certain perversity in the relationship between the two. I was at times to feel myself a misfit as I got on with doing what I badly wanted to do, with addressing readers, expressing opinions and arranging for others to express them, and this may have slowed me or stopped me in some of my tracks. Circulations were never to leap into being at the drop of my hat, though I did try to drop it. I was never in touch with readers, present to them, in the manner of Kingsley Martin. Kingsley was no dark horse. He was an editorial star and agonized conscience, a periodical giant straight out of the nineteenth century, who explained that he thought of the *New Statesman* as his mistress – with readers under the bed like reds, one might add, alert for every wince of the mattress. I was never able to manage that, or even to aspire to it. In never becoming widely-known for my opinions, I was, admittedly, no different from many other latterday editors. If I'd been in the habit of changing them, as Kingsley was, no one would have noticed; neither my thoughts nor my second thoughts got through. But many of my writers did.

When I left my last journal, I received only one letter from a stranger – the rest were from contributors and friends. A very low score for someone who'd been in the business for so long. The stranger's letter came from a man who lived near Windermere, Martin Jeffreys: he said he'd gained something from reading all, virtually, of the issues of the paper. Pleased to hear this, I was also pleased to hear from E. P. Thompson that he'd been glad to be treated, not just as a source of views on disarmament, 'as Mr Peace', but as someone interested both in politics and in literature.

Books and journals remain mutually responsive – just as politics and literature still do in most of those periodicals whose history incorporates a Thompsonian fusion of the two. Works of literature can still evolve from the pages of magazines. Andrew O'Hagan published a piece in the *London Review* shortly after I departed, at the time of the murder of two-year-old James Bulger in Liverpool by two ten-year-old kidnappers. Andy spoke autobiographically about the bullying and tormenting that went on among children in the Ayrshire of his upbringing, where his education was assisted, he believes, by reading the journal in which he was now writing about what happened there. The article, which told how he took part in the bullying, led to a book, *The Missing*, which is a meditation on British disappearances of modern times and in which his Ayrshire experiences are recalled.

Not long before this, a book about a son's relationship with his father was published. The author was Blake Morrison, poet and journalist, for whose doctoral thesis on the Movement I had acted as supervisor. Blake's book is a book about Blake every bit as much as it is a book about his father, and it has been followed in recent months by a book by him about the Bulger killing, *As If*, which is also a book about Blake's coverage of the trial and about Blake. At one point it mentions the haltingness and reticence of witnesses at the trial: 'I feel for them, in their taciturnity. I, too, used to dry up and die.' Statements of this kind have been awarded a period meaning by certain observers of contemporary writing.

In 1992 Nick Hornby brought out a book which has become associated with the other three in the minds of these observers. *Fever Pitch* is a book about football which is also a book about the writer's obsession with Arsenal Football Club, and about his relations with his separated parents, his girlfriends and himself. Its football madness isn't altogether mine (I've never had a team of my own, with the possible exception of Greaves's Chelsea and Blanchflower's Spurs and Bobby Moore's West Ham), and there were passages in the book which reminded me of the story told of Sophocles – that he felt that old age, by putting an end to sexual desire, had released him from a cruel master. But there can't be much doubt that *Fever Pitch* lives up to its reputation. And you don't have to have loved the old-fashioned surging lurch of the crowd on the terraces at Highbury to go for it.

Literary journalism has had its say about resemblances perceived between these books and some others of the time. Signs of the times were detected. Laddishness was imputed – men behaving badly, or like boys. And 'me-too-ism' was imputed – I too have done bad things or been a victim. There were reviewers who alleged that O'Hagan was flaunting his working-class street credentials in mourning his disappeared, and that Blake Morrison was writing about Blake Morrison when he should have been writing about James Bulger. For one journalist, the 'worst thing' about his book was that it was 'about Morrison' rather than the murdered boy or 'even' his assailants. Nick Hornby has been let off relatively lightly, though there are reviewers for whom an interest in football is laddish, and for whom, when spied among those who aren't members of the industrial proletariat, it rates as a sinister sign of the times. Hornby, too, has scornful words for the entrance into the crowd of university-graduate members of the middle class – like himself.

These authors have been linked to a head lad, or alleged lad. This is Martin Amis, whose novels and way of going on and of talking on television have been influential and representative, whose sombre baritone can be overheard, in replication, speaking into mobile phones on the tops of buses. Some of these lads, you might say, or I might say, are my lads, in the sense that I first met them when they were young, and like what they have been doing – which is no different in kind from what many other writers have done before them. What matters is not that they have written about themselves – in autobiographical accounts which can read like fiction, and in Martin Amis's novels, which can read like autobiography – but what they have had to say.

Atrocity has a long history, and a long history of silence on the subject, which helps us to feel when the time comes that there are some sorts of crime which have never been committed before. One aspect of this history of silence may be that there are matters which it is difficult to write about in a personal way without going wrong; and that there are matters we don't want to hear about, a reluctance which works to the detriment of those who undertake to deliver the message. Either way, the messenger is blamed, and especially if he strays into autobiography. I don't sympathize with the detraction heaped on recent messengers, part of which is premised on the delusion that there is something fundamentally new in their way of writing. But I can follow some of the objections which have been raised, and am exercised by the questions which have been asked or implied or begged. It seems significant that all three of the auto-biographers I have been discussing – Hornby, O'Hagan, Morrison – have published or intend to publish novels.

Novels are female, according to certain conceptions of gender and of literary history, and it's enjoyable that this alleged recent laddishness can be found to answer to descriptions of women's writing, and to feminist accounts of what women's writing is and should be like, and of the importance of personality and feeling. Men writing about themselves while also writing about something else is, in a sense, women's work. Feminists have caused offence by arguing – altogether intelligibly – that the personal is political, and the political personal, and they have suggested that it is good to wear your heart on your sleeve, to make clear who you are, and where you are coming from, in writing about something other than yourself. Their concern is associated with the desire to write about what only women can know about, and with the knowledge of a history of suppression in respect of women's voices: while this makes a difference here, it doesn't have to mean that there can be no affinities or identities between male and female writing. And their arguments represent the valorization of a reproach, to use the language of these debates. Women have, in the past, been blamed for having feelings and for showing them, and that story has not been abandoned.

Men are calm and stern and rational. Women are emotional, attached. There is a long-established school of thought which assigns the rise of the novel to the English eighteenth century and to the efforts of rational males, rising in the world and intent on realism. The novel was then invaded, according to certain traditional accounts, by the morbidities of the sentimental or hysterical female. It has been possible, therefore, to blame women for the novel while dispossessing them of responsibility for its creation, and to keep on blaming them for a number of other things besides. Henry James, so often a romantic writer, found fault with women writers for being romantic and silly, while Ruskin, writing about the pathetic fallacy, and about the phallus, referred to a victory of the intellect over the passions, whereby 'the whole man stands in an iron glow, white hot, perhaps, but still strong, and in no wise evaporating; even if he melts, losing none of his weight.' You might not expect a man like that to write novels. And yet this was a time when the novels that men and women were writing had become the principal literary form, one in which both passion and intellect were accommodated.

It's good to be reasonable, and it's good for historians (and indeed for autobiographers) to spend time checking their facts and their arguments, as well as saying where they are coming from. But women are reasonable too, and men have feelings which they can't do without, as Ruskin conceded. Men and women are in this thing together; many of the differences we perceive between men's writing and women's are imaginary, and the qualities espoused by these feminists are fully accessible to the male. Earlyish in my editorial life I published pieces by D. Lessing and B. Brophy in which unsigned passages were set for identification: sexing the author would give trouble, we thought. And it did. It proved hard to tell with any confidence, of these dark horses, which was female and which male. Here was a healthy slap at gender stereotypes.

There need be nothing wrong with the presence of the emotional and the autobiographical in non-fictional contexts, nothing wrong with its acknowledgment by the writer, and nothing wrong with construing it as a dimension of that writer's rationality. Meanwhile the unacknowledged presence of the autobiographical in fiction is a contested but also widely appreciated fact of literature. The turn towards fiction of these three lads can be considered a natural progression.

I trust it has been apparent that except in the sense that they are about what lads (and some lasses) do – tormenting, fighting, football – I don't believe that any of their previous books has to be considered laddish. There is, however, no shortage of laddishness at the present time – in response, who knows, to the heightened awareness of women's rights which has come about. On being advised that lad's monthlies were a growth area in the magazine field, and that some of them bore a cultural content, a knowingness, at least, about the arts of the young, I went and looked. Lifestyle and leisure magazines have been trading for long enough, but I had never known much about this sector, despite being, at some point in the Sixties, mistakenly sounded as a possible editor of *Time Out*. So I went and looked: maybe there was more to laddishness, and to magazines, than I knew. And there was. But I could have done without discovering it.

One of the titles is *Loaded*, and they are all loaded – with money, readers, and with text-constraining ads, each number a slidy, shiny tome. The April 1997 *FHM* (*For Him Magazine*) opened with an editorial 'letter' which began: 'I've never had much trouble with drunk women. Not because the women I dated in the past were all teetotal – far from it – but just because I've always been too pissed myself to notice.' The women in Wonderlad's magazine were trouble; they were grotesques bent on pleasuring men but also on marrying them. There was a lengthy piece which said how disgusting the old are.

'You've had your fun,' old guys were informed: 'now shut up and let us get on with it, and thanks for sorting the Krauts out.' And there was a very short review by a reputable journalist, of an autobiography by a footballer and gambler, the Leicester forward Claridge, a more interesting player than John Naughton conveyed. Implausible-seeming males wrote in for guidance on their blemishes and sexual complaints, and an agony uncle supplied it: 'Don't feel you must stop masturbating.' Lassified ads, of the sort pinned up in telephone booths, brought the bad dream to a close. Blame it on the Sixties? That earlier liberation is no doubt visible in such lucrative dreams.

I was a lad myself once. By this, I don't mean that I liked to play football when I was young, though I did like to. Every Sunday, in my effeminate hypochondria, I was to be seen tumbling about in a corner of Battersea Park, treading the bone-hard Royal Hospital pitch in Chelsea, wallowing through the morass of Wormwood Scrubs, as the spy George Blake came squirrelling down the prison wall on his scamper to Moscow. Football did come into it. But it isn't the bottom line of the bad-laddishness I'm now discussing: football fans, as distinct from football hooligans, are no more aggressive and male-chauvinist than a number of writers I could name, though it's true that the chants and howls you hear on the terraces are never going to help to make this distinction, between fans and fighters, utterly clear. Soccer songs, like rugby songs, aren't always lovely. They have been celebrated, and subverted, by the young poet Eleanor Brown, an Englishwoman who grew up in Scotland, where she was made to feel 'blamed for the beheading of Mary Queen of Scots':

> Your poetry belligerently asserts
> what nobody would trouble to deny:
> that you are the lads; that there you go;
> that yours will never be to reason why.

On the next page of her collection *Maiden Speech* she writes, with all of Hugo Williams's 'attack', about three drunken upper-class pigs:

> O grant them soon cirrhosis of the liver,
> our English God! Whom, on our English knees,
> We thank for public schools, and men like these.

What I mean is that when I was young I was taught 'masculinist' attitudes. All around was the notion of girls as different, and as prey, a night-out, what Burns called 'jads', and as excluded by nature from many of the opportunities available to young men, even those of the working class. Strange of me, in one sense, to have been in the least taken-in, since I rapidly began preferring the company of women to that of men, and discovering – in the words of Burns, of Rab the Ranter – that 'the Rights of Woman merit some attention'. And yet there I was – poisoned. The power of received opinion to stay in the minds of those who are keen to escape it is remarkable. In saying in this book what I had to say about the anti-semitism of Eliot and Graham Greene, I have been conscious of this, conscious of the many other good writers before the Holocaust who denigrated Jews. It's not easy to think of Keats doing this, though. You didn't *have* to be an anti-semite. And it isn't anachronistic to object to those writers of the past who were.

Football-liking lads together, as I think we were sometimes to feel, with due irony, in the thick of our travels, Ian Hamilton and I took flight to Australia in May 1987, in order to attend an international conference on literary journals, convened by Ian Donaldson and held at the National University in Canberra, a symposium and spree where Jeremy Treglown and Peter Porter would also be present. Ian Hamilton and I were booked by mistake in different parts of the plane: I was Business Class to Ian's Economy, and I used to stand at the top of a staircase in our airborne Odeon and peer for him among the huddled masses at my feet, a scene from Dante. This, I told myself, only joking, must be what major writers feel when they look down on minor ones. We stopped for a night in Singapore. Rattling from the airport towards the city, I engaged the taxi-driver in liberal talk about its political situation – until I felt a gruffness coming from my friend, who was to prove a benign but caustic travelling companion. He unbent, however, at the Taj Mahal of an Indian-owned hotel, where free saunas were on offer. I turned on the television in my room. The political situation appeared to involve government-service, air-hostess, American-sleek Asian sylphs, reading the news. We went down in the lift, to claim our saunas.

I found myself sitting for an hour, stripped, wallet in hand, beside a steaming kettle in a wooden booth. My sauna over, I stepped into the corridor. There, at an open door, stood Ian, robed, steamed, smoking a cigarette, and flanked by smiling jads who were hanging on his few words. Could these be former readers of the *New Review*? Where were the readers of the *London Review*? I could hardly be looking at a love nest, I presumed, but this was a lot better than a kettle. Economy Class had taken its revenge, as Ian stood on the threshold in the posture of Ruskin's transcendent lad – in no wise evaporating, melting, maybe, but losing none of his weight.

We zoomed off over the endless forests of Java to Australia, where lads are larrikins and 'larrikin' is a literary critical term. It seemed as divided as the old *New Statesman*: a vast desert hinterland, vying with a suburban south-east coastal strip. Melbourne, where we arrived, seemed nineteenth-century at moments, with a ghostly after-sense of the Frontier, and with some nice merchants' houses about the same age as my own, an architectural feature over which Ian didn't want to hear me exclaiming. The scene was even further than I'd anticipated from urban Britain, let alone from the crowds and tumult of Bombay, which I'd yet to get to, up there at the opposite end of the ocean. India and Australia have distinguished newspaper and periodical traditions – well portrayed, respectively, in a film of Satyajit Ray's and in the writings of Sylvia Lawson – and Australia's current literary condition seemed hale and disputatious. We also seemed to have arrived in a country where the men and women did not go about together.

Canberra has been said by Barry Humphries to have become a little sleazy. He was joking, as so often. A garden city of civil servants, deserted after dark in its homogeneous recentness. An air of filing-cabinet propriety. Low-density housing lassoed by empty motorways and parked about a pastoral landscape of pastel colours, soft-smudged with eucalyptus, loud with the song of vehement birds with names like Major Mitchell's Cockatoo.

The conference was attended by agreeable people of several sorts – among them, the cosmopolitan Grazia Gunn, later to marry the convenor, Ian Donaldson. The gathering concern with America which has been reported of Australia may have muted the country's traditional concern with the British literary culture, but, as the choice of speaker indicated on this occasion, it has not extinguished it. This was not an occasion, however, when a colonial deference was likely to be paraded. There were theorists in the audience who hailed from, but could hardly have approved of, the old country, and there were those in the audience who seemed to think that capitalist consumerism and English literature were finished, and that the true enemy lay on the moderate Left, among liberals, rather than in the conservative parties of the English-speaking world. And there were passages of arms when this conference on literary journalism seemed to have assembled in order to dance on its grave. I gave a lecture in which I boasted that the *London Review* was perhaps the only paper in Britain to oppose Thatcher's commitment to war over the Falklands, five years before. I sat down. Up rose a flaxen British Marxist feminist, domiciled in Australia, who asked why I had been so craven as to support the war. I was impressed by her not having listened. I had turned into Walter Allen on his visit to Cambridge in the Fifties – an object of reflexive suspicion for the priggish young.

In July of that year Ian Hamilton digested, in the course of a Diary piece for the *London Review*, the lecture he'd given at the conference on 'Why little magazines don't matter any more'. The Diary dealt with his experience of editing his magazine the *Review*, and is a valuable account of what literary journalism can be like when purpose and pleasure coincide.

> For a brief period, I told them, the *Review* had most of the things I'd want a little magazine to have: it had a group of unknown poets it admired, it had a 'kind of poem' it wanted to promote, and it had powerfully-placed enemies it was eager to attack. It had youth, it had a sense of humour, and – looking back on it from now – a bumptious kind of certainty that it knew all the answers. It also had some sense of history, connecting itself back to an earlier epoch that was out of fashion: the poems it argued for had their roots in Imagism but would pride themselves on having far more human content than their models. And it had a sense of its own necessity. Pop poetry was coming into vogue and the *Review* was going to put a stop to that.

In earlier days, said the Diary, the avant-gardists of the little magazines had been able to hold out against the mainstream for as much as a generation at a time. During his own editorial tenure, however, that had changed.

Mainstream magazines, quality newspapers, formerly bored by or sour about avant-garde activity, began to take an interest in such journals and to draw their contributors away. The *Review* suffered accordingly, he felt; there were poets and critics who, under the duress of these solicitations, sank into self-parody. The seducing and suborning may still be going on, but it looks as if there are too few little magazines still around – too few good ones, at any rate – for it to be worth the big papers' while to keep an eye out. And I doubt whether the big papers are all that interested any more.

The papers I worked for were none of them little magazines. Ian's efforts were closer to the single-handed than mine were; I was never tied that closely to the one 'kind of poem', and I am not – nor is Ian – as avant-garde as the Diary might perhaps suggest. But I would like it if it could be thought that some of the hopes and aims described there were mine too.

16. Amma and Mulberry

A FEW DAYS before my sixty-fifth birthday, in August
1996, I took a walk with my son Daniel's son Joseph, a
ball at our feet, through the Royal Hospital grounds in
Chelsea, with their red-coated veterans, their goal-posts,
and the lovely little secret park near by. These grounds
are where the Flower Show pitches its tents, and where
the match-making Ranelagh Pleasure Gardens stood in
the eighteenth century. Underneath lots of yellow locks,
two wary blue saucer eyes looked up, their large pupils
cocked for information. Was I a book-maker? asked
Joseph – not, he insisted, Joe. It was the sort of question
you might find in *Joe Miller's Jest Book*, the eighteenth-
century bestseller. I told him that I wrote books, and
thought to add: 'But I've been more of a magazine-
maker.'

This has been a book about his magazines by someone
who no longer has a magazine to mind, and is back where
he has been before at times – among the freelances, with
their dark talk of the yes and the no and the out-to-lunch
of editors – and who feels the loss. I fuss about my
health. I have made up, in the manner of my adolescence,
a forfending rhyme, which I bequeath to my detractors:

> No poor soul was ever iller
> Than Karl Fergus Connor Miller.

There are days when I am my tongue, my throat, my sinus, my anus. I have house-mite's chest. I spend as much time thinking of death as Kingsley Amis ever did. Nothing altogether new there, it's true. And I don't like to think of myself as retired. I have no desire to be the Chelsea pensioner I have become.

In the course of my birthday, primed with documents – passport, birth certificate, snaps – I went down to the post office to fetch my old-age pensioner's bus pass. One of my snaps would never do, and I disappeared into a curtained booth in the post office for a further likeness. I studied the instructions in the booth, the map of its few simple internal features, pressed buttons, and settled down to wait, and to read the works of Conor Cruise O'Brien. A rumbling sounded, but no portraits were sicked from what I took to be the appropriate feature. Time went on, and I then heard a voice saying, in a resigned sort of way: 'Come out, Mr Miller.' I came out of my closet to collect a strip of sad snaps from its outside wall.

This is what the old do, I told myself, or what Larkin's old fools do, this sitting-on in booths; I might be about to become the elderly party – witnessed by my daughter – whose hat had got caught in the closing doors of a compartment on the Underground, and who went on to the next stop on the Inner Circle at a stoop, not thinking to withdraw his head from the hat. I had forgotten that I used to make plenty of such mistakes when I was young. Meanwhile a frightened, hostile, identikit mad old sod stared out at me from my photocard. I seemed to have lost quite a bit of my devil, not to mention my confidence and my looks, since the last such photocard in 1979.

I returned to the house to meet a lawyer and draw up a will which leaves my stuff to my surviving spouse, three children and six grandchildren. I've had to face the disagreeable fact that my house can't be left without stressful complications to any single one of my children. So strangers will presently be sprawling in our ferny garden and trampling through our shafts of light.

Later in the day, I lay looking out of my bedroom window at the summer sky, sutured with vapour trails, that rose above the hospital next door, with its wounds and sores, wheelchairs and sticks, its tormented and angry cries. The hospital has been rebuilt; an Aids annexe has been added. The outside is an ugly fawn colour, a tessellation of rectangular Rich Tea biscuits. Inside, on a day like this, clasped by its promising blue sky, it will be radiant and spacious, I reflected, having not long since emerged from the place, on one of those catapult post-operative exits introduced by the Conservative Government for the protection of the National Health Service. Over the garden wall is a terrace where there are designer shrubs and palms, and a fountain with most of the qualities of a burst main, a terrace where patients and their pals walk and talk, and where a disturbed man, unseen, once kept drawling, for hours on end, in the tones of a debonair wartime wing-commander deep into gambling and drink: 'Good morning, Mulberry.' Like the Hindu god in *Passage to India*, Mulberry neglected to reply, or to budge from his bush or shrub.

I lay on my bed wondering what I had done with myself over all these years, and what to make of the bound volumes of the magazines of my millennium, which reach round my study wall for rather more than the length of an adult human being, and which enclose a region of my own human being. I had sometimes felt proud of what people wrote in these volumes: but often disappointed, as I now reminded myself, when I read what I wrote there myself, there or in books. Not long ago a seal was set on this recurrent sense of disappointment – during a visit with my wife to a combative friend in the country, whose opinions I value. He gave someone the impression of thinking that I was an editor and not a book-maker, and I took him to have said that my writings were no good. This was the biter bit: the literary criticism I'd published for so long had risen up to serve me right. The clays and cowpats of the surrounding hills and dales proved stickier than usual as I plodded about savouring this judge's sentence, so very like the sentences which I'd spent so much of my time publishing: naturally, I thought it was deserved. Something daunted, I nevertheless went on writing the present book. I found that I wanted to forget my friend's point, and to remember that it might be true.

As I lay on my bed, a further trouble presented itself. I have hurt people, I thought to myself. This is what people do, and I did it. And the worst of it was that the least of it was work, though work did indeed play a part. Talk of sacrifice can be hateful, in its so often seeming to relate to demands made of somebody else, its seeming to display the spirit which sent a generation to the trenches, and sent servicemen to Australia to test nuclear bombs and risk irradiation, without explaining the risk and without compensating them for their cancers. It can lead to the automatism of murder and suicide which has disfigured the Irish Republican tradition. But sacrifices have to be made, and there's a place for self-sacrifice, as there is for self-blame. In both of these last respects, my record is patchy, hurtful. The shrewdest criticism I heard of my editing was that I tried too hard, and that magazines must be brilliant, that they thrive on a stylish negligence, on error, improvisation and impromptu. But it would be equally true to say that my hard work on magazines was less like an ascetic exercise than a libidinous indulgence, and that this was one reason why I didn't work hard on my friendships. I made it to funerals, being a natural mourner, but I seldom rang the dead people up when they were alive, and however much I liked them, except to ask them for a thousand words by the end of the month.

When editors stop being editors, half of their friends vanish. This is expected. In my own case, it testifies both to the jostlingness and anxiety of a professional world and to an individual human deficiency – mine. No wonder Mulberry won't come. So there I was beneath a blue sky with my conscience troubling me. And my throat. Stuck in my sore throat, on such occasions now, are sore thoughts. It occurs to me that illnesses of the mouth and tongue are apt to happen to those who live by their words. I don't anticipate making a good death, and am surprised that someone so little in favour of organized religion – or, at any rate, of the blind, blaming, murdering, pain-prolonging sacrificial business that is more than half of the religion we know – should care about this, if I do care. I suspect that some part of the sentiment and superstition picked up during an early spell of exposure to a far from seductive Presbyterian piety has yet to leave me. But the only God I have ever felt like acknowledging in the course of my adult life bears a resemblance to that Mulberry.

Reviewers have been an unprotected workforce. They have been taken up and dropped – their writings have been cut and garbled – by editors who have made a fine art of negligence and indifference. I can't claim to have been innocent of such practices, any more than I can claim to have escaped the taint that spreads from the pursuit of judgment in newspapers and journals – from what Hans Keller thought of as the expression of a remunerated destructive disrespect. But I was seldom exposed, either as editor or contributor, to the system at its worst. Every so often, when darkness falls, I am to be found in a ruined chapel in East London, where I light a candle and give thanks, with all the religion that is left me, that I haven't spent my life as a freelance literary journalist working for papers where no one minds about literature.

In the autumn of 1995, I reviewed, in the *Times Literary Supplement*, Gore Vidal's show-off memoir *Palimpsest*: so I was pretty interested when, a few months later, also in the *TLS*, he reviewed, at unprecedented length and with unprecedented scorn, and in pride of place, John Updike's novel *In the Beauty of the Lilies*. The review was a calumny. It was that of a cynical, strenuously worldly, rival star. Vidal spent much of his ample space complaining about Updike's American patriotism during the Vietnam War and mocking the ineptitude of this patriotic novel. But despite the ominousness of its title, the novel is neither obtrusively patriotic nor obtrusively pious. What does stand out is the felicity and buoyancy of its thick descriptions of American life. It has in it, not God, but the God that lies in the detail of what happens in its New Jersey and Delaware. It is the work of a writer whose attitude towards the Vietnam War would not have offended the *Times Literary Supplement* of the time when the war was being waged, and might well have been sympathetically treated by the journal as it is now, had it been able to resist the snazziness of Gore Vidal's sneers. Soon afterwards my wife received a letter from a reviewer whom she did not know, and who had reviewed her book, *School for Women*, and discovered, when she saw the proof of the review, that an editor had removed 'the sections that made it plain how much I enjoyed the book'. Neither of these episodes is likely to have been free from the merely accidental, like many of the fouls that come about in football. Placed, however, as God contrived to place them, in conjunction, they suggest, if nothing else, the undesirability of praise, for editorial people, and the attraction of detraction.

The London literary scene described in Amanda Craig's novel of 1996, *A Vicious Circle*, is grounded in detraction, and so is the novel. What goes on is shown in a very poor light – the infernal glow of a satirical hostility. They are far from being sixty-five years old, these reviewers, though they are aging fast and dying young. Almost all of them went to Oxford or to Cambridge. They are either very rich or next-door to destitute. There are 'raddled and acidulous' female hacks on the scene, and there are 'savage' male hacks; elsewhere in London, 'tired-out hags' and their fourteen-year-old daughters queue up in National Health hospitals to give birth. This is a class-conscious Bohemia, with swift upward mobility for some. The hacks get to go to Andrew Evenlode's country house, nicely named Lode, which has peacocks and topiary. The main savage male hack, Mark, is 'a young Turk of the New Right'. Dyed eyelashes, snake's eyes, puny physique – clever, though. This Turk marries up into press-magnate opulence and influence, having abandoned a Belfast girl, Mary, who sorrows profusely, vows revenge, despises the literary world and becomes a successful reviewer. The novel itself reads like a revenge. The passage about a literary editor's grief on publishing a book of her own, arranging for its benign reception, and then failing with it, executes, very well, a rough justice, which may also be, in the sense of Francis Bacon's aphorism, a wild one:

> She blamed her publishers, she blamed bookshops, she blamed public libraries, she blamed her agent. She blamed the picture on the dust-jacket. She even blamed the hand-picked critics who had reviewed her. At the same time, she knew perfectly well that she had received an advance ten times what anyone else could expect simply because of her position.

Mark, the revenger's main concern, is said at the end to have been 'a small, mean sort of man', unworthy of Mary, and he is made to seem somehow to blame for the medical and subsistence-level nightmares which surround the scramblings of the Groucho Club hacks. Mary takes away from Mark's posh wife the man for whom the wife has learned to care, and 'everyone who's anyone comes to Mary's parties'. Having 'moved in the wrong circles', according to a decent friend, Mary continues to revolve there.

The novel has its resemblances to Aldous Huxley's *Point Counter Point* and Gissing's *New Grub Street*. It has Gissing's contrast between the shrewd operator and the struggling, dying artist – this one dies of Aids, having been adversely reviewed by Tabloid Mary, or rather Broadsheet Mary, and afterwards nursed by her. But it differs from these other books in taking very little interest in ideas or in the content of the imaginary books it mentions; there is nothing here that corresponds to the Lawrentian doctrines which are used, in Huxley's novel, to whack his London literary world. The novel does have one idea, though: it chronicles the effect on Grub Street of the Thatcher revolution. Cut-throat literary ambition might seem to have stepped up a gear since the Seventies. One character says that the British (as opposed to the Irish) don't like reading books, which means that the reviewer who makes it his business to tell them not to read them is sure to excel; and most of the reviewers here are believed to hate them. Awards to industry have been bestowed for less.

The novel was very promptly reviewed by a writer of note, who hailed it, I'm told, as the best English novel, or thereabouts, since the war. No intention to assist Amanda Craig with this clearly extravagant claim need be presumed; other writers altogether may have been in mind. There may have been a wish to get a rise out of the appropriate people – those enemies that writers, and the clever, tend to have. Publishers rose, among others, and the statement was solemnly weighed at Mary's parties. The writer of note was the novelist cheeky A. N. Wilson, who then called attention to his retirement from the post of literary editor of the London *Evening Standard* by announcing that Seamus Heaney was a parish-magazine poet who would never have made a name for himself if he hadn't been Irish.

Not all reviewers are clones of the reviewers in this novel. I went for years at a time without meeting anyone quite like Mark, though I always knew he was somewhere about. The novel presents the aetiology (Craig makes lavish use of medical terms) of a vocational disease or deformation, and the symptoms it examines are those in particular of literary journalists battling it out on mass-circulation newspapers whose editors prefer 'lifestyle' and interviews to reviews. Craig's reviewers – who might remind one of the Craig's dragoons of Heaney's Belfast war song to the air of 'Dolly's Brae' – represent only a corner of the literary world, which is no more restricted than it has ever been to the London area. Nevertheless, her novel has things to say about the literary struggle as it is experienced more generally, and contains graphic testimony to what there is in the literary world which is worth quitting or avoiding, and which even the most scrupulous writers must find it difficult to avoid entirely.

You'd think people might be put off by the realities travestied – though not always by much – in the novel. But they still come forward, anxious to write their books and articles, and to take the risk of having to live or die by an editor's, publisher's or reviewer's opinion, and by the public opinion, of how hot they are. Seen in the light of these anxieties, literature is a commitment which can look like the explorer Sir Ranulph Fiennes setting out, disguised as the elderly Solzhenitsyn, to shamble across the Antarctic wastes with kidney stones passing through his body. Death, despondency and despair – Wordsworth's words for the fate that threatens the lives of poets – hang over all lives; but there's something about the activity of writing which might make it seem a little odd that, having started and succeeded, or failed, it can be difficult for writers to stop.

In the mid-Eighties Alan Taylor's powers began to weaken and he was to develop Parkinson's disease: but his practice as a reviewer was not going to fade away into the dark if Alan had anything to do with it. He was one of several gifted historians with whom I was lucky enough to work – such people as Hugh Trevor-Roper, M. I. Finley, Rosalind Mitchison, Michael Howard and John Vincent – and it was bleak to watch historians of later generations shoving him into the dark with their valedictions when biographies were published after his death.

In September 1984, when he sent in a Diary to the *London Review*, I found myself reacting, indeed overreacting, to a text that seemed more like a hallucination than the account of a hallucination. A stay in hospital had flung the historian into the past, a more remote past than the one he used to write about. Had the dream melted by the time he came to write the Diary? Had the philtre worn off?

Most of my life seems to have been passed in some part of the North of England and at different periods. My first stretch was in Roman Britain, when I lived in York and was afterwards stationed on the Wall. These experiences were very instructive to me as an historian.

The Romans did not remain long. Nor did I waste much time at the court of King Arthur. The outstanding figure of my attraction was the king, though I did not manage to encounter him often. This was the period when I spent most of my time on the Yorkshire moors. I got lost pretty often, though always rescued by other wanderers. Gradually I moved into a more civilised existence. The centre of my life was now Harrogate, a place I have never visited in my life. I had difficulties here obtaining regular copies of the *Manchester Guardian*, which did not surprise me at all.

I took a taxi out to his house in Tufnell Park, to check that he was all right, and that his enchantment, his Alice-like tumble down a time-warp, had slipped into the past by the time he chose to write the piece. And so it proved. The piece testifies to the existence of the human imagination, which historians can be inclined to discount, and which Alan, in his many lucid intervals, was never one for proclaiming. He had believed in his hospital bed that he'd been translated, and after his discharge I had believed it of him too, in a sense, and for a while. In that restricted sense, a dream had come true, as dreams sometimes do.

Around 1989, the agnostic philosopher A. J. Ayer reported, during his last months, an out-of-the-body experience: it may have been felt by some that he'd discovered his soul, having all along preferred to believe in his ego. Both A. J. P. Taylor and A. J. Ayer had potent egos, egos that refused to stop – I was with the philosopher once when, after a Spurs success at White Hart Lane, we were threatened with injury by a Glasgow Rangers supporter, who failed to interrupt what Ayer was saying. And their out-of-the-body experiences originated, I feel, in this refusal to stop – both in mind-altering illness and in the old Adam of a native obstinacy. It wouldn't do to get carried away by them. But they have their meaning, and their poignancy, for any student of the writers concerned, both of them as skilled as they were popular, both of them resented for that by their peers.

Two years after his time-travelling, a letter arrived from Alan enclosing a fragmentary review of Nigel Hamilton's life of Field Marshal Montgomery, a favourite subject of Alan's ('Hitting them for six', an expression of Montgomery's, was the *New Statesman* heading on a piece by him about what the general did to the Germans). The covering letter read:

> I am sorry to send this in so late. It was heavy going and I have been ill into the bargain. I think I have now made it interesting after a delay . . . Please send me some more books if you think it is any good. It is so hot today I am writing in shorts.

The review was unfinished and not always clear. But it becomes wholly clear at the point where it tells how, when Montgomery received a 'great prize from Miss Foyle, the keeper of the famous Book Shop', Alan was asked to award it:

> When I arrived he was sitting by himself. I said to him: 'I know you. You are the great general.' He replied: 'I know you. You are the great historian.' I hesitate to decide whether either of us got things right.

No, he didn't. Alan was not a hesitant man, and his vanity was never a secret, any more than Freddy Ayer's was. I am not seeking to expose it by quoting from the article which his strong will, sitting in its hill-walker's shorts in the June sunlight, had fought to produce. It had always been one of the attractions of his Diaries.

The last years of Jonathan Miller's mother Betty, a biographer of Robert Browning and a good novelist, were shadowed by ill-health, starting with a pneumonia and ending with Alzheimer's, of which she died, too young, in 1965. Jonathan told me, in our thirties, impressing me very much, of how her editor at the *TLS* had become aware of a gradual loss of edge in the pieces she was sending him. Betty was like an ark full of amiable animals. There was a horse in there, a fox, a giraffe, red-setter tints to the hair and face, and she had lips that seemed to tremble in response to the world around her, of which she was sometimes said to have been fearful. A friend, Isaiah Berlin, has talked of her 'moral charm', and of her melancholy and her beautiful manners, and another friend, Rosamond Lehmann, talked of the 'stressing of sensuous impressions' in her novel about the Home Front in the Second World War, *On the Side of the Angels*, in which yew trees sharpen the air with a 'rasp of sap', and there's a bar with a heavy curtain over the door, where the drinkers take pleasure in waiting to see 'what the beating and bulging would this time bring forth', a vigil both sensuous and comic.

The book has her moral charm, and it's also exciting. A dark stranger in Commando uniform flutters a community of medical officers and their womenfolk, quartered in a Gloucestershire town. Imperfect marriages are accepted by two sisters, for one of whom, in such a death, there may lie victories of the mind and spirit. The book has the extra charm of being very much of its period. The carnival effect of putting on a uniform is explored. Officers refer to their wives in French, as *madame* – a company-director uncle of mine used to do this, and so did Betty's psychiatrist husband. Those were the days when psychiatrists were known as trick-cyclists, when bicycles stood upright and almost human at kerbs, propped on a pedal, and when cigarettes were 'selected' from cases and tins, and smoked as if England expected it.

Betty and her sensuous impressions are missed to this day by those who knew her or her writings. She belonged to a circle of female friends which included Naomi Lewis – an authority on children's books among others, and a saviour of London's wounded pigeons, who reviewed frequently, and very well, for Terry Kilmartin at the *Observer* – and Stevie Smith, author of a doggerel poem about the horrors of a mother's love and of the spoilt child, a poem attended by a tale of female solidarity which deals with the antics of the small Jonathan Miller on a shingle beach beside the 'bulging sea'. Hughie was 'devoured by restless energy, he must do his train noises (or whatever it was), and he must have an audience'. Unlike Stevie. It might seem that this was a circle in which you were never too young to be reviewed. Hughie ends up angry, speaking of his sister in the language of a novel by Ivy Compton-Burnett. She has 'displaced me', he cries, 'in my mother's affection, as soon as she was born this is what she did'.

Literary starts and finishes have not been uncommon in the extended family, most of them Jewish, which I entered when I married. My wife's grandfather, Redcliffe Salaman, wrote a pioneering work on the social history of the potato (a reissue was nepotistically discussed in the *London Review*, delightfully too, by Angela Carter); his daughter-in-law, Esther, from Zhitomir in the Ukraine, was a novelist and autobiographer; her sister Fania wrote a memoir of her friendship with Wittgenstein; a third sister, Miriam, was married to Redcliffe's son Raphael, who gave himself to the history of agricultural technology. My wife's mother is a painter, still, at eighty-eight; her father, Robert Collet, was a pianist who wrote on music (Couperin, Berlioz, Liszt); another Aunt Esther, Esther Hamburger, teaches, and writes about, singing. Her own concerns – feminism, bilingualism and the teaching of literature – have shaped a series of books. Writing relatives, these – musicians, painters, doctors, Bedalians, few of them football-mad. My son-in-law, Ardu Vakil, follows the game. But this has not prevented him from publishing a novel about growing up, a Parsi,

anciently a Persian, in Bombay, where Parsis are sometimes called India's Jews. His daughter Tara, turned
three, has already grown up. 'You're not going to like
this,' she was heard to say at an early point. She is
working on a first novel.

Ardu's wife, my daughter Georgia, is a solicitor and
has informed views about the woe there is in the writing
of books; his sister Shireen is married to my son Sam,
who works for the World Service of the BBC and has
started to write one; my son Daniel lives with his wife
Yvonne and their two children in Hackney, painting away
softly the while. When I met these Parsis they looked to
me like the courtly figures in the Mughal paintings that
Vidia Naipaul hangs on his walls. Their cool garments of
emerald and lime and white samite were not upstaged by
Rebecca's barbaric vest and simarre of Persian silk in the
book Tony Blair is rumoured to admire, *Ivanhoe*. How
exotic, and how exogamous, it all was. 'What country is
he the prince of?' I snarled, forseeing my daughter's
departure. But when I got to his family's Bauhaus villa
on Juhu beach in Bombay, I found the same books on the
shelves as had been on my own in adolescence. There by
the pale Arabian Sea was Quiller-Couch's *Oxford Book of
English Verse*, which had lain by the North Sea on my
Scottish shelf, thumbed, and inscribed with exclamations.
And now here was Ardu, having English-versed it in his
youth, first-noveling it, and making his literary start, in
London, with *Beach Boy*, which reveals an adolescence
very different from that of my children — total strangers
to the interest in food displayed by the samosa-struck boy
in the book — and yet, in so many ways, very much the

same. It has the priests, and the circling mortuary vultures, of the Zoroastrian religion, together with a worship of the stars of Hindi movies and of the Western rock scene; it alludes to *Great Expectations* and has its own Miss Havisham; and it has the universal feature of a father's death.

The world is smaller now, and more closely knit; most countries are more responsive to one another than they were when I opened the 1939 edition of Quiller-Couch's anthology. Indian literary starts have become a growth area for anyone in this country who reads books, and an even more prolific phase in the long history of Anglo-Indian cultural relations has begun. Indians have done what the Irish have done: they have taken possession of the colonial language, and have shown a gift for turning it into literature. 'English' has long been, and is now generally recognized as, an amalgam of English English, in its considerable variety, Hiberno-English, in Seamus Heaney's expression, Scots English and Indian and American English, among others. The imperial or metropolitan definition of the language, hanging out its appendage of shameful foreign and provincial accents, is well on the way to being gone with the winds of change that did for the Empire. Or so I hope. All my life, in my multiple or muddled nationality, I have had a taste for English-speaking writers who flourished at a remove from London, and have owed much to the passage to India which began for me, in the late Fifties, with the stories of Narayan. The South African stories of Dan Jacobson, and his novella *A Dance in the Sun*, shone a similar light when I came to know them at about the same time.

My own situation in life, while including the polar opposite of any literary start, can occasionally seem like the beginning rather than the end of the line. I have come to experience reversions – not to Camelot or Hadrian's Wall – but to the way I once was, to past states, to a vulnerability and fluster, for instance, outlived in middle age but graphically illustrated all over again in that photo booth, and to an earlier conversational blurting. An ancestor of my wife's, an eighteenth-century Dissenting patriarch, Samuel Collet, who is portrayed by my coincidentally-named son Sam in a piece he is writing, said at the age of eighty-five: 'I know I write as a child, and talk as a child; for I am a child.' I am a child too at times, and I suppose I should admit that, with nothing like the sanction of Samuel Collet's longevity, this is a childish last chapter.

Such reversions and regressions do little to shake, however, indeed tend to confirm, the sense I have of a perseverance, of the same old self, the same old face, fallen as it now is when exhibited in post offices: of a continuous and indivisible entity much preoccupied, over the years, with the duality of man. This is not to cancel or amend what has been said in this book about dual purposes and complexity of motive, about the dilemmas, respites and escapes of the individual life, which can turn one person into two. But my own life has kept me conscious both of an empire of duality and of an enduring individual idiosyncrasy. I am old, and I am also the same old thing.

A recent coincidence – one of those intriguing co-incidences and symmetries to which I referred in an earlier chapter – has helped to make me suppose so.

When, at the age of twenty, I was doing my National Service in Hamburg, as a broadcaster for Army Radio, I dreamed a dream. I was in a barracks which was like a spired cathedral honeycombed by booths and cubby-holes opening at moments into high halls, and which was like a prison. I was alone, but there were unseen companions somewhere in the vicinity, soldiers like myself, for all I knew, and I was in a fever of wanting to be just like them. It had been the same when I first went to school: I'd have gone to the ends of the earth to draw lines with the same kind of ruler as the other children. Here once more in my cathedral and barracks and jail I ran high and low, hoping for a way of belonging to the company that was hidden from me.

All my life I have been frightened of doctors, and now I had to go and see one in this dream. I might be suffering from a contagious illness. A killing growth might have to be cut from me. And perhaps I would cut myself off for good from my friends by being singled out for this operation. I began to realize that I might be more afraid of the doctor than of the disease, that I would rather hide it than be publicly treated for it.

The interview with the doctor was a nightmare. He was the first person I'd met in that barracks or jail or cathedral. *Ex cathedra*, the Medical Officer, who proved a match for the least appealing of the medicos in Betty Miller's novel. He was dressed in white overalls, with unsettling civilian clothes showing beneath them, those, perhaps, of a Harley Street psychiatric consultant, licensed to cut, rather than your ordinary regimental doctor. He was on the short side. His hair had withdrawn from a plump forehead, and grew dark and thick in a sweep back over either ear. His eyes were soft, womanly, intent. Over his forehead was tilted, like a halo that had slipped, a shiny steel saucer, the better to see me with. He had the air of an overgrown criminal cherub whose name was Alphonse, or Aldous. 'You are to be operated on immediately,' said Alphonse, or Aldous. I protested, indignant that I hadn't been examined beforehand. 'It's not up to you to go asking questions,' he said, as if I were one of those servicemen who suffered a poisonous nuclear posting to Australia. 'You're not beyond discipline just because you're sick.'

The operation took place. I walked into this white wall. The first thing I felt when I came out of the anaesthetic was that part of my face was missing. It couldn't be my eyes. I was seeing with them. A cheek? An earlobe, an eyelid, a lip? The cathedral reared up around me as I hurtled in search of an answer through its barrack-rooms and jail. I found myself holding a large framed mirror up to my face, and saw that the wing of my right nostril had been ever so carefully cut away according to the lines of my nose. Only a morsel of flesh was gone, though. From my right, I reckoned, my nostrils would scarcely seem more than distended, and not quite ludicrously enough for me to seem permanently indignant or passionate. From the left, there was no change in my appearance. Full face, I'd look merely lopsided. The barracks, the jail, the cathedral, and angel-eyed Alphonse or Aldous, vanished from my mind. People, my hidden friends, would be hard-pressed to notice the change. I was not disfigured. My face was free to proceed towards its appointment with that unsightly photocard, all of forty-five years later.

In 1995, a few months before the snap was taken, my dream came true. The very same fears and fascinations, the same wish to hide my disease, the same old tug between apartness and belonging, returned, so far as they'd ever been away. The occasions of my waking life of the time are perceptible in the dream, as is a reading of the stories of Kafka and of Freud. It seemed at the time to be telling me the story of my life, or of some of it. And now here it was again. The castration anxiety – Freud-sponsored or spontaneous – which may seem to figure in the dream had been swept up into an actual exploratory operation: it was as if the old op recorded during my National Service, broadcast with rich incongruity to the British Army of the Rhine, and thereafter forgotten, had returned. Up my nose they went with their knives – as I squinted at their turbans and shiny steel saucers – in order to remove a small piece of my person, like a word of praise excised from a book review, and to perform a biopsy. By the end of it, as before, I'd lost something; presently there would be nothing left to lose. It then became apparent that before administering that last snub there would be time for life to spring one or two more of its well-known incidental reverses. I was wheeled back to my bed, and chose to enter a different world or other mood, for respite, by raising my two arms a foot above my sinus, that I might clutch and read Ian Hacking's book on multiple personality, *Rewriting the Soul*. But the first sentence that met my eye was about autopsies, and injuries to the head. Escapes are like that.

And changes are like that. Now you see them, now you don't. Have they happened? Human subjectivity seems programmed to find them imponderable. Times change, and don't change. New is old, or may appear to be. Just as the changing person may feel the same as ever. Literature may be felt to have lightened up in response to a new technology; but old books could be buoyant too.

A further new development, whereby admiration of the great writer has been denounced and may have abated, is no less elusive, but has been read by some as proof positive of a literary decline. My own response to this development has been made clear, in the course of a book parts of which are suffused in paradox. It describes a search for good writers, a concern with artistic merit, and with its subjection to the hostility of critics. But it also contains its own hostile critical accounts, and suggests that there is more to it all than the importance of important writers. It is capable of the thought that art is for everyone who wants it, that everyone who wants it does it, and of the thought that the human mind can hardly help it, in the sense that there is and has to be an art of living. These last thoughts have gained ground in recent times, but they have also been resisted: 'minor' and 'popular' are repressive terms which have yet to lose their currency. We have long been taught to use them, to think in this way, to go for the rare birds, the fit few, of a better class of artist. It is the way in which Mike Leigh's films were initially held by critics to be downmarket, and suspected for their element of improvisation, an element which lends support to the democratic idea of a diffused or universal artistry. Also supportive is the information that audiences throughout the world have welcomed his picture *Secrets and Lies* as the affecting work of art that it is. The Oscar-winning, higher-kitsch film of the book *The English Patient*, a film in which the well-favoured and the titled rise above death and disfigurement, and a photogenic corpse is none the worse for prolonged exposure in a desert cave, is, I admit, popular too at this point, and will no doubt take precedence in the folk memory of publicists.

It follows that the talk against élitism which occurs in this book can't be thought – in the light of this further development – to belong to a period which has now gone. Jamesonism is no longer young, and we've been listening for years to news of this or that levelling stupidity, this or that more or less ludic assault on the book and on Western civilization and its dead white males. But the canon has not been deserted. It has shown itself, indeed, to be susceptible of change and renewal. The objections I have raised on the subject are no more out of date than they are such as to make me sorry that a literary culture which is in this sense canonical has survived. My position is, as I am painlessly aware, contradictory, since I believe that excellence is a good thing, but that too much of it, in some of the forms to which we have been accustomed, is not.

Modernism was still an excitement, still news, when I was a boy. It is now history, and was followed by a period of stability in which the example of the Modernist writers ceased to be commanding, while remaining influential, and which has not been disrupted by the largely factitious turmoil of the Post-Modern. In October 1970, Patricia

Beer published in the *Listener* a poem called 'Self-Help' which shows no obvious debt to Modernism, which would seem to be on good terms with the poetry Larkin wrote, and enabled others to write, in the middle of the century, and which has the interest of articulating one of the century's principal changes of heart. As a girl in the West Country, she had learnt to strive by reading Samuel Smiles's Victorian manual of that name, in praise of all that a selection of notable males had managed to achieve and overcome. Her poem now places her in London, where there are 'bathless flats', and problem children who smash their neighbours' milk bottles. The people around her 'live now'. They are unlike Smiles's 'resolute contenders'. They are

> Unlike my father and my grandfather
> Who worked so hard and never helped themselves,
> And unlike me in another sense who might
> Have come straight out of *Self-Help* on my worst days,
> Practising lawful self-advancement, preaching
> It, enjoying its rewards. And through
> The white comfortable mist a wind blows holes,
> Lays bare the quagmire reaching for us all,
> Whispers how soon we could be shouting 'Help.'

Women are spoken for in the poem, where the nineteenth-century game of 'Help the Genius' is mentioned – the genius in the house, that's to say, a house that has yet to fall down; but men are spoken for too, though great men are not in favour. The poem attests to a change of outlook in the matter of women's rights, a change which is actually happening, which is neither imaginary nor completely imponderable, and which has taken a long time to get to the point it has reached; it is perhaps the least equivocal of the benefits which this expiring millennium has produced. But the governments of this country have never given it their ungrudging support, and everywhere in the world it still has a long way to go. All the time, moreover, there come turnings-back, reversals, restorations of the veil.

As a university teacher I was exposed to the give-and-take of the feminist advance to a degree that I wouldn't have been had I remained mewed up in the ivory tower of a newspaper. I remember the cold glances of some female feminist students, and could imagine at the time the scorn that would have answered the lisping patriarchal suggestion that I was one of them myself. Nevertheless, I was and am. My pantheon, so far as I have one, enshrines the courage of those twentieth-century women who have fought for their rights, the suffragettes and their successors, in this country and in others, the shy dinner ladies and factory workers of recent years, lobbying arm-in-arm for equal pay and equal opportunities, the Iranian women who threw off the chador and have been forced back into it.

There were few female literary editors in my day. Most of them, latterly, were Claire Tomalin and Miriam Gross. Claire succeeded me, and her husband Nick, at the *New Statesman*, and shone there, as elsewhere, in that capacity, before yielding to the attractions of biography. Women writers were important to the magazines I worked for – among them, Doris Lessing, Angela Carter,

Nell Dunn, Emma Tennant, Gabriele Annan, Anita Brookner and Penelope Gilliatt. But it wasn't till I got to the *Listener* in the Seventies that the presence of women writers – not all of them feminists in any strictly political sense – became self-conscious, in some measure politicized. Then, though, it did – thanks, in particular, to the efforts and ardour of Brigid Brophy. Another woman whom I was always eager to publish was by no means strictly political, though she did speak up for Mrs Shakespeare and for her presence in her husband's sonnets. This was the critic Barbara Everett – mistress of the alarming compliment, and of refinements and preliminaries, who is able to step through them to saying the hitherto unsaid, to saying things that are as much literature as they are criticism. They abolish the distinction.

The old man in Chekhov's 'A Boring Story' both appears to have and professes to lack a 'ruling idea'. I don't think I have one of these. I am certainly not an adherent – forsaking all others – of any code or creed, if that can be thought to form part of what Chekhov is driving at here. I support the Labour Party, and am more conscious of political leaders than I can altogether account for. But I don't want the Labour Party to tell me who I am. And I don't want to resemble the Party spokesman who, on the eve of the '97 Election, responded to news of a Tory plan to privatize the Inland Revenue by complaining that the selling price was too low. At that point I was with those who intended to vote for Tony Blair, but who were not sure that he would make a good prime minister, having made a very good leader of the Opposition. We went on to hope that the leadership would improve in office on their Thatcherite pre-election publicity, and would settle the worries aroused by an intensely tactical campaign. My hopes as a political onlooker have often been disappointed. I regret that Denis Healey did not become leader of the Labour Party, and that John Smith was leader for so brief a spell. Would I live to regret that starry Blair had become prime minister?

These were my guarded feelings as I looked forward to a Labour victory. They were to be transfigured, though, when the time came to count the votes. On May the First I went out into World's End, Chelsea, to stand in another of my neighbourhood booths and make my cross. This time I did not have to be prised from the booth; I didn't have to be helped to cast my hopeless vote. It was a tactical vote against the certain winner, against old-lad Alan Clark of Saltwood Castle; as I cast it, I remembered my dealings, thirty years ago, with his very haughty dad Kenneth, Lord Clark of Civilization, whose story of art sent the *Listener*'s sales soaring. Night then fell, and I was unable to withdraw my eyes from the television screen, well past my bedtime into the early hours of the morning, as a Labour triumph of unexampled profundity unfolded. I was moved. Moved? I was caught up in the wave of delight that broke over Britain. It felt like the end of a bad old world. A light brighter than the false dawn glimpsed by Dick Crossman in the Sixties had appeared in the sky.

One by one, several of the worst people in the House of Commons were turned out. And as I watched, the victors seemed time and again to be decent young women.

Tory Euroscepticism outdid itself by claiming, much in the manner of old-style Labour Left recrimination over their party's insufficiency of socialism, that the Tories had lost because they hadn't been Eurosceptical enough, and went on to inflict a further defeat on the Party by rejecting for the leadership easily its most eligible politician, Kenneth Clarke, a less ducally forbidding bearer of the name. Another contender for the leadership, Michael Howard, was denounced by his former colleague at the Home Office, the Gothic spaewife Ann Widdecombe, who said what others had said less startlingly – that he has 'something of the night' in him. This might look like the Medieval night which used to include the Jews. Would she have spoken in the same way if Howard had come from a long line of East Anglian farmers?

The BBC's estranged correspondent Martin Bell, standing as an independent against the cash-for-questions Tory Neil Hamilton, looked ill at ease with an assignment that might have come to pieces in his hands. The recent convert to a 'journalism of attachment' described himself, on this occasion, as anti-party, 'not a *joiner*'. He talked of 'trust' and 'honour'. And he won. Nearly 20,000 people, though, voted for the known hustler he was challenging. Blair the campaigner was efficient and graceful. There were moments that recalled the ease and elegance displayed, before he became President of America, by New Labour's admired Bill Clinton – a body-language that refused to burden the people with dogma. He was at his best among his Sedgefield helpers; some Old Labour faces noticeable here, amidst all the talk of newness, not unfamiliar from past campaigns.

The vote was a vote to get the Tories out, and the Labour campaign appeared to expect that. They stuck to offering reassurances while making very few pledges, and who could say that it didn't work? Pledges and policies were considered divisive, and one of the reasons why the result was called stunning may have been that it left people not knowing what had happened to them. What happened next, in an informal way, proved to include an indication that the Government would be going ahead with an acceptance of the Social Chapter of the Maastricht Treaty, with its minimum wage; it also included, less wonderfully, a suggestion by the Heritage Secretary that Britain would be holding on to the Elgin Marbles, docked from somebody else's heritage. A fortnight after the election, the policies announced in the Queen's Speech seemed well worth supporting – with the exception of the education proposals. Labour is to be as tough on schools and teachers as it is due to be on crime: a rapid-reaction enforcement of standards and hit-listed 'failing schools' are on their way.

Labour's plans for Scotland, revealed later in the summer, delighted me less than they did Neal Ascherson, the veteran romantic separatist. I believe in the mixed Britain of the present time, in its different faces, races and traditions, in the attempt by its people – against the odds, as it often appears – to get these together, in their attempt to live together, overtaken by the aftermath of empire, on their narrow little zig-zag island. I used to hope for a greater regional autonomy in Britain. But Labour's law-making, tax-adjusting Scottish assembly looks too much like a division of the country into north and south; no other part of the island has so far been offered such powers. This is a devolution which could weaken the authority and stability of the Westminster Government, at a time when sovereign states still have to protect themselves, and when this one is subject to the direction, as never before, of excellent Scottish politicians, such as the Royal High's Foreign Secretary, Robin Cook. It is likely to turn up, on all sides, the volume of ethnic and nationalist cant. There are brave hearts south of the border too, recoilers from Europe and from each other and from the recoiling Scots. Few people in Britain want it to break up. But it has become possible to reflect that stranger things have been happening.

The thin edge of the wedge may in the end produce an approximation to the 'purely Scotch' Scotland which Henry Cockburn remembered from his youth, but which was in part a fiction of his maturity. It may produce a return to a serene ethnicity that never was. I remember from my own youth an Edinburgh school which was divided into four 'nations': Picts, Scots, Britons and droopy Angles. We were a mixture, thereby arbitrarily sorted out, but with some regard for the history of the country. As an Angle, I wore a round school lapel-badge rimmed in light blue. As a Hiberno-Scot from London (not Angle but Anglo), I am with Tam Dalyell, MP for West Lothian, in failing to feel that Scotland would be better-off as a small separate country burdened with a very large lapel-badge. But it seemed that many of those resident in Scotland who voted successfully for devolution in the September referendum were willing to risk it, to risk what they are likely to think is unlikely to happen, in saying yes to the proposals. Meanwhile, Labour's partner in devolution, the Scottish National Party, is more than willing to risk it. They are all for it, and over half of them are for holding a Scottish referendum on the abolition of the Monarchy. They are one good reason among others for disbelieving Labour's claim that devolution will strengthen the Union.

Will the death of Princess Diana, and the mass mourning it occasioned, strengthen the Union, or the Crown? A day or two before the funeral a dinner was held in a London house, on the street known as Embassy Row, near where she lived in Kensington Palace. Some guests had been taken aback by the national excitement over her death. Was it not perhaps a little overdone, wondered their excellencies. All those flowers that had been brought to the palace, those cards with their simple, misspelt messages, placed with the bouquets by 'Mary from Bolton' and many more. But no one seemed to mind when the ambassador's wife told how her neighbour had remembered her birthday and sent her a present. Diana had a gift for giving people presents, while appearing to like the people she met, and not just the stars and prominenti. She liked the miserable and vulnerable, and they liked her in return – partly for being vulnerable herself. Others, of course, were irritated by her, and dined out on her mistakes. After her death Diana and her fairy-tale were described as 'tawdry' by the familiar figure of a London contributor to the *New York Review of Books*.

The diplomatic guests had seen nothing yet. A trance descended on the population, and London's gates seemed besieged, Buckingham Palace stormed, by blooms and bouquets, heaps and drifts of them. Large quantities were imported from Turkey, where my wife was to hear that the royals had plotted Diana's death, like so many sultans. This was a memorable summer, and these were strange days, with portents winking at you like lights, some of which have since gone out. Her brother's words in Westminster Abbey were much more than a retaliation against predatory newspapers and the sullen House of Windsor. Quality papers were quick to describe Earl Spencer's speech as mad and mendacious, but most people, including Mary from Bolton and myself, were moved by it, just as most people, many of us republicans, were saddened by his sister's death. None of what happened, however, moved me to foresee the fall of the House of Windsor which its current disrepute has been thought to portend.

The funeral was not – for all the overruling of the Royal Family which it was taken to contain – the beginning of the imminent end of British kings and queens. It was more of the same sort of thing. 'Your Majesty's self is but a ceremony,' Philip II of Spain was informed by one of his bolder ambassadors. Majesty is its ceremonies, and it is also the stardom at which Diana excelled, to a point well beyond the capacity of any Windsor. Both attributes were displayed and worshipped at the funeral, and lots of the mourners must have felt: the Monarchy is dead – long live the Monarchy. Let there be a Charles III after all, or a William V instead. But then, only a few days later, the Scots went and devolved themselves. A new Scotch millennium was hailed. The sentimental loyalty to royalty which has long subsisted in

Scotland did not prevent them from making a statement that is more likely to harm than it is to strengthen the Crown. And then again, soon after that, the Welsh chose a lesser devolution. But only a quarter of them voted in its favour; only a quarter voted for the Assembly they are about to receive. Tony Blair hailed this as a victory for democracy.

Some of the democracies we refer to, and take for granted, are more peculiar than others. Britain's democrats will upset a number of calculations by holding onto their royal family, while Blair's grass-roots Welsh victory is, in more ways than one, an illusion. During the devolution debate, regional autonomy was at times confused with local government, and credited with its more attractive features. Those, however, who see the point of a properly attentive, even-handed central bureaucracy, of the kind which has served this country well, will not be anxious for more of the purposes and practices associated with the local democracy available in City Halls.

Referendum voters in Scotland who saw themselves as declaring for a free country would do well to learn from whatever offhand old centaur they are able to consult that there are no free countries, though some countries are freer than others, and to learn from Socrates, who said only this morning on a T-shirt passed in the street not far from my polling-station that 'no man is ever truly free.' Sovereignty, as opposed to devolution, would release the Scots from future submissions to British general election results, but it isn't clear what it would do for the solution of problems which post-war Northern politicians have been in a position to address but in which they have failed to take an interest. It could be said that Scotland needs to escape from drug dependency rather more than it needs to escape from England, and that neither escape will be easy to achieve. Scottish Anglophobia sharpened in revulsion from the England of Thatcher and Major, but I don't believe that many Scots people share it, in its more atavistic forms, or look forward to nursing it behind the battlements of a nation state. And there are over three-quarters of a million of them living south of the border, a sixth of the home-based Scots-born population. Not many of these absentees 'hate the English', presumably; not all of us can be considered ripe for repatriation. But we are Scots for all that, and some of our best friends are Scots. We are glad – those of us who think so – that Scotland is no less Scottish now than it was a hundred years ago. And yet we have other friends who are English. Why can't the Scots and English live together in peace on the same island? Hating the English is bad for the human spirit, and so would a phobic separation be.

The 1997 General Election was decided by voters who must often have felt that Labour could hardly do worse than the previous government – faultlessly characterized after the election, by a Conservative, as 'given to cruel and shallow sophistries'. Then, at that same point, a Cassandra appeared on television, and in tears, to say: 'It's all going to go to pot.' A cry from the depths of an old anguish of the Left. Would their governments work? Would they be left-wing?

Those people who are awake to the values of fairness and community have gained a self-styled one-nation government which is expected to care about these values, half-baked though the oratory on the subject has been, and for all the reassuring talk there has been of incentives and individual success. But a large number of the electors in Martin Bell's Tatton don't know what fellowship is, and there are plenty of others like them. The newspapers which came round to Blair will desert him, and Labour rule won't have to wait long for the trouble to start. Nevertheless, I live in hope that this will be, and will be seen to be, a good government. Some hopes have succumbed to the fear that there's such a thing as a Blair oligarchy, or court, which will do what it can for the deserving rich, for the windfall state of millionaires and misery. But the signs are in mid-autumn that the electorate has yet to decide that it has all gone to pot.

Politics is a way of life for fairly few, of whom I've not been one. Even in the aftermath of a euphoric election, I don't regret that I haven't been capable of living by, or for, the regenerations promised, and sometimes achieved, by elected governments. Like Martin Bell, I tell myself that I am no joiner, and we need neither of us be suspected of flatly misleading ourselves in this respect. But then it's also true that practically everyone is a joiner of something. There goes the shy celebrity Martin Bell, 'the man in the white suit', into the club-like House of Commons, with its friends and enemies and enemy friends, and the stare of a mass public. And there I went into journalism.

Journalists are exposed, just as politicians are, to the attention and opinions – to the suffrage – of other people, who include the members of their own profession. I have never been very keen on other people myself, without wishing or thinking them dead; I am like many other people in that way, not all of whom are writers. And I am someone who believes that fellowship is possible, and who can even remember what it could be like at times, but who can't help thinking of it now as problematical, if not outlandish. Nevertheless – that most Edinburgh of words, as Muriel Spark once made it seem – I went into journalism, and I supported Labour in the hope that they would attempt what party-political activity makes it very difficult to accomplish. With due allowance for the realities of a society deeply suspicious of itself on class grounds and subject to secession tremors, I hoped that Labour might bring people together, and that Labour in Europe might lead to a country that was less divided internally, and less hostile to other countries. Their plans for Scotland can't be seen, from that point of view, as a sure step forward.

What has always appealed to me most is my family, my friends, the magazines I have joined with others in endeavouring to get right, and the books I have read. In harking back to the middle ground of my life, it is books, every bit as all but a handful of human beings, that I tend to remember – books and the people of the past who wrote them and about whom I have written. I feel that I know Henry Cockburn and Louisa Stuart as well, see them as clearly, as I do many of my dead or absent friends.

I have gone back, as you can tell, to lying on my bed and looking out of my window. In my hand nestles a coffee-coloured ivory netsuke from nineteenth-century Japan. A netsuke is a fastening used to tether an ornament or a medicine casket to a kimono. This one is, to my eye, talismanic. It is a beautiful carving which depicts Amma, a blind masseur, with a lump or bump on his skull, moving forward on his stick, accompanied by a woman, who carries their mats, which look to me a little like page-proofs or galleys. Amma's face wears an equivocal smile, which may be a suffering or struggling grimace. The woman's face is utterly impassive. Amma's end could be in sight, but he is holding on, I think, pushing on, persevering. I have to hand it to him. The carving has in it a hint of the marital bond and complex struggle. These two people are like apparitions, who have emerged from the darkness which retains the maker of the image, their *sculptor ignotus*. My great artist is unknown, and will never be known.

Index